HOW
FISCHER PLAYS
CHESS

David N. L. Levy

FONTANA/COLLINS

This Fontana edition is published in association
with William Collins, Glasgow, 1975

© David N. L. Levy 1975

Made and Printed in Great Britain by
William Collins Sons & Co. Ltd Glasgow

FOREWORD

It is only natural that every chess author should wish to write a book about Bobby Fischer. This enigmatic genius has elevated the game to hitherto unimaginable heights, reaching the front pages of the world's newspapers and more than doubling the number of registered players in the Western World.

Fischer's popularization of the game he loves has also had a pronounced effect on chess literature. Since December 1970 when he began his successful journey on the road to the World Championship title, more chess magazines have been born, more newspapers have published chess columns, and many more chess books have appeared on the market than ever before over the same time span. It surprises me that only a small handful of these books have been about Fischer and I was delighted when Mark Collins asked me to write a book analysing Fischer's style of play.

In this volume I have traced the development of Fischer's style, beginning from the time when his games were first recorded in tournament bulletins. I have discussed his preference for certain openings and variations and shown how, eventually, he cured himself of a fatal stylistic malady – his persistence in playing unsuccessful lines.

As well as performing the essential function of illustrating my various arguments, the games and positions that I have included are both instructive and entertaining in their own right. Some of the games are well known but most of them are not. I have deliberately kept to a minimum the number of games that also appear in Fischer's outstanding work *My Sixty Memorable Games*. For this reason the reader is unlikely to have seen many of these games before.

I should like to thank Katia Young who translated many annotated games from Russian (and one or two from Serbian) and who also translated from Russian the article by Spassky in which he gave his first impressions of Fischer. I should also like to thank Bernard Cafferty for translating Suetin's essay on Fischer's style from the Russian edition of *My Sixty Memorable Games*. The photographs of Fischer in Havana in 1956 and 1966 were kindly loaned to me by the Cuban International Arbiter and chess journalist Carlos Palacio, who must also be thanked for introducing me to José Casado, thereby enabling me to be the first to publish the game Fischer-Casado (game 2). Naturally I wish to thank Señor Casado for supplying me with the score of that game.

I should like to thank my wife, Jacqueline, for making many useful suggestions during the editing of my typescript.

Lastly, on behalf of chess players everywhere, I must thank Bobby Fischer himself. The beauty of his games, the clarity of his play, and the brilliance of his ideas have made him an artist of the same stature as Brahms, Rembrandt, and Shakespeare. I hope that my book will help readers towards a greater appreciation of his art and a greater understanding of how it has been achieved.

DNLL

London
July, 1973

CONTENTS

1

THE EARLY YEARS

There can be no doubt that Bobby Fischer is the most superlative chess player that has ever lived. His results up to the time that he defeated Spassky in Reykjavik indicate that his playing strength had already surpassed zeniths reached by Alekhine, Botvinnik, Capablanca and Lasker who had all occupied the World Champion's throne before him. Fischer is a more controversial figure than Alekhine or Staunton. He is more dedicated to the game than were Capablanca and Steinitz. He is also fast becoming the most prolifically biographed player in the history of the game.

The first important step in Fischer's chess career was taken before he had even laid eyes on a chess set. When he was five his mother, Regina, having moved from Bobby's birthplace of Chicago to California and then Arizona, brought Bobby and his sister Joan to New York, the Mecca of American chess. In his first book *Bobby Fischer's Games of Chess* he recalls that he learned chess 'early in 1949' i.e. when he was five or just turned six. He and Joan taught themselves the moves from the instructions that came with a chess set that she had bought in a local candy shop.

For the next two years Fischer played against his sister, with boys that he had taught or just by himself. 'It was the game I liked best because it was the most difficult one of all.' By the time he was almost eight his mother felt frustrated for her child without an adequate opponent. She wrote to the chess columnist of a Brooklyn newspaper and was invited to bring her boy along to a local club where Max Pavey, a former Scottish Champion, was giving a simultaneous exhibition. At the Brooklyn club that evening Bobby lasted only a quarter of an hour against Pavey but the club president, Carmine Nigro, invited him to become a regular member and attend their weekly meetings.

The great importance of Bobby's being in New York lay in its abundant chess centres and its stimulating atmosphere. The city boasts a host of cafés and chess salons where the game can be played to all hours. In these often seedy gathering places are nurtured many of America's talented young chess players. Bobby played regularly at the Brooklyn club, on the concrete tables in Washington Square Park, and at the Hawthorne Chess Club, a training camp for young players which met in the home of John W. Collins. Almost all of his spare time was devoted to the game that he had already adopted as his own. 'Only once in my life did I work at something other than chess. When I was ten years old in Brooklyn, seven of us began to work in a bar, putting the chairs on the tables and sweeping the floor after the customers had left. We fantasized about how much we would be paid by the bartender. When he put his hand in his pocket he brought out a big wad of bills but he only gave us a dollar between seven of us. This was the first frustration of my life and after that I began to detest meanness.'

Bobby's rise to fame was in no way meteoric. He played and studied for four more years before he was strong enough to compete in even the most modest tournaments. And then, in 1955, his name began to appear in the lists. Not among the prizewinners at first but this did not matter. The important thing was that he was being tested, being given a chance to air the knowledge that he had acquired during those first years of study.

The scores of five of Fischer's games have survived from 1955, all played in the US Junior Championship at Lincoln, Nebraska. Even at that early stage in his career these games exhibit some of the most significant hallmarks of his present style:

(1) The preference for positions with clearly defined strategic aims.
(2) The taste for dynamic openings e.g. the Rauser (Yugoslav) Attack against the Sicilian Dragon.
(3) An aptitude for most King's Indian type positions.
(4) A readiness to experiment with something of his own in an almost forgotten variation. e.g. FISCHER–AMES, Lincoln 1957. 1 P—K4, P—K4; 2 N—KB3, N—QB3; 3 N—B3, N—B3; 4 B—B4, N×P; 5 B×P ch, K×B; 6 N×N, P—Q4; 7 N(K4)—N5 ch, K—N1; 8 P—Q4 (8 P—Q3, P—KR3; 9 N—R3, B×N – 9...B—KN5 is also good; 10 P×B, Q—B3, is good for Black); 8...P—KR3; 9 N—R3, B—KN5; 10 P×P (10 Q—Q2, B×N(R3); 11 P×B, N×P, is good for Black. The text is Fischer's improvement on existent theory), 10...N×P; 11 N—B4, and the game was eventually drawn.

For a twelve-year-old boy I particularly admire the economy of his moves in the following King's Indian, played in the third round at Lincoln.

---

1 THOAMSON–FISCHER
US JUNIOR CHAMPIONSHIP 1955

King's Indian Defence

1 P—Q4, N—KB3; 2 P—QB4, P—KN3; 3 N—QB3, B—N2; 4 P—K4, P—Q3; 5 N—B3, O—O; 6 B—Q3, B—N5!. This is the most logical way of reacting to the misplacement of White's KB.

7 O—O, N—B3; 8 B—K3, N—Q2; 9 B—K2

By intensifying the pressure against White's QP Fischer has gained a tempo for his K-side attack.

9...B×N; 10 B×B, P—K4; 11 P—
Q5, N—K2; 12 B—K2, P—KB4; 13
P—B4?

Unthematic. He should try 13 P—B3,
when, if Black exchanges pawns he only
helps to increase the scope of White's
bishops, while the advance ...P—B5
followed by ...P—KN4 lacks the
support of Black's QB and White will
probably be able to create sufficient
Q-side counterplay. Now Black's position
quickly springs to life.

13...P—KR3; 14 B—Q3, K—R2; 15
Q—K2, BP×P; 16 N×P, N—KB4;
17 B—Q2, P×P; 18 B×P, N—K4;
19 B—B2??

The worst of many evils. Possibly 19
B×N was the best chance.

19...N—Q5; 20 Q—Q2, N×P;

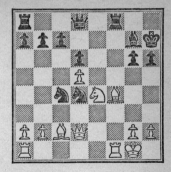

21 Q—B2

'We die that we may die no more' –
Herman Hooker.

21...R×B; 22 Q×R, N—K7 ch; 23
K—R1, N×Q; 24 Resigns

During the first seven months of 1955 Fischer played some thirty tournament
games. Possibly his failure in the Junior Championship was a big blow to his
ego but whatever the reason he did not compete any more that year. There
have been three periods in Fischer's career when he withdrew from com-
petetive chess only to return a more formidable opponent. The months
August to December 1955 represented his first dormant period. He hiber-
nated an inconspicuous young player and awoke an embryo master. His
first event of 1956 was the Greater New York City Championship, a seven
round Swiss system tournament with fifty-two players in which Bobby tied
for fifth place with Jackson and Saidy, behind Lombardy and Mengarini
(1st equal) and Fuerstein and McKormick (3rd equal). He won the class B
trophy and this success among strong opposition was such that when touring
Cuba with the Log Cabin Chess Club the following month he was considered
able enough to be invited to give a simultaneous exhibition.

Fischer's exhibition at the Capablanca Club in Havana took place on
February 26th 1956, prior to his thirteenth birthday. A photograph taken
of this, his first display, shows him opening 1 P—K4 on all (visible) boards.
The game in which he is about to move is a Sicilian Defence. The next (to
his right) a Ruy Lopez, Steinitz Defence Deferred. Then another Lopez,
another Sicilian, two more Ruy Lopez, a Giuoco Piano and then the
Exchange Variation of the Ruy Lopez, which he was to bring into prominence
in master chess a decade later in an Olympiad held less than a mile from the
spot where he gave this exhibition. One more Ruy Lopez is distinguishable,
but of the other boards nothing can be made out.

This restricted choice of openings is unusual for a simultaneous exhibition.
Normally the master will essay the whole spectrum of chess openings if only
to make things less tedious for himself. But Bobby, even in an exhibition,
seemed determined to prove that in chess there is only one truth and that at

the very beginning this truth is 1 P—K4. Apart from an early eighteen-month flirtation with the Reversed King's Indian he remained totally dedicated to the king's pawn openings for the next fifteen years, and at the time of his winning the World Championship in 1972, 1 P—K4 was still his first string.

Only one game score (so far unpublished) survives from that Havana evening and I am including it solely for historical reasons. The game itself is of no intrinsic value and is rather dull.

2 FISCHER–JOSE ARANGO CASADO

Sicilian Defence

1 P—K4, P—QB4; 2 N—KB3, N—QB3; 3 P—Q4, P×P; 4 N×P, N×N; 5 Q×N, P—Q3; 6 P—QB4, P—K4; 7 Q—Q3, N—B3; 8 N—B3, B—K3; 9 B—N5, B—K2; 10 B—K2, P—QR3; 11 P—QN3, O—O; 12 O—O, R—K1; 13 QR—Q1, Q—R4; 14 R—Q2, QR—B1; 15 B×N, B×B; 16 R(1)—Q1, KR—Q1; 17 N—Q5, B×N; 18 Q×B, Q×Q; 19 R×Q, B—K2; 20 P—B3, P—KN3; 21 P—B5.

A strange move. Did Fischer not notice 21 . . . R×P; 22 R×R, P×R; 23 R× R ch, B×R, when the game is a dead draw?

21...K—N2
What is this? Is Black playing to win? 22 K—B2, R—B3; 23 P—N3, P—B3; 24 P—B4, K—B2; 25 K—K1, P—QN4; 26 P—QN4, K—K1; 27 P× KP, P×BP; 28 P×KBP, B×P; 29 P×P, B—K2; 30 R×R ch, B×R; 31 R—Q6, R×R; 32 P×R, B—R4 ch; 33 K—Q1, B—N5; 34 P—K5, B—B6; 35 P—K6, B—K4; 36 P—Q7 ch, K— K2; 37 B—N4, B—B2; 38 K—B2, P— N5; 39 K—Q3, K—B3; 40 K—B4, P—QR4; 41 K—B5, P—R4; 42 B— R3, P—N4; 43 K—B6, B—Q1; 44 B— N2, P—QR5; 45 B—Q5, B—R4; 46 K—N7, P—R6; 47 K—B8, K—K2; 48 B—B4, B—Q1, Draw agreed

1956 was Fischer's breakthrough year, the year that he first became nationally acclaimed and internationally reported. His first few results in '56 were mixed but at the US Junior Championship he took first place and the prize of a portable typewriter. From Philadelphia he flew immediately to Oklahoma City, where, in the US Open Championship, he faced his toughest opposition so far. His result: tied for fourth behind Bisguier and Sherwin (1st equal) and Steinmeyer (3rd). Faithful to his beliefs, he still stuck to a rigid choice of openings. As Black he defended 1 P—Q4 with the King's Indian.

3 DONOVAN–FISCHER
US OPEN CHAMPIONSHIP 1956

King's Indian Defence

1 P—Q4, N—KB3; 2 P—QB4, P—KN3; 3 N—QB3, B—N2; 4 P—K4, P—Q3; 5 N—B3, O—O; 6 B—K2, QN—Q2; 7 O—O, P—K4; 8 P—KR3, P—B3; 9 B—K3, Q—K2; 10 Q—B2, P—QR3; 11 P—QR4, R—K1; 12 P×P, P×P; 13 P—R5, N—R4.
Starting the attack.

14 KR—Q1, N—B5; 15 B—KB1, N—B1; 16 P—B5, N—K3; 17 N—QR4, N—N4; 18 N×N, Q×N; 19 K—R2, B—K3

White's complete domination of his QN6 square is looking ridiculously redundant.

20 P—KN3

Accepting a sacrifice that gives Black the K-side dark squares in return for the piece. In fact White's extra piece is of no consequence since his knight plays no further part in the game.

20...B—R3, so that after 21 P×N, P×P, 22 B—Q4 would accomplish nothing.

22 B—B1, Q—R5;

23 R—R3, QR—Q1; 24 R(3)—Q3, R×R; 25 R×R, B—N2!
So that...B—K4 is always in the air.

26 P—N3, P—B4!; 27 R—KB3

Frees the queen from defence of KBP.

27...P×P; 28 Q×P, B—B2; 29 Q—B2, R—K8; 30 B—B4, Q—N4; 31 B×B ch, K—B1!; 32 R—N3, P×R ch; 33 P×P, Q×B; 34 Q×Q, R×Q; 35 B—K6, R—K8; 36 B—B8, R—K7 ch; 37 K—R1, R—K2; 38 K—N2, K—K1; 39 P—R4, K—Q1; 40 B—N4, R—K6; 41 Resigns

And against 1 P—K4 he has never deserted his first love.

4 GROSSGUTH–FISCHER
US JUNIOR CHAMPIONSHIP 1956

Sicilian Defence

1 P—K4, P—QB4
Fischer's first (recorded) Sicilian.

2 N—KB3, P—Q3; 3 P—Q4, P×P; 4 N×P, N—KB3; 5 N—QB3, P—QR3
And it's a Najdorf!

6 B—K2, P—K4; 7 N—N3, B—K2; 8 B—K3, O—O; 9 Q—Q2, P—QN4;

10 P—B3, B—K3; 11 P—N4?
Of course he should castle first.
11...P—Q4!; 12 P—N5?
This only makes things much worse. He
had to try 12 P×P.
12...P—Q5; 13 P×N, B×P!; 14
O—O—O, P×B; 15 Q×Q
If 15 Q×P ??, then 15...B—N4.
15...R×Q; 16 N—B5, N—B3; 17
N×B, P×N
The triplets are not so very detrimental –
they control so many key squares.

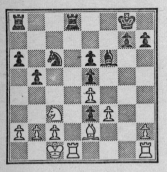

18 KR—B1
But White is lost anyway. Collins

suggested that he could have put up a
better fight with either 18 P—QR3
(which can be met by 18...N—Q5
followed by ...KR—N1, ...P—QR4
and ...P—N5), or 18 KR—N1, P—N5;
19 N—R4, N—Q5; 20 R—N2 (which
seems to fail to 20...B—R5 followed
by...B—B7 etc).
18...P—N5; 19 N—R4, N—Q5; 20
R×N, R×R!
Better than 20...P×R; 21 P—KB4,
when White has some counterplay based
on N—B5 and/or B—B4 in conjunction
with P—B5.
21 B—Q3, R(1)—Q1; 22 K—Q1, B—
N4; 23 K—K2, B—B5; 24 P—KR3,
R—QB1; 25 R—Q1, R—B3; 26 P—
N3, K—B2; 27 P—R4, K—B3; 28
P—R5, P—R4; 29 N—N2
Losing by force. But if (say) 29 R—
QB1, K—N4; 30 R—KN1 ch, K—R3;
31 R—KR1, R×P ch!; 32 B×R, R—
Q7 ch and 33...R×B, White is totally
lost.
29...R×B!; 30 Resigns
It is easy to see that all possible recap-
tures are futile, e.g. 30 N×R, R×P ch;
31 K—K1, B—N6 ch, and 32...P—
K7 ch.

As White, Bobby usually chose to play the King's Indian Reversed,
which we discuss fully in the next chapter. See page 18.

It was not until 1957 that the Lessing J. Rosenwald Trophy Tournament
officially became the US Championship, but it was already the premier
event of the American chess calendar. Entry was only by invitation and
limited to twelve players. Fischer was invited to participate as the current
US Junior Champion, an automatic qualification for entry until the 1959/60
tournament when Robin Ault ignominiously lost every game and the rule
was discreetly abandoned.
    The 1956 Rosenwald Tournament took place in New York in October.
In the first round, with the black pieces against Bisguier, Fischer got a very
bad opening and was wiped out, the only time that he was to lose to Bisguier
in their first fifteen games!

5 BISGUIER–FISCHER
ROSENWALD TOURNAMENT 1956

King's Indian Defence

1 P—Q4, N—KB3; 2 P—QB4, P—
KN3; 3 N—QB3, B—N2; 4 P—K4,
P—Q3; 5 P—B4, O—O; 6 N—B3,
P—B4; 7 B—K2, P×P; 8 N×P, N—
B3; 9 N—B2, B—Q2?
A serious mistake. After this passive
move White gets a good form of the
Maroczy bind against the Sicilian
Dragon. Correct is 9...P—QR3; 10
O—O, P—QN4, or 9...B—K3, fol-
lowed by...P—QR3 and...P—QN4.
    10 O—O, R—B1; 11 B—K3, N—
QR4; 12 P—QN3, P—QR3; 13 P—
K5!
Black is not allowed time for ...P—
QN4, the move he would like to play.
    13...P×P; 14 P×P, N—K1; 15 N—
Q5
Threat 16 B—N6.
    15...R—B3; 16 N—Q4, R—B1; 17
    N—B2, R—B3; 18 N(Q2)—N4
Initiating a long, forcing sequence that
wrecks Black's position.
    18...R—K3; 19 B—N4, R×P; 20
B—N6, Q—B1; 21 B×B, Q×B; 22
B×N, P—K3; 23 N—Q3, R—R4; 24
N(Q3)—B4, R—B4; 25 B—N4, P×
N; 26 B×R, B×R; 27 Q×B, K×B;
28 Q—R8 ch, K—K2; 29 R—K1 ch,
K—Q1; 30 N×QP, Q—B3; 31 Q—
B8, Q—Q2; 32 R—Q1, R—B3; 33
Q×N ch, Resigns

Another of Fischer's losses in this event was to Reshevsky, the tournament
winner. In one of the quiet variations of the King's Indian he was out-
manoeuvred and when he lost on time in a hopeless position there were ten
moves still to make. But time trouble has never bothered Fischer. His forty
moves have usually been made with plenty of time to spare and in recent
years it has not been uncommon to see him using less than ninety of the
allotted 150 minutes. This loss to Reshevsky is, in fact, one of only two
known examples of Fischer exceeding the time limit.

The sensation of this Rosenwald Tournament was Bobby's game against
Donald Byrne. He offered the exchange at move thirteen and later gave up
his queen to win a rook, two bishops and a pawn. The game was hailed as a
masterpiece, Kmoch going so far as to call it 'the game of the century'. In
my opinion, however, the game, attractive though it is, can in no way be
held in such high exaltation. It was merely the fact that the combination was
created by a thirteen-year-old boy that brought the game so much publicity.
Had it been played in the Barnet League between two sixty-year-old men it
is doubtful whether it would have been considered worthy of publication.

6 D. BYRNE–FISCHER
ROSENWALD TOURNAMENT 1956

Grünfeld Defence

(by transposition)

1 N—KB3	N—KB3
2 P—B4	P—KN3
3 N—B3	B—N2
4 P—Q4	O—O
5 B—B4	P—Q4
6 Q—N3	P×P
7 Q×BP	P—B3
8 P—K4	QN—Q2

More active is 8...P—QN4; 9 Q—N3, Q—R4, e.g. 10 B—K2, P—N5; 11 N—Q1, P—B4; 12 O—O, B—QR3, with a good game for Black. Bisguier–Benkö, US Championship 1963/64.

9 R—Q1

If 9 P—K5, N—Q4!; 10 N×N, P×N; 11 Q×P, N×P! – Fischer.

9 ...   N—N3

10 Q—B5?

A curious move, putting the queen on an exposed square for no apparent reason. Correct was 10 Q—N3.

10 ...   B—N5

Already Black has a lead in development.

11 B—KN5?

Almost a beginner's error, moving a piece for the second time before completing his development. The idea is to put pressure on Black's KP but this plan merely helps Black to launch an attack against White's king. 11 B—K2 was normal and best.

11 ...   N—R5!

Neatly exploiting the vulnerability of White's K4 square and the misplacing of White's queen.

12 Q—R3

12 N×N, N×P, is hopeless for White, e.g. (i) 13 Q×KP, Q×Q; 14 B×Q KR—K1; 15 B—K2, R×B; 16 O—O, P—QN4, followed by 17...N×N, winning a piece; or (ii) 13 Q—N4, N×B;

14 N×N, B×R; 15 K×B, B×P; 16 Q—Q2, B×BP, with a winning material advantage – Fischer.

12 ...   N×N
13 P×N   N×P!

Demonstrating the futility of White's eleventh move – the capture of Black's KP is both forced (in order to maintain material equality) and fatal.

14 B×P   Q—N3!
15 B—B4

Not 15 B×R, B×B; 16 Q—N3, N×QBP!; 17 Q×Q, P×Q; 18 R—R1, R—K1 ch, with a winning attack – Fischer.

15 ...   N×QBP
16 B—B5

If 16 Q×N, KR—K1, and Black has a pawn for nothing.

16 ...   KR—K1 ch
17 K—B1

17 ...   B—K3!

'... will be talked about for centuries to come' – FRANK BRADY

'This is the counter that raises this game to an immortal level.' – ROBERT WADE

'...a stunning masterpiece of combination play...' – HANS KMOCH

'Men do not know why they award fame to one work of art rather than another ... they think to justify the warmth of their commendations by discovering in it a hundred virtues, whereas the real ground of their applause is inexplicable – it is sympathy.' – THOMAS MANN

Since 17...N—N4? loses to 18 B×P ch, K×B; 19 Q—N3 ch, B—K3; 20 N—N5 ch, etc. the text is forced. Black's move is not in any way a sacrifice – it wins material by force and guarantees him a draw by perpetual check at the very least. So the eulogies would appear to be rather exaggerated.

18 B×Q

18 B×B loses by force to 18...Q— N4 ch; 19 K—N1, N—K7 ch; 20 K— B1, N—N6 dbl ch; 21 K—N1, Q— B8 ch; 22 R×Q, N—K7 mate, and 18 Q×N, to 18...Q×B!.

18 ...	B×B ch
19 K—N1	N—K7 ch
20 K—B1	N×P dis ch

21 K—N1	

If 21 R—Q3, P×B; 22 Q—B3, N×N.

21 ...	N—K7 ch
22 K—B1	N—B6 dis ch
23 K—N1	P×B
24 Q—N4	R—R5 !
25 Q×P	

25 Q—Q6, N×R; 26 Q×N, fails to 26...R×P, and death on back rank.

25 ...	N×R

Black has a winning material advantage as well as a killing attack. The remainder of the game is a massacre.

26 P—KR3, R×P; 27 K—R2, N×P; 28 R—K1, R×R; 29 Q—Q8 ch, B— B1; 30 N×R, B—Q4; 31 N—B3, N— K5; 32 Q—N8, P—QN4; 33 P—R4, P—R4; 34 N—K5, K—N2; 35 K— N1, B—B4 ch; 36 K—B1, N—N6 ch; 37 K—K1, B—N5 ch; 38 K—Q1, B— N6 ch; 39 K—B1, N—K7 ch; 40 K— N1, N—B6 ch; 41 K—B1, R—B7 mate

When first published in the Soviet Union this game was accompanied by derision of the profuse publicity that it had brought the thirteen-year-old. 'They showed the game and they said "He's a very fine, talented young player but all this publicity that he's getting is sure to do damage to his character." And then, sure enough, from then on, they started attacking my character. They had never even met me or knew anything about me. And this kind of attitude really turned me off.'

Thus began Fischer's antipathy towards the Soviet chess hierarchy and its methods, a feeling that was later to grow into a combination of contempt and hatred.

2

HOME-MADE OPENINGS

Chess books should be used as we use glasses – to assist the sight; although some players make use of them as if they thought they conferred sight. CAPABLANCA

Perhaps the most typical characteristic of young chess players is their almost insatiable appetite for learning 'book' opening variations. By knowing in detail the sharpest and latest lines they are assured of a certain number of points simply through the relative ignorance of many of their opponents. Unfortunately, this tendency to rely on a profound understanding and thorough knowledge of the openings that they play, has produced in some Western countries a whole generation of chess 'masters' whose excellent theoretical knowledge obscures a void in areas more fundamental to the art of chess. Commenting on the narrowness of the Soviet team's victory in the 1970 Olympiad, Victor Korchnoy observed: '. . . dozens of chess bulletins, magazines, newspapers and books are being issued in the West and Soviet chess publications are widely distributed abroad. Western chess players are not only better informed than Soviet players but also have an opportunity of constantly improving their knowledge of openings . . .

'. . . What is left is, of course, a great superiority in the understanding of chess, which does not disappear even with growing age. That is why our country has many top rate Grandmasters while other countries have only one or two. That is why we still beat foreign chess masters.'

One of the marks that distinguishes the opening play of the book masters from that of their less artificial colleagues is the desire and ability of the real player to innovate, while the memory banks are content to churn out what they know, rarely producing a theoretical improvement of any great significance. With Fischer this talent for innovation was colossal from the very beginning of his international career. He developed variations that had previously been considered inadequate. He produced innovations of enormous significance (see his game against Botvinnik p.79). He persevered in the quest for theoretical truth even when it brought him repeated disaster.

King's Indian Reversed or King's Indian Attack

Although he was continually enriching his book knowledge young Bobby's mind was by no means infertile or unimaginative. For a year and a half from mid-1956 his favourite opening complex was the King's Indian Reversed (which later became known as the King's Indian Attack). The attraction of the opening was obvious – he was so taken with the flexibility and resilience of the King's Indian Defence that it was most appetizing to have the same set-up with a move in hand. At Oklahoma City in five out of his six games with white Fischer opened in this way. He would play 1 N—KB3, 2 P—KN3, 3 B—N2, 4 O—O, 5 P—Q3, 6 QN—Q2, followed by P—K4 and expansion in the centre or on the Q side. But although his results with this system were generally impressive (the opposition was none too strong), the positions that he obtained from the opening were not. Some examples:

FISCHER–GROSS, US Open Championship 1956
1 N—KB3, N—KB3; 2 P—KN3, P—Q4; 3 B—N2, B—B4; 4 O—O, P—K3; 5 P—Q3, B—B4; 6 QN—Q2, N—B3; 7 P—QR3, P—QR4; 8 Q—K1, B—KN3; 9 P—K4, P×P; 10 N×P, N×N; 11 P×N, O—O. White has no advantage whatsoever. The game was quickly drawn.

FISCHER–POPEL, US Open Championship 1956
1 N—KB3, N—KB3; 2 P—KN3, P—KN3; 3 B—N2, B—N2; 4 O—O, O—O; 5 P—Q3, P—Q3; 6 P—K4, P—B4; 7 QN—Q2, N—B3; 8 P—QR4, P—QR3; 9 N—B4, R—N1; 10 P—R5, B—K3; 11 N(B3)—Q2, P—Q4; 12 P×P, B×P; 13 N—N3, B×B; 14 K×B, N—Q5; 15 N×N, P×N; 16 B—B4, R—B1; 17 B—K5, Q—Q4 ch; 18 Q—B3, Q×Q ch; 19 K×Q, N—Q4. White has some pressure, but not very much. Black had no difficulty in drawing.

A few weeks later he tried a K-side attack for the first time.

FISCHER–FOX, Canadian Open Championship 1956
1 N—KB3, N—KB3; 2 P—KN3, P—Q3; 3 B—N2, P—KN3; 4 O—O, B—N2; 5 P—Q3, O—O; 6 P—K4, P—K4; 7 QN—Q2, P—B3; 8 P—B3, Q—B2; 9 N—R4, P—QR4; 10 P—KB4, QN—Q2; 11 P—B5, N—B4; 12 N—N3, N×N; 13 P×N, N—Q2; 14 P—KN4, R—K1; 15 Q—B3, N—B4; 16 P—B6, B—B1

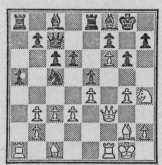

In his efforts for an all-out attack, White has somewhat compromised his position on the Q side and in the centre. There seems to be no way for him to make any further genuine progress with his attack or to take advantage of the dark square weaknesses around Black's king; but Fischer finds a good practical try.

17 N—B5 !, P—Q4 !. 17...P×N; 18 NP×P, N×NP would be much too dangerous for Black: 19 B—K3, N×R; 20 Q—R5, N—B7; 21 B—R6, K—R1; 22 Q—N5 (threatening simply 23 B×B), B×B; 23 Q×B, R—KN1; 24 R—B3, and Black is helpless against the threat of 25 Q×P ch and 26 R—R3 mate. But the text is the start of an excellent defensive plan, opening up the Q file and Black's QR2—KN8 diagonal.

18 Q—N3, P×P; 19 P×P, K—R1; 20 Q—R4, Q—Q1, 20...P×N; 21 NP×P, N×NP loses as before. **21 N—N7.** If the knight retreats, 21...N× NP will lead to an eventual win for Black. 21 R—B3 would have been a better chance, e.g. 21...N×KP; 22 R—KR3, B—B4 ch; 23 B—K3 (not 23 N—K3 ?, Q—Q8 ch; 24 B—B1, Q×KNP ch, forcing the exchange of queens), 23...B×B ch; 24 N×B, N×KBP; 25 R—KB1 (25 R—Q1, B— Q2; 26 R×B, is not so good), 25...K—N2; 26 R(R3)—B3, R—K3; 27 P— N5, N—R4; 28 R×P ch, K—N1; 29 N—N4, with an overwhelming attack. But on 21 R—B3, Black can play 21...P×N; 22 NP×P (if 22 R—R3, Q— Q8 ch; 23 B—B1, Q×KNP ch), 22...Q—Q8 ch; 23 R—B1, Q—K7! (threat 24...N—Q6 followed by ...N—B5); 24 R—K1, Q—QB7; 25 R— K3, N—Q6: 26 R—KR3, B—B4 ch; 27 B—K3, B×B ch; 28 R×B, N—B5, and Black wins. Did Fischer really see all this over the board or did he think that the text was decisive?

21...B×N; 22 P×B ch, K—N1. On 22...K×P; 23 B—N5 is deadly, e.g. 23...Q—N3; 24 B—K3 or 23...Q—Q2; 24 B—B6 ch, K—N1; 25 Q— R6, N—K3; 26 R—B3. **23 Q—B2, Q—K2; 24 B—N5.** Otherwise comes 24...N—K3, consolidating. **24...N—Q6; 25 Q—Q2[1], Q—Q2; 26 QR— N1.** Or 26 QR—Q1, Q×P. **26...Q×P; 27 B—R6, N—B5; 28 B×N, P×B; 29 R×P, Q—R4; 30 QR—KB1, B—K3; 31 Q—KB2, R—K2; 32 P—B4, Q—K4; 33 R—B6, K×P; 34 P—R4 ?** But in any case, a pawn down with nothing to show for it, White was losing. **34...B—B4!; 35 R×B, P×R; 36 P×P, P—B3,** and Black eventually won.

Probably disillusioned by the apparent inadequacies of this home-made opening system, Fischer became generally reluctant to play the Reversed King's Indian against strong opposition (it did appear from time to time in his Swiss system tournament games). But there was one exceptional case. He had noticed that Black's defensive set-up was much less flexible when the second player had included ...P—K3 in his opening moves, and that this move weakened Black's KB3 square, rendering him more vulnerable to an attack on the dark squares. So, from time to time, Fischer employed his King's Indian Attack against the French Defence or after the move sequence 1 P—K4, P—QB4; 2 N—KB3, P—K3, and it is in this form that the system became internationally popular during the mid-1960s.

The earliest example of Fischer playing this kind of attack came in his very first game in a US Championship.

---

[1] Some sources give this move as 25 Q—K3, but then (i) 25...Q—B4 solves all of Black's difficulties and (ii) after the game continuation, 25...Q—Q2, White could win a piece by 26 QR—Q1.

7 FISCHER–FUERSTEIN
US CHAMPIONSHIP 1957/8

King's Indian Attack

1 P—K4, P—QB4; 2 N—KB3, P—K3;
3 P—KN3, N—KB3; 4 P—Q3, P—Q4;
5 QN—Q2, B—K2; 6 B—N2, O—O; 7
O—O, N—B3; 8 R—K1, Q—B2.
For the speedier plan of advancing the
Q-side pawns without first playing in the
centre, see game 51.

9 Q—K2, R—Q1 ?
Unthematic in view of White's next
(inevitable) move, which closes the
centre. Better is 9...B—Q2 or 9...P—
QN4.

10 P—K5, N—K1; 11 P—B3
Depriving Black's QN of the Q5 square
before transferring the Q2 knight to the
K side.

11...P—QN4 at last. 12 N—B1, P—
N5; 13 B—B4, Q—R4 ?
Another time-wasting move. Fischer
suggests 13...P×P; 14 P×P, R—N1.

14 P—B4, N—B2; 15 P—KR4, Q—
N3; 16 P—R5, P—N6; 17 P—R3,
P×P
Possibly 17...N—Q5 would have pro-
duced more counterplay.

18 P×P, B—R3; 19 N(B1)—R2,
QR—B1; 20 P—R6, P—N3

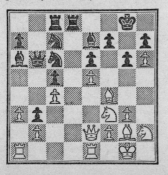

Now White has a clear plan – to take
advantage of the dark-square weaknesses by N—N4, etc. Meanwhile, Black
has absolutely no counterplay. This is a
direct result of his wasted tempi earlier
in the game.

21 B—N5, N—Q5; 22 Q—K3, B×B
The Q5 knight is needed for the defence:
22...N—B7; 23 Q—B4 leaves Black
helpless.

23 Q×B, N—K1
If 23...N—B7, then 24 N—N4!, N×R
(either); 25 N—B6 ch, K—R1; 26 N—
Q7!, winning.

24 N—N4, N—B4; 25 QR—B1, Q—
B2; 26 N—Q2, R—Q5
Otherwise 27 N—K4 and 28 N(K4)—
B6 ch.

27 N×P, R×P; 28 QR—Q1, R—
R5; 29 R—K4!, B—N4
29...R×R; 30 B×R does not reduce
the pressure on Black's K side, because
the subsequent exchange of his B4 knight
highlights Black's dark-square weaknesses.

30 R—QB1, Q—N3; 31 N—Q2
On its way to K4 and KB6.

31...R×R; 32 N×R, B—Q6
There is no adequate defence. Black
cannot hold the dark squares without
exchanging queens (32...Q—Q1), and
thereby losing his QRP.

33 N(N4)—B6 ch, K—R1
If 33...N×N; 34 N×N ch, K—R1; 35
P—KN4, N—Q5; 36 N—K4!, Q—Q1;
37 R×P winning – Fischer.

34 P—KN4, B×N; 35 B×B, N—Q5;
36 N×N, Q—Q1; 37 Q×Q, R×Q;
38 N—Q6, N—K7 ch; 39 K—B1,
N×R; 40 N×P ch, K—N1; 41 N×R,
N—N6; 42 K—K2, N—Q5 ch; 43
K—Q3, K—B1; 44 N—B6, and Black
Resigns

The Reversed King's Indian provided the young master with a useful, amorphous opening weapon. It was sufficiently unanalysed in the books to make it excellent 'rabbit bashing' material for the American Swiss system tournaments which gave Fischer much of his early experience. Yet the opening was sound enough to make it a viable second string against the occasional master (and even Grandmaster). But in top-class competition viability is not enough. To win strong tournaments consistently it is necessary to have a repertoire of openings that have some depth to them; openings that set problems lasting well into the middle game and even later. Fischer's first home-made system just did not fit the bill and so, except for the occasional airing, this system rarely saw the light of day in his games after the end of 1957.

But the same cannot be said of Fischer's other early theoretical contribution.

6 B—QB4 against the Sicilian

Opening variations in master chess tend to follow fashions, swaying in popularity according to the latest spate of games. Someone finds a 'new' move which changes the assessment of a variation and suddenly that variation is seen with less frequency. Those who practised it with a kind of paternal affection try to revive their pet by administering various plausible antidotes (new new moves). If they fail they leave it dying and adopt another variation or a completely different opening. Later, possibly years later, some antidote *is* discovered and the corpse can then safely be resuscitated without any fear of contagion. Thus chess theory evolves along a spiral path, ever richer in its practical background though often showing an old (i.e. new new!) face.

The task of the innovator is perilous and can often be a thankless one. If his new idea is a failure, the rewards for his efforts consist of a zero on the score-board and a mention in some theoretical article with a question mark hung next to his brainchild. Then what? He doesn't give up but finds some improvement for the next time. Perhaps then, or the time after, or the time after that, his idea will be given some credence, but in the interim he will still be suffering the punishment of the zeros. (Of course there are times when a variation is considered good enough for a draw, but if its supporter is the player of the white pieces a draw is, in some way, almost as severe a defeat as an actual loss.)

At the international level almost all Masters and Grandmasters are credited with some of these new moves. But few of them are responsible for reviving whole opening systems. The only example in the 1970s is Larsen's vitalization of 1 P—QN3 which was virtually unheard of before he adopted it. And if there is risk in playing a new move what of testing a whole new system? Larsen is a fearless individual who continued to support 1 P—QN3 even when it brought him absolute disaster. Less than a month after losing with it against Spassky in seventeen moves he repeated the same variation (plus improvement of course) against the same opponent and got a good game.

The principal danger in patronizing a whole new system is that there are so many uncharted variations within it, any of which might be discovered to be rather unpleasant. In this realm Fischer is as fearless as Larsen. If he believes in a move, a variation, or a system, he will continue to play it even though it may cost him dear in points. His stubbornness in this respect will be referred to again more than once in this volume.

6 B—QB4 against the Sicilian was the first Fischer patent which had any big impact on chess theory. Before he championed this move it was almost never tried against the Najdorf Variation, while in its other setting (after 5...N—QB3 instead of Najdorf's 5...P—QR3) the move had met with only slightly more support. [After the move 6 B—QB4 there are some slight transpositional possibilities between the two variations, but such transposition is rare so I shall continue to distinguish between them when discussing 6 B—QB4.]

6 B—QB4 against the Najdorf Variation

The Najdorf Variation of the Sicilian Defence became popular shortly after the Second World War. The attack based on 6 B—QB4 was scarcely seen before 1950 and not analysed until the mid-1950s. Fischer probably first read of the move in Lipnitsky's book *Questions of Modern Chess Theory* (published in Moscow in 1956) to which he refers in his notes to a game with Sherwin from the 1957/8 US Championship.

The Sherwin game opened 1 P—K4, P—QB4; 2 N—KB3, P—Q3; 3 P—Q4, P×P; 4 N×P, N—KB3; 5 N—QB3, P—QR3; 6 B—QB4, P—K3; 7 O—O, P—QN4; 8 B—N3, P—N5, and now Fischer played 9 N—N1 as recommended by Lipnitsky. In his notes he comments: 'Where should the knight go – to R4 or N1 ? I. O. Lipnitsky, in his book *Questions of Modern Chess Theory*, highly recommends the move played. But it seems that after 9...N×P ... Black maintains his extra pawn with a good game. But if 9 N—R4, N×P; 10 B—K3, with a strong attack.' Two years later in a famous debacle against Tal (game 19), Fischer chose 9 N—R4, and quickly reached a tremendous position, only to lose through indecisive play.

Fischer's debut with 6 B—QB4 came in the 1957 US Open Championship at Cleveland. He had started the year with a series of uninspiring results (he even failed to qualify for the Manhattan Club Championship finals). But after winning the US Junior title for the second time (and another portable typewriter) he tied with Bisguier for first place in the 1957 US Open, winning the title on one of those stupid, artificial tie-breaking systems that are too frequently applied even though they prove little or nothing. [With the Sonneborn system for example, a player scores more for beating high-scoring opponents than low ones but he does not suffer a greater penalty for losing to low-scoring opponents than to high-scoring ones. Is this logic?]

Fischer's play at Cleveland was more convincing than before, and he went through the tournament undefeated.

8 FISCHER–WITTE
US OPEN CHAMPIONSHIP 1957

Sicilian Defence

1 P—K4, P—QB4; 2 N—KB3, P—Q3; 3 P—Q4, P×P; 4 N×P, N—KB3; 5 N—QB3, P—QR3; 6 B—QB4, P—K3; 7 O—O, B—Q2 ?

Passive. The bishop belongs on QN2.

8 B—N3, B—K2; 9 B—K3, O—O; 10 P—B4, Q—B2; 11 P—N4 !, K—R1

11...R—Q1; 12 P—N5, N—K1; 13 P—B5 is even more unpleasant for Black because 13...P—K4; 14 N—Q5 costs him a piece.

12 P—N5, N—N1; 13 P—B5, P—K4; 14 N—Q5, Q—Q1; 15 N—KB3, B—QB3

If 15...N—QB3; 16 B—N6, Q—B1; 17 N×B, and 18 Q×P.

16 B—N6, Q—B1; 17 N×B

Much stronger than 17 N—B7, N—Q2; 18 N×R, Q×N, and 19...B×KP.

17...N×N; 18 Q×P, Q—K1

Everything is hopeless.

19 B—B5, P—QN3; 20 P—B6, N—N3

If 20...P×B; 21 P×N, R—N1; 22 N×P, and the roof caves in.

21 P×P ch, K×P; 22 Q—B6 ch, K—N1; 23 B×R, Q×B; 24 QR—Q1, and White won.

In September 1957 Fischer played an eight-game match with Rudolfo Cardoso, Junior Champion of the Philippines, who had come to North America to compete in the World Junior Championship in Toronto. (Fischer could hardly complain that it was Lombardy and not he who had been selected to represent the USA in Toronto – Lombardy was already a recognized master and he won the world title with a 100% score in the finals.)

In three out of his four games with White Fischer opened 1 P—K4 and the Filipino defended with the Najdorf Variation. The first two games transposed to the Sozin Variation, one of them being decided by a direct K-side attack.

9 FISCHER–CARDOSO
SECOND MATCH GAME 1957

Sicilian Defence

1 P—K4, P—QB4; 2 N—KB3, P—Q3; 3 P—Q4, P×P; 4 N×P, N—KB3; 5 N—QB3, P—QR3; 6 B—QB4, P—K3; O—O, B—K2; 8 B—K3, O—O; 9 B—N3, N—B3; 10 P—B4, N—QR4

10...Q—B2; 11 Q—B3, B—Q2, is more solid.

11 Q—B3, Q—B2; 12 P—N4, N×B

If 12...N—B5; 13 P—N5, N—Q2; 14 N—B5 !, P×N; 15 N—Q5, Q—Q1; 16

B×N, with a tremendous game for White. (The sacrificial motifs N—B5 and N—Q5 are always in the air in the Sozin Variation.) On 12...P—QN4; 13 P—N5, N—Q2, White can sacrifice a piece for two pawns and a strong attack: 14 N×KP!, P×N; 15 B×P ch, K—R1; 16 N—Q5, Q—Q1; 17 Q—R5.

13 RP×N, R—N1
Since 13...P—QN4 loses a pawn to 14 N(either)×NP.

14 P—N5, N—Q2; 15 P—B5, N—K4; 16 Q—N3, K—R1
A waste of time because the brunt of White's attack will come along the KR file rather than the KN file. 16...P—N4 was correct, gaining a tempo on the game continuation.

17 N—B3, N×N ch; 18 R×N, P—N4; 19 Q—R4, P×P; 20 P×P, Q—B3; 21 QR—KB1, B—N2; 22 B—Q4, P—N5
If 22...Q×R; 23 R×Q, B×R; 24 Q—R3, B—N2; 25 P—N6, P×P; 26 P×P, P—R3; 27 Q×P ch.

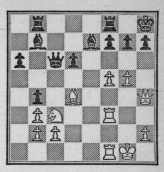

23 B×P ch!, K×B; 24 Q—R6 ch, K—R1; 25 P—N6, Q—B4 ch; 26 R(B1)—B2, P×P; 27 P×P, Q—KN4 ch; 28 Q×Q, B×Q; 29 R×R ch. R×R; 30 R×R ch, K—N2; 31 P×P, Resigns

The second time he faced 6 B—QB4, Cardoso was crushed positionally, but at the third attempt he produced a defence which almost netted him the full point:

FISCHER–CARDOSO, Fifth Match Game 1957, Sicilian Defence
1 P—K4, P—QB4; 2 N—KB3, P—Q3; 3 P—Q4, P×P; 4 N×P, N—KB3; 5 N—QB3, P—QR3; 6 B—QB4, P—K3; 7 O—O, P—QN4; 8 B—N3, B—N2; 9 B—N5, QN—Q2; 10 B×P?!. It was eventually discovered that 10 R—K1 gives White an excellent game. See for example Fischer–Rubinetti (page 143). 10...P×B; 11 N×KP, Q—B1. 11...Q—N3 may be better, e.g. 12 B—K3, Q—B3; 13 N—Q5, R—B1. 12 N×B, R×N; 13 Q×P, Q—B3; 14 QR—Q1, Q×Q; 15 R×Q, O—O—O, and although the game ended in a draw it is very doubtful whether White's pawns counterbalance Black's extra piece. Fischer was obviously dissatisfied with this game for in the last encounter of the match in which he had the white pieces he switched to the King's Indian Reversed (and won again).

Cardoso's troubles with the Najdorf Variation did not, incidentally, arise only when he had the black pieces. In the first game of the match Fischer played the Najdorf and, after 6 B—KN5; 7 P—B4, B—K2; 8 Q—B3, he chose the Gothenburg Variation (8...P—R3; 9 B—R4, P—KN4; 10 P×P, KN—Q2). Cardoso did not play the crucial line that had made the variation infamous in 1955 but we can be fairly sure that against it Fischer already knew the improvement that he put into practice against Gligoric at the Portoroz Interzonal the following year (page 38).

The Sozin Variation

With his penchant for 6 B—QB4 against the Najdorf Sicilian, it is hardly surprising that Fischer was also attracted to the same move in another similar position. After 1 P—K4, P—QB4; 2 N—KB3, P—Q3; 3 P—Q4, P×P; 4 N×P, N—KB3; 5 N—QB3, N—B3, the move 6 B—QB4 introduces what was once known as Leonhardt's Variation, after its German originator, but which Soviet chauvinism renamed after the Leningrad player and theoretician Vyeniamin Sozin. The strategy behind the Sozin is fundamentally the same as in the corresponding line of the Najdorf. White's KB augments his grip on the centre, and bears down on Black's K side where the attack will come. One of the tactical motifs associated with both variations is the possibility of the sacrifice of White's bishop at K6 in return for two or three pawns, and an attack against Black's king, which will be kept in the centre.

Fischer rarely had an opportunity to play the Sozin Variation in his early days. The Najdorf and Dragon Variations were, and still are, the most popular forms of the Sicilian among the dynamic American players. And in the international arena he did not face the defence so often. His reputation as a Sicilian killer and his dogmatic approach to the more subtle problems of the French and Caro-Kann Defences, combined to persuade his opponents that playing the Sicilian against Fischer exhibited certain suicidal tendencies. But more about that later.

What conclusions can be drawn about Fischer's style from the character of these two home-made opening systems? His disillusionment with and rejection of the King's Indian Attack typifies a dislike of the opaque, an aversion for positions that offer flexibility to the opponent and that lack a singular theme. The twin Sicilian Variations are much more clear-cut in their aims – grip the centre then attack on the K side. Not unduly subtle perhaps, but then the Sicilian is not the most subtle of openings. Since the story of Fischer's style is a tale of clarity and directness, it is not surprising that 6 B—QB4 runs right through it.

3

HIS EARLY REPERTOIRE

I have already referred to the narrowness of Fischer's repertoire. In his own country this was not something that could hamper him to any great extent, because he very quickly became much stronger than almost all his rivals and the opening did not, therefore, play such an important part in his games.

But when he started to play abroad he was no great worry for the strongest Grandmasters. It was not in talent that he was lacking but in the fresh approach that is required in the opening phase of each game in a strong tournament. Although he was a clever innovator in his youth and a brilliant and prolific one later in his career, his international naissance already showed some kind of theoretical staleness. He played the same lines again and again, even when they were not wholly successful, thereby making himself an easy opponent for whom to prepare.

I cannot emphasize enough the enormous importance of the openings in top-class international competition. Modern Grandmaster technique is so finely balanced, that without having some advantage from the opening it is only with extreme difficulty or by luck[1] that one of them can overcome another. This is why any study of a Grandmaster's style must necessarily involve a close look at his opening repertoire.

We have already been introduced in some detail to two of Fischer's early opening preferences. In this chapter we examine the full extent of his remaining repertoire at the time when, as a boy of fourteen, he won the US Championship, to earn the title of International Master and to qualify for the 1958 Interzonal. We see, too, the effect of his whole repertoire on his performance at Portoroz, where he narrowly qualified for the 1959 Candidates' Tournament thereby becoming, at fifteen, the youngest Grandmaster in the history of chess.

The Closed Ruy Lopez

For all modern Grandmasters who open 1 P—K4 as White the Ruy Lopez must be the main theoretical weapon. The other symmetrical KP openings have been almost entirely theoretically exhausted and none of them promises White any advantage if his opponent knows his onions. But the 'Spanish Torture' is different. The problems that it poses are more subtle than those of the King's Gambit, more lasting than those of the Giuoco Piano, and rather difficult to solve, even for a Grandmaster. The Closed Ruy Lopez has been played so often in master chess that in their monograph on the opening Wade, Blackstock, and Booth required 256 pages to do it justice, and that for a position arising after White's ninth move!

Fischer adopted the Lopez sporadically during his King's Indian Attack phase. He was not always at home in some of the lesser-known variations (surprising, because he surely studied all the obscure byways), but he showed a remarkable understanding of the intricacies of the Closed Defence.

---

[1] A word usually used in chess in association with a big mistake but possibly also meaning a few smaller ones.

10 FISCHER–RINALDO
US OPEN CHAMPIONSHIP 1957

Ruy Lopez

1 P—K4, P—K4; 2 N—KB3, N—QB3;
3 B—N5, P—QR3; 4 B—R4, N—B3;
5 O—O, B—K2; 6 R—K1, P—QN4; 7
B—N3, P—Q3; 8 P—B3, O—O; 9 P—
KR3, N—QR4; 10 B—B2, P—B4; 11
P—Q4, Q—B2; 12 QN—Q2, B—Q2;
13 N—B1, KR—K1; 14 N—K3.
The older method. Nowadays 14 P—
QN3 is preferred.
   14...P—N3; 15 B—Q2, B—KB1; 16
R—QB1, B—N2?
Correct is 16...N—B3, when 17 N—
Q5, N×N; 18 P×N, can be met by
18...N—R4; 19 P×KP, P×P; 20 P—
QN3, B—N2; 21 P—B4, N—N2.
   17 P—QN4!

The difference. Now Black's QN is
driven from QR4 for good . . .
   17...N—B3; 18 N—Q5!, N×N; 19
P×N, N—K2
. . . so it must retreat to a more passive
square.
   20 QP×BP, N×P
20...P×P, leaves White with a passed
QP.
   21 B—N3, N—B3; 22 P×P, Q×QP;
23 N—N5, R—KB1; 24 B—K3!, Q×
Q; 25 R(K1)×Q, P—R3
Otherwise 26 B—B5.
   26 N—K4, N×N; 27 R×B, QR—B1;
28 P—QB4, N—N4; 29 B×N, P×B;
30 P—B5, Resigns
There is no defence to the plan of P—
B6, P—B7, B—Q5 and B—N7.

The Sicilian Dragon

All modern masters employ the Rauser (Yugoslav) Attack against the
Dragon and the directness of White's attacking plan certainly conforms to
Fischer's taste. But his early experiences against the Dragon were by no
means happy ones. Fischer has never been at ease when his opponent has
had counterchances, and when playing for mate against the Dragon White
must be prepared to put up with some discomfort from Black's Q-side
counter-attack.

11 FISCHER–WARNER
US JUNIOR CHAMPIONSHIP 1955

Sicilian Defence

(Fischer's first recorded game)

1 P—K4, P—QB4; 2 N—KB3, N—
QB3; 3 P—Q4, P×P; 4 N×P, N—B3;
5 N—QB3, P—Q3; 6 B—K2
He hasn't yet adopted 6 B—QB4.

6...P—KN3; 7 B—K3, B—N2; 8
P—B3
Mixing the Classical and Rausre
systems.
   8...O—O; 9 Q—Q2, P—QR3; 10
O—O—O. Q—R4; 11 K—N1, R—
Q1; 12 P—KN4, N×N; 13 B×N,

B—K3; 14 Q—K3?
Unthematic. More natural would be 14
P—KR4 or 14 B×N, B×B; 15 N—
Q5, Q×Q; 16 N×B ch, with a level
ending.
    **14...N—Q2; 15 P—B4, B×B; 16
Q×B, N—B3; 17 P—B5, B—Q2; 18
P—KR4?!**
Better 18 P—N5.
    **18...B—N4!; 19 B—B3, QR—B1;
20 N×B?**
Giving a helping hand to Black's attack

by half-opening the QR file.
    **20...P×N; 21 P—R5, R—B5; 22
Q—K3?**
22 Q—Q3 was essential so as to protect
both the KP and QBP.
    **22...R—R1; 23 P—R3, Q—R5; 24
P—B3, N×KP; 25 B×N, R×B; 26
Q—R6, R—K7; 27 R—Q2??**
If 27 R—QB1, Q—N6. The only chance
was 27 Q—B1.
    **27...R×R; 28 Q×R, Q—K5 ch; 29
Resigns**

This game may have implanted in Fischer's subconscious an exaggerated
fear of the Dragon's flames, for the next time that he faced the defence
(against Mednis in the Rosenwald Tournament) he did not play the strongest
continuation (which involved Q-side castling) when, in the opening, he
could have achieved a clear advantage:

    1 P—K4, P—QB4; 2 N—KB3, P—Q3; 3 P—Q4, P×P; 4 N×P, N—
KB3; 5 N—QB3, P—KN3; 6 B—K3, B—N2; 7 P—B3, O—O; 8 Q—Q2,
B—K3?; 9 N×B, P×N. Now White's best is 10 P—K5, N—K1; 11 P×P,
P×P; 12 O—O—O, when Black's Q-side counterplay is much too slow.
Instead Fischer played 10 B—QB4, Q—B1; 11 B—N3, N—B3; 12 N—K2,
K—R1!; 13 N—B4, P—Q4!; 14 N×KP, Q×N; 15 P×P, N×P; 16 B×N,
Q—K4; 17 B×N, Q×NP!; 18 R—Q1, P×B; 19 B—Q4, B×B; 20 Q×
B ch, Q×Q; 21 R×Q, and the game was eventually drawn.

Over a year later Fischer faced the Dragon again and delayed Q-side
castling until the last possible moment! This paranoid fear of a counter-
attack can be traced all through Fischer's career and it gives rise to the
Soviets' main criticism of his style – that he likes to play 'without an opponent'.

French Defence
Fischer hardly ever met the French before 1959. The probelms that he faced
when playing against the Winawer Variation (he always chose 3 N—QB3
with only one exception) are discussed in chapter 4.

Caro-Kann Defence
This defence, like the French, has caused Fischer many difficulties throughout his career, and it is surprising that more Grandmasters did not choose
it or the French as their regular anti-Fischer weapon. Although he has tested
the whole range of systems against the Caro-Kann, Fischer has yet to find
one that suits him. His earliest choice was the Two Knights Variation, which
he employed until 1959, when he only made an even score with it in the
Candidates' Tournament.
    Fischer's early international encounters with the Caro-Kann almost

certainly suffered from a lack of home experience. In the USA the Caro-Kann has never been a popular defence, and Fischer met it only once (that we know of) before he first played in a tournament abroad.

12

FISCHER–KAMPARS
NORTH WESTERN OPEN CHAMPIONSHIP 1957

Caro-Kann Defence

1 P—K4, P—QB3; 2 N—KB3, P—Q4; 3 N—B3, B—N5; 4 P—KR3, B×N; 5 Q×B, P—K3; 6 P—Q4, N—Q2

6...N—B3 may be more accurate.

7 B—Q3, P×P; 8 N×P, KN—B3; 9 O—O, N×N; 10 Q×N

10 B×N, N—B3; 11 Q—Q3, was played by Gligoric in 1948 without him achieving any advantage from the opening. Fischer's plan guarantees him the advantage of the two bishops but it costs him some tempi.

10...N—B3; 11 Q—K3, N—Q4; 12 Q—B3, Q—B3; 13 Q×Q, N×Q; 14 R—Q1, O—O—O; 15 B—K3, N—Q4; 16 B—KN5, B—K2; 17 B×B, N×B; 18 B—K4, N—Q4; 19 P—KN3, N—B3; 20 B—B3, K—B2; 21 K—B1, KR—K1

White's advantage is so minimal that the draw on move thirty-seven was already virtually assured.

King's Indian Defence

This has always been Fischer's favourite defence to 1 P—Q4 although from time to time he has defended the Queen's Gambit and played the Nimzo-Indian and Grünfeld Defences. His early perseverance with the King's Indian, which was despite some horrible results against strong players, is one of the best examples of Fischer's theoretical stubbornness. From the twenty-five recorded King's Indians that he played prior to the Portoroz Interzonal, he scored 13½ points (54%) compared with a score of over 79% in all his other games as Black. Why this disparity? I believe that the answer lies in Fischer's contempt for 1 P—Q4 as an opening move. (He once wrote 'I have never opened 1 P—Q4 on principle'.) Such an attitude can only be dangerous, because contempt clouds the judgement and leads to irrational decisions over the board.

One of Fischer's particular dislikes is the Sämisch Variation, in which White's fundamental aim is to launch an attack against the black king. Sometimes Black seeks counterplay on the Q side and/or in the centre. Another plan, the one adopted by Fischer in the following game, is for Black to start a quick pawn advance on the K side before White can mount his attack. In either case Black's king often has many anxious moments, and it is probably from this that stems Fischer's antipathy to the Sämisch Variation. He just abhors seeing his king vulnerable to attack.

13 AVRAM–FISCHER

LOG CABIN INDEPENDENT OPEN CHAMPIONSHIP
1957

King's Indian Defence

1 P—Q4, N—KB3; 2 P—QB4, P—KN3; 3 N—QB3, B—N2; 4 P—K4, P—Q3; 5 P—B3, P—K4; 6 P—Q5, N—R4; 7 B—K3, O—O; 8 Q—Q2, P—KB4; 9 O—O—O, P—B5; 10 B—B2, B—B3; 11 KN—K2

More active is 11 Q—K1, preparing for P—KN4 without allowing the reply ...P×P e.p. followed by ...B—N4 ch.

11...B—R5

Unnecessary. Black would do better to commence his Q-side attack by ...P—QR3 and ...P—QN4.

12 B—N1, B—K2; 13 K—N1, N—Q2; 14 N—B1, K—R1?!

Black's strategy here is too slow. He should be attacking on the Q side.

15 N—Q3, P—QR3

At last.

16 Q—QB2?!

White does not understand the position – he is attacking on the wrong flank.

16...R—B2

Better 16...N(2)—B3, followed by ...B—Q2.

17 N—K2, Q—B1; 18 Q—B3, P—KN4

Another unthematic move.

19 P—B5, P×P; 20 P—KR4

20 N×KP ??, N×N; 21 Q×N ch, B—B3, and the queen is trapped.

20...R—N2; 21 P×P, R×P; 22 R×N !?, R×R; 23 N(K2)×P, R—R8; 24 N—K6, Q—B3; 25 B—K3

If 25 N×P(B7), R×B; 26 N×R, B—Q3, followed by ...P—N4 and ...B—N2, winning the knight.

25...B—Q3; 26 N—B2, R—R4; 27 B—K2, N—B1??

Much stronger was 27...P—N4 !, and if 28 P—B4, then P×P !. Now White wins a pawn and Black's position collapses.

28 N×N, B×N; 29 P—B4, R—R7; 30 P×P, Q—N3; 31 B—B3, P—N3; 32 B—B4, R—R5; 33 P—KN3, R—R7; 34 Q—K1, B—R3; 35 P—K6, B×B; 36 P×B, P—KR4; 37 N—Q3, P—R5; 38 Q—B3 ch, Q—N2; 39 N—K5, B—N2; 40 B—R5, R—KN1; 41 P—K7, Q×P; 42 N—N6 dbl ch, K—R2; 43 N×Q, Resigns

Portoroz

The 1957/8 US Championship was also a Zonal Tournament, the official FIDE[1] qualifying event at the first stage of the World Championship cycle. Two Americans qualified for the Interzonal, but Reshevsky, who had been runner-up to Fischer in the US Championship (New York), did not play, and his place was taken by Sherwin. As this was Bobby's first trip to Europe (and he was still only fifteen), his sister went along with him. Lombardy was also there, playing the rôle of Fischer's second.

On the way to Portoroz Bobby and Joan flew to Moscow, where he visited the hallowed rooms of the Central Chess Club and played some blitz games with Petrosian, Vasyukov, and some other top Soviet players. Fourteen years later when Vasyukov was Taimanov's second in the Candidates' match

[1] Fédération International des Échecs.

in Vancouver, he and Fischer reminisced about this friendly blitz contest and even argued about who had won.

After Moscow came a short period of training in Belgrade, where Bobby played a few games with Janosevic and Matulovic, and where he met Gligoric for the first time. Among the Grandmasters Gligoric has always been one of Fischer's best friends. He recalls that as they relaxed one day by the side of the river Sava, Fischer quizzed him about various opening lines. '. . . and I didn't remember them. Probably he thought that I was hiding the lines but I didn't do that. He asked me about the Gothenburg Variation and I didn't remember, so (in the Interzonal) he used that line against me!'

The Interzonal was by far the strongest event in which a fifteen-year-old had ever played. And with twenty rounds it was almost twice as long as the tournaments Fischer was used to at home. The very thought of competing with so many giants would bring trepidation to most young players. And a bad result, even in such company, can produce such a demoralizing effect as to retard the development of a young master by a year or two during his critical, formative period. But none of this worried Bobby. He arrived in Portoroz brimming with confidence, intending to qualify for one of the six places in the Candidates' Tournament by the simple expedient of drawing with the Grandmasters and beating the 'patzers'. And that, with a good slice of luck added, is more or less what he did!

At Portoroz Fischer started with a quiet draw against Neikirch, and a win (from a totally lost position) against Fuster who had played the Sämisch Variation against Bobby's King's Indian Defence. Two rounds later he was again facing the Sämisch, this time in the hands of Benkö who was not quite so obliging about letting Bobby off the hook.

---

14 BENKÖ–FISCHER
INTERZONAL TOURNAMENT, PORTOROZ 1958

King's Indian Defence

1 P—Q4, N—KB3; 2 P—QB4, P—KN3; 3 N—QB3, B—N2; 4 P—K4, P—Q3; 5 P—B3, P—K4; 6 KN—K2, O—O; 7 B—N5

Fuster–Fischer, in an earlier round went 7 B—K3, P—B3; 8 Q—Q2, QN—Q2?! (8. . .P×P; 9 N×P, P—Q4!); 9 P—Q5, P×P; 10 N×P, N×N; 11 Q×N, N—B4?!; 12 O—O—O, with a clear advantage for White.

7. . .P×P

7. . .P—KR3; 8 B—K3, P—B3 is also bad for Black because White's Q—Q2 will come with gain of tempo.

8 N×P, N—B3; 9 N—B2, B—K3; 10 B—K2, P—KR3; 11 B—R4, P—KN4; 12 B—B2, N—K4; 13 N—K3, P—B3; 14 O—O, Q—R4!; 15 Q—Q2!

After 15 Q×P, KR—Q1; 16 Q—R3, Q×Q; 17 P×Q, White's extra pawn is worthless.

15. . .KR—Q1; 16 KR—Q1, P—R3; 17 P—QR4, Q—B2

17. . .Q—N5; 18 N—B2!

18 P—R5, P—B4; 19 P—R4!, Q—

K2; 20 P×P, P×P; 21 N—B5 !,
B×N; 22 P×B, P—N5

How else to save the KNP? 22...N—
R2; 23 N—Q5 is horrible for Black.
23 B—R4, Q—B1; 24 P×P, N(K4)×
NP; 25 B(2)×N, N×B
26 Q—N5 !
Not 26 B×R ?, B—Q5 ch.
26...N—B3; 27 R—Q3, N—R2; 28
Q—N4, P—B3; 29 N—Q5, Q—B2;
30 R—K1, R—K1; 31 R(3)—K3, R—
K4; 32 B—N3, R×R; 33 R×R, R—
K1; 34 R—K6, N—N4; 35 R×QP,
R—K5; 36 R—Q8 ch, K—R2; 37 B—
B4, B—R3; 38 R—Q7!, R—K8 ch;
39 K—B2, N—K5 ch; 40 K×R, Q×
R; 41 Q—N6 ch, Resigns

After this loss to Benkö, Fischer continued his 'draw with the Grand-masters' policy by sharing points with Bronstein and then Averbakh. And then came Larsen, comparatively new to the rank of Grandmaster, who tried his hand at the Dragon Variation. The Dragon, as it happened, was an excellent weapon to try against Fischer for psychological reasons (see page 29), even though it is rather unlikely that the Danish Grandmaster knew of Fischer's previous games against it. But the particular variation chosen by Larsen, although in vogue at the time, was not difficult for Fischer to refute.

15 FISCHER–LARSEN
INTERZONAL TOURNAMENT, PORTOROZ 1958

Sicilian Defence

1 P—K4	P—QB4
2 N—KB3	P—Q3
3 P—Q4	P×P
4 N×P	N—KB3
5 N—QB3	P—KN3
6 B—K3	B—N2
7 P—B3	O—O
8 Q—Q2	N—B3
9 B—QB4	

The modern variation (at that time).
More usual was 9 O—O—O.

9 ... N×N?

In the early days of the system begin-

ning with White's ninth move this exchange was considered Black's safest course. With much hindsight we can now state that 9...N×N? leads to almost certain defeat for Black and that 9...B—Q2 is the correct move. For a detailed discussion of the whole variation the reader is referred to my book *The Sicilian Dragon* (Batsford).

10 B×N	B—K3
11 B—N3	Q—R4
12 O—O—O	P—QN4

12...P—QR3; 13 P—KR4, P—QN4;
14 K—N1, KR—B1; 15 KR—K1 is also very much to White's advantage.

Tal–Portisch, Oberhausen 1961.

13 K—N1　　　　　P—N5

If 13...KR—B1; 14 KR—K1!, B×
B; 15 BP×B, P—N5; 16 B×N!, P×
N; 17 B×BP, B×B; 18 P×B, R×P (or
18...Q×BP; 19 Q×Q, R×Q; 20 R—
QB1); 19 R—K3, R(1)—QB1; 20 R×R,
Q×R; 21 Q×Q, R×Q; 22 R—QB1!,
R×R ch; 23 K×R, White wins the
pawn ending because of his 2:1 Q-side
majority. It is the evaluation of this and
similar endings that has caused 9...N×
N to disappear from master chess.

14 N—Q5　　　　　B×N

15 B×B?!

Correct is 15 P×B!, as Tal played
against Larsen at Zurich 1959, when
White has the advantage of the two
bishops and pressure against Black's
backward KP, e.g. 15...Q—N4; 16
KR—K1, P—QR4; 17 Q—K2!, Q×Q;
18 R×Q, P—R5; 19 B—B4, KR—B1;
20 P—QN3!, with a clear advantage to
White.

15 . . .　　　　　QR—B1?

Surprisingly enough this natural reply
is the losing move. Correct is 15...N×
B; 16 B×B (Fischer had intended 16
P×N, Q×QP; 17 Q×P, which cannot
be dangerous for Black), 16...N—B6
ch!; 17 B×N, P×B; 18 Q×BP, Q×Q;
19 P×Q, KR—B1, when White's advantage is minimal.

16 B—N3　　　　　R—B2

17 P—KR4　　　　Q—QN4

18 P—R5!　　　　KR—B1

If 18...N×RP?; 19 B×B, K×B;
20 P—N4, N—B3; 21 Q—R6 ch, K—
N1; 22 P—N5, N—R4; 23 R×N, P×R;
24 P—N6, P×P; 25 Q×P ch, winning.
And on 18...P—R4 comes 19 P×P,
P×P; 20 B×N, P×B (or 20...B×B;
21 Q—R6); 21 Q×QP.

19 P×P　　　　　P×P

20 P—N4　　　　P—R4

21 P—N5

Not 21 B×N, B×B; 22 Q—R6, P—
K3, and Black can continue with...Q—
K4.

21 . . .　　　　　N—R4

If 21...N—K1, as recommended by
Vasyukov, 22 B×B, N×B; 23 R—R6!
and there is a mating attack along the
KR file.

22 R×N!　　　　　P×R

No better is 22...B×B; 23 Q×B,
P×R; 24 P—N6, P—K3; 25 Q×QP.

23 P—N6　　　　　P—K4

24 P×P ch　　　　K—B1

25 B—K3　　　　　P—Q4

The threat was 26 Q×QP ch.

26 P×P　　　　　R×KBP

27 P—Q6　　　　R—KB3

28 B—N5　　　　　Q—N2

29 B×R　　　　　B×B

30 P—Q7　　　　　R—Q1

31 Q—Q6 ch

In fact 31 Q—R6 ch leads to mate in
three, but the text is quite sufficient:
31...K—N2; 32 R—N1 ch, etc. So...

31 . . .　　　　　Resigns

So Fischer had scored a psychological triumph, winning with almost
consumate ease against the Dragon. But his theoretical armoury was still to
be subjected to further tests. Against Olafsson, three rounds later, Fischer
tried the Queen's Gambit Declined for the first time in his career, doubtless
disillusioned (temporarily) with the King's Indian. The result of this
experiment – disaster.

16 OLAFSSON–FISCHER
INTERZONAL TOURNAMENT, PORTOROZ 1958

Queen's Gambit Declined

1 P—QB4	N—KB3
2 N—QB3	P—K3
3 N—B3	P—Q4
4 P—Q4	B—N5
5 P×P	P×P
6 B—N5	P—KR3
7 B—R4	P—B4
8 P—K3	N—B3
9 R—B1	

Inferior alternatives are (i) 9 B—QN5, Q—R4; 10 B×QN ch, P×B; 11 B×N, B×N ch; 12 P×B, Q×BP ch; 13 N—Q2, P×B; 14 R—QB1, Q—Q6, with chances for both sides. Portisch–Fischer, Bled 1961; and (ii) 9 B—K2, P—KN4; 10 B—N3, N—K5; 11 R—QB1, Q—R4, with the more active position for Black. Bazan–Fischer, Mar del Plata 1960.

9 . . .   P—B5

Not new and not good. Black should play more actively with 9...P—KN4; 10 B—N3, Q—R4; 11 N—Q2 (11 B—K2, N—K5 transposes to Bazan–Fischer), 11...B—K3; 12 P×P, P—Q5; 13 P×P, O—O—O, with active piece play compensating for the sacrificed pawns. Bletchzin–Usov, Leningrad 1961.

10 B—K2	B—K3
11 O—O	O—O
12 N—Q2	B—K2

This is Fischer's improvement on the game Stahlberg–Filip, Helsinki Olympiad 1952 which went: 12...P—R3; 13 P—B4, N—K2; 14 P—N4!, with a strong K-side attack.

13 P—QN3 ?!

Fischer had expected his opponent to continue in the same vein as Stahlberg, i.e. with 13 P—B4, when he had intended 13...N—Q2; 14 B×B, Q×B; 15 P—KN4, P—B4.

13 . . .   P—KN4 ?

Bad timing. He should play 13.∴.B—

QR6!, and if 14 R—N1 then 14...P—KN4; 15 B—N3, Q—R4 (16 Q—B2, N—QN5); or if 14 R—B2, then 14...N—QN5; 15 P×P, N×R; 16 Q×N, B—K2, when White has insufficient compensation for the exchange.

The text exposes Black's king so much, as to provide White with the necessary compensation for the material that he sacrifices.

14 B—N3	B—R6
15 R—B2 !	N—QN5
16 P×P	N×R
17 Q×N	P×P
18 N—N5	B—QN5
19 N—B7	

Also good is 19 N×BP.

19 . . .	B×N
20 N×B	P×N

21 B×P !

A strong zwischenzug. If now 21...B—N5, then 22 Q—N6 ch, K—R1; 23 Q×RP ch, N—R2 (or 23...K—N1; 24 B×P ch, R—B2; 25 Q—N6 ch); 24 B—K5 ch, R—B3; 25 B—Q3, Q—K2; 26 B×R ch, Q×B; 27 Q×N mate.

21 . . .   Q—K1

If 21...Q—B1, then 22 Q—N6 ch, K—R1; 23 Q×RP ch, K—N1; 24 B—N3, K—B2!; 25 B—K5, Q—Q1; 26

R—Q1, B—N5; 27 P—Q5, P×P; 28
P—B4 !

22 Q×B	N—K5 !
23 Q—Q3	N×B
24 RP×N	R—B3
25 Q—K4	

White's play on the light squares
amply compensates for his slight
material deficit.

25 . . .	R—QB1
26 B—N3	Q—Q2
27 R—Q1	R—K1
28 P—B4 ?!	

Stronger was 28 Q—K5. After the
text Black is allowed time to improve the
position of his queen.

| 28 . . . | Q—R2 ! |
| 29 Q—K5 | |

Also possible was 29 Q—B3.

| 29 . . . | Q—B4 |
| 30 P—N4 | |

Not 30 Q—Q6, because of 30...Q—
K5 with counterplay.

30 . . .	Q×Q
31 QP×Q	R—B2
32 P—B5	

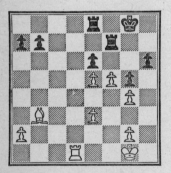

| 32 . . . | R—B2 |

A better defence was 32...K—B1 !,
e.g. 33 P—K4, R—B2, or 33 R—Q6,
P×P; 34 B×R, K×B; 35 R—B6 ch,
K—N2; 36 R×BP, P—N4; 37 K—B2,
P—N5; 38 K—B3, P—QR4; 39 K—
K4, P—R5, with fair drawing chances
in the rook ending. But not 32...P×P ??

at once, because of 33 R—Q7, R—KB1;
34 R×P, K—N2; 35 R×R ch, R×R;
36 B×R, K×R; 37 P×P, winning
easily.

| 33 R—Q6 | R—B4 ! |

If 33...R—B3; 34 B×P ch (not 34
B—R4, P×P), 34...K—B1; 35 K—B2,
R×R; 36 P×R, R—Q1; 37 P—Q7, K—
K2; 38 K—B3, P—N4; 39 K—K4, K—
Q3; 40 K—Q4, and White wins by advancing his KP to K5 and then infiltra-
ting with his king either to Q5 if Black
retreats...K—K2, or to KB5 if Black
plays...K—QB3.

If 34...R(1)×B, then 35 R×R(K6),
R×R; 36 P×R, K—B1; 37 K—B2, K—
K2; 38 K—B3, K×P; 39 K—K4, with
a won pawn ending.

34 B×P ch	K—B1
35 B—N3	R(B4)×P
36 R×P	R×KP
37 R—KN6 ?	

Correct was 37 R—KB6 ch, K—K2;
38 R—KN6, because now Black has a
drawing resource at his disposal.

| 37 . . . | R(1)—K5 ? |

Missing 37...R×B; 38 P×R, R—
K5; 39 R×P, R—N5; 40 P—B6, K—
B2; 41 R—KB5, R×KNP; 42 R—B3,
P—R4, drawing.

| 38 R×P ? | |

Once again allowing the sacrifice
mentioned in the last note. The correct
procedure is 38 R—N8 ch, K—K2; 39
R×P, R×B (or 39...R—N6; 40 R—
N7 ch, K—B3; 41 R—N6 ch, K—K4;
42 B—Q1); 40 P×R, R—N5, and now
White has the important move 41 R—
N7 ch (compare the previous note),
which speeds up the advance of his
pawns.

38 . . .	R—N6 ?
39 R—N8 ch	K—K2
40 P—N5	R—K7
41 B—Q5	K—Q3
42 B—B3	R×RP
43 P—B6	K—K3
44 R—K8 ch	Resigns

If 44...K—B2; 45 B—R5 mate.

This unfortunate loss can largely be attributed to Fischer's choice of defence. In playing the QGD he was challenging his opponent on a battle-field well trodden by Olafsson but never experienced by himself. After destroying a fine position by an impetuous thrust (13...P—KN4?), Fischer needed to play with great accuracy to save the game but he later compounded his error through a lack of endgame technique. Despite its mistakes, however, this was a most interesting encounter.

The Portoroz tournament was dominated throughout by Mikhail Tal, the brilliant twenty-two-year-old Latvian, who two years later was to wrest Botvinnik's World Championship title away from him. With the black pieces Tal could normally be expected to play the Sicilian against 1 P—K4, but when he came to play Fischer in round twelve Tal had evidently decided to play it safe and not to give the 'Sicilian killer' the type of position he handled best. The opening was a Ruy Lopez and rather a dull one. Fischer had a little pressure but nothing to speak of, and Tal had no real difficulty in steering the game to a draw.

The narrowness of Fischer's qualification at Portoroz can be judged from the events of the penultimate round. Fischer was drawn to play Cardoso whom he had crushed so convincingly a year earlier. Fischer had White, and Cardoso played the Caro-Kann so, naturally enough, Fischer adopted his pet Two Knights Variation.

---

17 FISCHER–CARDOSO
INTERZONAL TOURNAMENT, PORTOROZ 1958

Caro-Kann Defence

1 P—K4, P—QB3; 2 N—QB3, P—Q4; 3 N—B3, P×P; 4 N×P, B—N5; 5 P—KR3, B×N; 6 Q×B, N—Q2
An interesting pawn sacrifice. The normal move is 6...P—K3.

7 N—N5
Stronger is 7 P—Q4 or 7 B—QB4.

7...KN—B3; 8 Q—QN3?
Correct is 8 P—Q4.

8...P—K3; 9 Q×NP, N—Q4
Black has ample compensation for the pawn. If now 10 P—Q4, N—N5; 11 B—Q3, R—QN1; 12 Q×RP, R—R1, with a draw by repetition.

10 N—K4, N—N5; 11 K—Q1, P—KB4; 12 P—QB3, R—QN1
A tempting alternative was 12...P×N; 13 P×N, N—K4; 14 P—N5, B—K2;

15 P×P, O—O; 16 P—B7, Q—Q5, e.g. 17 B—R6, B—Q3, or 17 P—B8(Q), QR×Q; 18 Q×B, QR—Q1; 19 Q×KP ch, K—R1, followed by ...R×P.
    13 Q×RP, P×N; 14 P×N

14...B×P?
14...R×P, followed by 15...B—B4, gives Black a very strong attack because his rook can quickly come into play on the Q file, e.g. (14...R×P); 15 P—QN3, B—B4; 16 Q—R6, R—Q5; 17 Q×P, O—O; 18 Q×Pch, K—R1, and

Black's whole army is active. Now, the pendulum begins to swing the other way.
15 Q—Q4, O—O; 16 B—B4, N—B4; 17 Q×Q, R(N1)×Q; 18 R—B1, R—Q5; 19 P—QN3, B×P; 20 K—K2, B×B; 21 QR×B, and White eventually won.

Had Cardoso made the most of his opportunities in this game Fischer would not have finished in the first six places, and the Grandmaster title would not yet have been his. Just to prove that reaching a good position against Fischer was no fluke, the Filipino annihilated Bronstein in the final round, pushing the Soviet Grandmaster out of the group of qualifiers.

When the last round started it was clear that a draw would assure Fischer of at least a tie for one of the places in the Candidates' Tournament. Most experienced players would play safe under these circumstances, especially in view of the fact that Fischer's last round opponent, Gligoric, needed only a draw to be absolutely certain of qualifying. But caution has never been the hallmark of Fischer's play. With the black pieces he chose the infamous Gothenburg Variation about which he had quizzed Gligoric a few weeks earlier.

18 GLIGORIC–FISCHER
INTERZONAL TOURNAMENT, PORTOROZ 1958

Sicilian Defence

1 P—K4	P—QB4
2 N—KB3	P—Q3
3 P—Q4	P×P
4 N×P	N—KB3
5 N—QB3	P—QR3
6 B—KN5	P—K3
7 P—B4	B—K2
8 Q—B3	P—R3
9 B—R4	P—KN4

The Gothenburg Variation first appeared one fateful day in 1955 when three Argentinians were drawn to play the black pieces against three Russians at the Gothenburg Interzonal. All three games opened in the same way. The Argentinians had prepared this variation as a surprise weapon but all three were annihilated with uniform ease. After

that triple disaster the variation was naturally not at all popular, yet Fischer had such great faith in an improvement suggested by Keres that he was willing to test this ultra sharp line in such a crucial game.
10 P×P   KN—Q2
After 10...P×P; 11 B×NP, QN—Q2; 12 B—Q3, N—K4; 13 Q—K2, White has a sound extra pawn and the better position. Ragozin–Pilnik, Czechoslovakia 1956.
11 N×P   P×N
12 Q—R5 ch   K—B1
13 B—N5 !
The most active square for the bishop. A game Khasin–Nikitin, semi-final 26th USSR Championship, went instead 13 B—B4, N—K4; 14 N—Q5, P×N; 15 O—O ch, K—N2; 16 B—KN3, QN—

B3; 17 B×QP, P×P; 18 R—B7 ch, N×
R; 19 Q×N ch, K—R3; 20 P—KR4,
R—B1; 21 P×P ch, B×P; 22 Resigns.

13 . . .   R—KR2 !

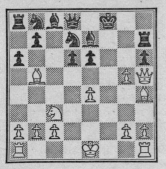

A strong defensive move (suggested
by Keres) which simultaneously activates Black's rook and prepares to
shield his king. In the Gothenburg
trilogy Panno played 13...N—K4
against Geller and lost quickly after 14
B—N3, B×P? (14...R—KR2 is still
probably adequate for a draw); 15
O—O ch, K—K2; 16 B×N, Q—N3 ch;
17 K—R1, QP×B; 18 Q—B7 ch.
Najdorf (against Keres) and Pilnik
(against Spassky) both tried 13...K—
N2 ?; 14 O—O; N—K4; 15 B—N3,
N—N3; 16 P×P ch, R×P, and they
too were crushed by White's attack.

Although the text move was suggested
in the bulletins of the Gothenburg
Interzonal, its invention has frequently
been incorrectly attributed to Fischer.

14 Q—N6 ?

Already a mistake. Best was the
natural continuation 14 O—O ch. Keres
then analyses 14...K—N1; 15 P—N6,
R—N2; 16 R—B7, B×B; 17 Q×P;
R×R; 18 P×R ch, K×P, and now
White should take the draw by 19 R—
KB1 ch, B—B3; 20 Q—R7 ch, K—K1;
21 Q—N8 ch, etc.

14 . . .   R—B2
15 Q×RP ch   K—N1
16 Q—N6 ch

After 16 P—N6 ?, B×B ch; 17 P—
N3, R—N2; 18 P×B, P×B, White has
nothing to show for the two pieces.

16 . . .   R—N2
17 Q×P ch   K—R1

At last Black's king is safe and he is
ready to unravel his Q side so as to make
use of his extra piece. White still has
some play but his four pawns are not
well situated to provide compensation.

18 B×N

On other bishop moves 18...N—K4
or 18...N—N3 will be strong.

18 . . .   N×B
19 O—O—O   N—K4
20 Q—Q5   B—N5

Now Black has a strong initiative.

21 QR—B1

If 21 R—Q2 ?, R—KR2 !

21 . . .   B×P ch?

Relinquishing his initiative. 21...R—
B1 maintains the tension, and sets up
pressure on another front.

22 B×B   Q×B ch
23 K—N1   Q—K2
24 Q—Q2   B—K3

Preventing N—Q5.

25 P—KN3   R—Q1
26 R—B4   Q—N4
27 Q—B2   K—N1
28 R—Q1   R—KB2
29 P—N3   Q—K2
30 Q—Q4   N—N3
31 R×R   Q×R
32 Q—K3   Draw agreed

And so at fifteen, Fischer had become the youngest ever Grandmaster.

4

WORLD CHAMPIONSHIP CANDIDATE

Among the unique aspects of Fischer's performance at Portoroz was the fact that he had had no previous international experience. Obviously it was vital for the fifteen-year-old schoolboy to grab every opportunity of meeting strong international players before he returned to Yugoslavia in the autumn of 1959. But because he was a schoolboy the first (and probably best) testing ground was denied him – he was unable to play in the Munich Olympiad because of his classes at Erasmus High School.

Winning his second US Championship title was no great effort, nor did it really help Bobby to develop his talent. His first two competitions in 1959 were also of little practical use. In a weak Mar del Plata tournament he tied for third place, and at an even weaker event in Santiago de Chile he shared fourth to sixth places, finishing ahead of a group of inferior South American players. (One of them, an unknown named Carlos Jauregui, beat Fischer using the Sämisch Variation against the King's Indian and then vanished back into obscurity much as Munoz did after his equally surprising win in the 1960 Olympiad [see page 59].)

The best lesson that Fischer was taught during his first visit to South America was on the subject of the Winawer Variation. His teacher in this instance was Ivkov, one of the co-winners of the Santiago tournament. Fischer, as White, played weakly in the opening, leaving his king without a safe place to hide. He then further compromised his king position by advancing his KNP and KRP in an attempt to create play where there was none, finally being forced into sacrificing a pawn for nothing to prevent Black from exploding the centre in front of White's king.

For most of his career the Winawer Variation has caused Fischer discomfort whenever he faced it. Part of the reason is probably his disbelief in its viability: 'I may yet be forced to admit that the Winawer is sound. But I doubt it!' But we may be sure that the principal cause lies in the counterattacking nature of the defence. Just as Fischer disliked playing against the Sicilian Dragon and the Sämisch King's Indian, so he would be averse to any opening variation that gave his opponent attacking chances. Eventually, this conflict of antipathy versus disbelief was to be resolved through perseverance in favour of Fischer's own judgement rather than his fears. Those who dared to employ the Dragon against him after the early 1960s did so only at the cost of a point. And as he showed in the first game of his match with Larsen (see page 147), he is now adequately equipped to deal with the problems of the Winawer Variation. But before he became the Winawer's master, Fischer was to lose many points to the defence. Examining his record against the Winawer we find that from fifteen games against opponents of master strength Fischer scored nine points (60%), well below his average score with White against master players and only slightly above the 57% to 43% average lead that White holds over Black in international competition.

Only a fortnight after the Santiago tournament Fischer competed at Zurich, where he tied with Keres behind Tal and Gligoric in a strong field of sixteen. His play at Zurich was generally of a higher calibre than had been seen at Portoroz, and in his wins over Keres and Unzicker (both were Closed Ruy Lopez) he demonstrated the technique of a super-Grandmaster.

The 1959 Candidates' Tournament

I doubt that Fischer honestly believed that he could win the Candidates' Tournament at his first attempt, even though Tal later ridiculed Fischer for being just so optimistic. 'Fischer, at the outset, dreamed of becoming champion of the world. But he would have had better chances in playing, first, for the Junior Championship.' His failure to win at Portoroz, at Mar del Plata, at Santiago, and at Zurich, must surely have made him realize the hopelessness of his task in Yugoslavia. But perhaps not. The tales of how he cried after losing a game and how Larsen, his second, read him stories from a Tarzan book, amply reflect his immaturity at that age. Possibly he *was* just sufficiently naïve to expect that he could succeed in a field that included four top Soviet players.

The tournament was different from anything that Bobby had played in before. Instead of there being a number of comparative rabbits in the field there were eight strong Grandmasters and no other players. Each of the eight met each other four times, twice with each colour. The winner of this twenty-eight round marathon would earn the right to challenge Botvinnik. In 1956 and 1959 no one objected to this system of qualification, but three years later it was a different story (see page 75).

Fischer's performance in Yugoslavia can hardly be called bad by most standards, but it was certainly much worse than he had expected. There were three main reasons for his 'failure.' His disastrous score against the Soviet players in general (five out of sixteen), and against Tal in particular (four losses); his inability to score heavily against the non-Soviets; and his rigid opening repertoire, in particular his inflexible attitude to the Caro-Kann Defence. In short, he was neither strong enough nor sufficiently well prepared (in an all-round sense), to be able to shine among the world's very strongest players.

The best illustration of the extent to which he was outclassed is the quartet of games which he lost to Tal. After the tournament Fischer complained to Gligoric that he had reached a winning position in every one of these games, a false claim if ever there was one. In fact Fischer did not hold the advantage at any stage in their first three encounters. In the fourth game he came very close to victory but even then it passed him by, and he overplayed his hand.

19 FISCHER–TAL
CANDIDATES' TOURNAMENT, BELGRADE 1959

Sicilian Defence

1 P—K4	P—QB4
2 N—KB3	P—Q3
3 P—Q4	P×P
4 N×P	N—KB3
5 N—QB3	P—QR3
6 B—QB4	

What else?

6 . . .	P—K3
7 B—N3	P—QN4

In an earlier round Tal had played 7...B—K2; 8 P—B4, O—O against Fischer, and after 9 Q—B3, Q—B2; 10 O—O, P—QN4; 11 P—B5, P—N5!, Black had seized the initiative. Tal most probably chose the text move because he was afraid of 10 P—N4 or 10 P—B5.

8 P—B4

For 8 O—O, see the game Fischer–Rubinetti (page 143).

8 . . .   P—N5 ?!

Fischer got such a fine position in this game that this win of a pawn has hardly ever been seen again in master chess. The normal continuation is 8...B—N2; 9 P—B5, P—K4; 10 N(Q4)—K2, QN—Q2; 11 B—N5, B—K2; 12 N—N3, P—KR4!, with roughly equal chances.

9 N—R4

Not 9 P—K5?, P×P; 10 P×P, P×N; 11 P×N, Q×P; 12 P×P, Q—R5 ch, with a good game for Black.

9 . . .   N×P

Less risky is 9...B—N2.

10 O—O   P—N3!

Other possibilities are: (i) 10...N—KB3; 11 Q—B3, P—Q4; 12 P—B5!, P—K4; 13 R—K1, P—K5; 14 Q—N3!; (ii) 10...B—N2; 11 B×P!, P×B; 12 N×P, Q—K2; 13 P—B5; (iii) 10...B—K2; 11 P—B5, P—K4; 12 B—Q5; and (iv) 10...P—Q4; 11 P—B5, R—R2 (not 11...B—Q3; 12 P×P, P×P; 13 Q—N4!); 12 B—K3, B—Q3; 13 Q—N4,

N—KB3; 14 Q×P, R—N1; 15 Q—R6, P—K4; 16 N—K6, P×N; 17 B×R, P×P; 18 N—N6!. All seem to be horribly bad for Black.

At the time it was thought that the text was a mistake but in view of more recent history it is probably Black's best chance.

11 P—B5!   NP×P
12 N×BP!

12 . . .   R—N1

Szeles–Sax, Hungary 1972 went 12...B—QN2; 13 N—R6, B×N; 14 Q—R5!, Q—K2; 15 B×B, R—N1 (threatening 16...R×P ch; 17 K×R, N—B3 dis ch); 16 P—N3, N—Q2; 17 QR—K1, with a strong attack, but White eventually lost.

12...P×N? would naturally be wrong on account of 13 Q—Q5, R—R2; 14 Q—Q4, forking both rooks. But Fischer gives 12...P—Q4; 13 N—R6, B×N, as a better defence than the text.

13 B—Q5

Possibly better was 13 Q—R5, N—KB3; 14 Q—B3, R—R2; 15 N—N3, and 16 B—K3.

13 . . .   R—R2

Not 13...P×B; 14 Q×P, B×N (14...R—R2??; 15 Q×N ch, and the rook cannot play to K2); 15 R×B, R—

R2; 16 Q×N ch, R—K2; 17 Q×P, R—K7; 18 B—N5 !, R×B; 19 R×R, Q×R; 20 Q×N ch, Q—Q1; 21 Q× Q ch, K×Q; 22 P—B4, and White wins the ending with his extra pawn.

14 B×N?

Correct is 14 B—K3 !, e.g. 14...N— B4; 15 Q—R5 !, R—N3; 16 QR—K1 !, with a terrific attack – Kevitz.

14 ... P×N
15 B×P

Probably too slow. Stronger was 15 B—Q5, followed by B—K3 and Q—R5 with tremendous pressure. But not 15 B—K3, R—K2; 16 B—N6, Q—Q2; 17 B×P, because of 17...Q×N; 18 B×B, Q—B3 !, winning a piece because of the mate threat.

15 ... R—K2 !

The key to Black's defence.

16 B×B Q×B
17 B—B4

Also possible was 17 R—B2 (guarding KN2 and blocking the KN1—QR7 diagonal) and if 17...Q—B3; 18 P—B3.

17 ... Q—B3
18 Q—B3 Q×N

After 18...Q×Q; 19 R×Q, R—K7; 20 R—B2, the ending is very good for White.

19 B×P Q—B3 !
20 B×N Q—N3 ch
21 K—R1 Q×B

22 Q—QB6 ch?

22 QR—K1 ! is undoubtedly correct, e.g. 22...K—Q2 (or Q1); 23 R— Q1 ch, K—B2; 24 Q—B4 ch, K—N2;

25 R—Q6 !, Q—B2 (25...Q—B1 ?; 26 Q×NP ch, K—R1 – so far this analysis is by Vukovic – 27 Q—R5 ! and Black is helpless against the double threat of 28 R—Q8 and 28 R×P ch, e.g. 27... K—N2; 28 Q—N6 ch, followed by 29 R—Q8. The move 27 Q—R5 ! was dreamed up by Haygarth during a sleepless night on a cross-Channel ferry!); 26 Q×P ch, K—B1; 27 R× RP, Q—N2 drawing – Fischer.

Inadequate defensive tries are (22 QR—K1) R×R; 23 Q×P ch and 24 R×R; 22...R—N2; 23 Q—B6 ch; and 22...R—N3 ?; 23 Q×P ch, K—Q2; 24 R—Q1 (not 24 Q×P, R—Q3, when Black can defend), 24...R—Q3; 25 R×R ch, K×R; 26 R—B6 ch, winning – Fischer.

After the text it is White who must fight to save himself.

22 ... R—Q2
23 QR—K1 ch

If 23 QR—Q1, then Q—B2; 24 KR— K1 ch, B—K2; 25 Q—R8 ch, R—Q1.

23 ... B—K2
24 R×P

Or 24 R—Q1, Q—B2; 25 Q—R8 ch, Q—Q1; 26 Q—B3, R—N3 !, and Black wins.

24 ... K×R
25 Q—K6 ch

If 25 Q×R, then Q—Q3.

25 ... K—B1
26 Q×R(Q7)

After 26 R—KB1 ch, K—N2; 27 R— B7 ch, K—R1; 28 Q×R, R—Q1 !; 29 R×P ch (or 29 Q—N4, Q—K4), 29... K×R; 30 Q×B ch, K—N3, and there is no draw.

26 ... Q—Q3
27 Q—N7 R—N3
28 P—B3 P—QR4
29 Q—B8 ch K—N2
30 Q—B4 B—Q1 !
31 P×P P×P
32 P—KN3 ?

After 32 P—QR3, Black can force the exchange of queens by 32...Q—Q7, since 33 R—KN1 (33 Q—Q2 is the only move) loses to 33...B—N3.

Correct is 32 Q—K4, with a probable

draw. Remember that once Black has exchanged his QNP all endings will be drawn because the bishop controls the wrong colour squares for the KRP.

32 . . .	Q—QB3 ch
33 R—K4	Q×Q
34 R×Q	R—N3 !

34. . .B—K2 only draws after 35 R—B7, K—B2; 36 R—N7 and 37 P—QR3.

35 K—N2	K—B3
36 K—B3	K—K4
37 K—K3	B—N4 ch
38 K—K2	K—Q4

| 39 K—Q3 | B—B3 |
| 40 R—B2 ? | |

40 P—N3 was the only hope.

| 40 . . . | B—K4 |
| 41 R—K2 | |

The sealed move. White is quite lost.
41. . .R—KB3; 42 R—QB2, R—B6 ch; 43 K—K2, R—B2; 44 K—Q3, B—Q5 !; 45 P—QR3, P—N6; 46 R—B8, B×P; 47 R—Q8 ch, K—B3; 48 R—QN8, R—B6 ch; 49 K—B4, R—B6 ch; 50 K—N4, B—R8; 51 P—QR4, P—N7 !; 52 Resigns

The other Soviet players were not quite so convincing against Fischer, but they still made a fairly hefty plus score, helped largely by good results on the black side of the Two Knights Variation of the Caro-Kann Defence. Between them they scored two wins and three draws in this variation.

20 FISCHER–PETROSIAN
CANDIDATES' TOURNAMENT, BLED 1959

Caro-Kann Defence

1 P—K4, P—QB3; 2 N—QB3, P—Q4; 3 N—B3, B—N5; 4 P—KR3, B×N; 5 Q×B, N—B3; 6 P—Q3, P—K3; 7 P—KN3, B—N5; 8 B—Q2, P—Q5
Another equalizing method is Pachman's suggestion 8. . .Q—N3 (now 9. . .P—Q5 is a real threat); 9 O—O—O, P—Q5; 10 N—K2, B×B ch; 11 R×B, QN—Q2.
9 N—N1, B×B ch
For 9. . .Q—N3 see the next game.
10 N×B, P—K4; 11 B—N2, P—B4; 12 O—O, N—B3; 13 Q—K2, P—KN4 ?!
Petrosian was probably afraid of 13. . .O—O; 14 P—KB4, but after 14. . .P×P; 15 P×P, R—K1, Black does not have a bad game.
14 N—B3 ?!
White could have obtained a dangerous initiative by 14 P—KB4, NP×P; 15 P×P, Q—K2; 16 N—B4, N—Q2; 17

Q—N4. Fischer's plan is less aggressive.
14. . .P—KR3; 15 P—KR4 !, R—KN1
On 15. . .P—N5; 16 N—R2, P—KR4; 17 P—B3, White has an attack brewing in the KB file.
16 P—R3, Q—K2; 17 P×P, P×P; 18 Q—Q2, N—Q2; 19 P—B3, O—O—O; 20 P×P, KP×P !
The K4 square will be useful for Black's knights. 20. . .BP×P; 21 P—QN4, Q—B3; 22 KR—B1, K—N1, would be marginally better for White.
21 P—QN4 !, K—N1; 22 KR—B1
Although White seems to have the more dangerous attacking prospects his position is slightly inferior because of the inactivity of his minor pieces. His bishop in particular can play no useful part in the attack.
22. . .N(B3)—K4
Not 22. . .P×P ?; 23 P×P, Q×P; 24 Q—R2 (threatening 25 R×N).

23 N×N, Q×N; **24** R—B4, R—QB1; **25** QR—QB1

25 R—N1 is only strong if Black replies 25...P—N5; 26 P×P, N×P; 27 Q—N4, with an excellent game for White. But on 25...R—B2 ! Black's Q side is held together, and White's R—N1 is a wasted move.

25...P—N5; 26 Q—N2, R(N1)—Q1; 27 P—R4 ?

A weak move. Correct was 27 B—B1, followed by B—K2, activating White's bishop and protecting his QP which soon comes under attack. From now on Petrosian takes complete control.

27...Q—K2 !

After this simple move White's QP and QNP both come under pressure.

28 R—N1

If 28 P×P, N—K4 !; 29 R×P, N×P. 28 R—Q1 would keep the material equilibrium, but at the cost of getting a passive position: 28...N—K4; 29 R×

BP, R×R; 30 P×R, Q×P, and Black has a big advantage.

28...N—K4; 29 R×BP, R×R; **30** P×R, N×P; **31** Q—Q2, N×QBP; **32** Q—B4 ch, Q—B2; **33** Q×NP, N×RP; **34** P—K5, N—B4; **35** Q—B3, P—Q6 !; **36** Q—K3, P—Q7; **37** B—B3, N—R5; **38** Q—K4, N—B4; **39** Q—K2, P—R3; **40** K—N2, K—R2; **41** Q—K3

The time trouble is over and Petrosian seals his next move. The win is only a matter of time.

41...R—Q6; 42 Q—B4, Q—Q2; **43** Q—B4, P—N3; **44** R—Q1, P—R4; **45** Q—B4, R—Q5; **46** Q—R6, P—N4; **47** Q—K3

Or 47 Q—B8, Q—B2; 48 Q—R8 ch, K—N3.

47...K—N3; 48 Q—R6 ch, N—K3; **49** Q—K3, K—R3; **50** B—K2, P—R5; **51** Q—QB3, K—N3; **52** Q—K3, N—B4; **53** B—B3, P—N5; **54** Q—R6 ch, N—K3; **55** Q—R8, Q—Q1; **56** Q—R7, Q—Q2; **57** Q—R8, P—N6 !; **58** Q—QN8 ch, K—R4; **59** Q—QR8 ch, K—N4

Not 59...K—N5; 60 B—B6.

60 Q—QN8 ch, K—B5 !; **61** Q—N8, K—B6; **62** B—R5, N—Q1

Black can also win by 62...P—R6; 63 B×P, Q—Q4 ch; 64 K—N1, Q—B6, but Petrosian prefers to keep his extra pawn.

63 B—B3, P—R6; **64** Q—B8, K—N7; **65** Q—R8, N—K3; **66** Q—R8, P—R7; **67** Q—R5, Q—R5 !; **68** R× P ch, K—R6; **69 Resigns**

---

21 FISCHER–KERES
CANDIDATES' TOURNAMENT, ZAGREB 1959

Caro-Kann Defence

1 P—K4, P—QB3; **2** N—QB3, P—Q4; **3** N—B3, B—N5; **4** P—KR3, B×N; **5** Q×B, N—B3; **6** P—Q3, P—K3; **7** P—

KN3, B—N5; **8** B—Q2, P—Q5; **9** N—N1, Q—N3 !; **10** P—N3

On 10 P—B3, both 10...B—K2 and 10...B—R4 are quite satisfactory for Black.

10...P—QR4!
Simple chess. White's Q side is now under considerable pressure.

11 P—R3, B—K2; 12 B—N2, P—R5
Also good is 12...Q—B4, followed by the manoeuvre ...N—R3—B2—N4—B6.

13 P—QN4, QN—Q2; 14 O—O, P—B4; 15 R—R2 ?!
A passive move. Necessary was 15 P—B4, and if 15...P×P e.p., then 16 N×P, P×P; 17 P×P, or 15...P×NP; 16 P×P, B×P; 17 B×B, Q×B; 18 N—R3. In either case White's position is more active than in the game.

15...O—O; 16 P×P, B×P; 17 Q—K2
Better is 17 Q—Q1.

17...P—K4; 18 P—KB4, KR—B1; 19 P—R4, R—B3; 20 B—R3, Q—B2; 21 P×P, N(Q2)×P; 22 B—B4, B—Q3 !; 23 P—R5, R—R4 !
All of Black's pieces are now poised for the attack on White's king.

24 P—R6, N—N3; 25 Q—B3, R—R4 !; 26 B—N4, N (N3)×B !; 27 B×R
Or 27 P×N, R—R5.

27...N(B5)×B; 28 P—N4, B—R7 ch; 29 K—N2, N×NP; 30 N—Q2, N—K6 ch; 31 Resigns

A fine example of Fischer's difficulties with the non-Soviets is the first of his games with Olafsson, in which the Icelandic Grandmaster used the excellent psychological ploy of adopting Fischer's own favourite move against the Najdorf Variation.

---

22 OLAFSSON–FISCHER
CANDIDATES' TOURNAMENT, BLED 1959

Sicilian Defence

1 P—K4, P—QB4; 2 N—KB3, P—Q3; 3 P—Q4, P×P; 4 N×P, N—KB3; 5 N—QB3, P—QR3; 6 B—QB4(!), P—K3; 7 P—QR3
But this twist of Bronstein's is not so dangerous. The idea is to preserve the KB against the knight manoeuvre ...N—QB3—QR4 (or ...QN—Q2—B4). Another point of the text move is that it prevents the advance ...P—QN5, which is a crucial counter-attacking motif in many lines. The disadvantage is that it costs White a vital tempo.

7...B—K2; 8 O—O, O—O; 9 B—R2
If 9 P—B4, P—Q4! or 9...N×P!

9...P—QN4; 10 P—B4, B—N2; 11 P—B5, P—K4; 12 N(Q4)—K2, QN—Q2

If 12...N×P, then 13 N×N, B×N; 14 N—N3, B—N2; 15 Q—N4 (or 15 P—B6!), followed by N—R5, with a strong attack for the pawn(s).

13 N—N3, R—B1; 14 B—N5
In the game Robatsch–Fischer, Havana 1965, White tried to improve with 14 B—K3. The game continued 14...N—N3; 15 B×N, Q×B ch; 16 K—R1, Q—K6!; 17 N—Q5, B×N; 18 B×B, B—Q1; 19 P—QR4, B—N3; 20 P×P, P×P; 21 R—R6, P—N5; 22 N—R5, N×B; 23 Q—N4, P—N3; 24 P×N, R×P; 25 P×P, RP×P; 26 N—B6 ch, K—N2; 27 N—R5 ch, K—R3 !; 28 N—B6, R—B7; 29 R(6)—R1, R—QR1 !; 30 Q×QNP, K—N2; 31 Q×P, Q—K7; 32 N—K8 ch, R×N; 33 R(B1)—K1, Q—N5; 34 Resigns. After the game Robatsch telephoned Fischer (who was playing by telex from New York) to ask

him where he had gone wrong, and was dumbfounded at being told that the whole variation is worthless!

14. . .N—N3; 15 N—R5

15. . .R×N

Although successful in similar positions this sacrifice does not work here *because* Black has an extra tempo! The paradox lies in the move 14. . .N—N3, which left Black's KB3 square more vulnerable than usual. A good alternative to the text is 15. . .N—B5.

16 P×R, N×N

On 16. . .N×P, White must play 17 P—B6! and not 17 B×B, Q×B; 18 Q—N4, because of 18. . .Q—N4, when Black has a good game for the exchange. Or if 16. . .B×P; 17 N×NP!, K×N; 18 B×N ch, K×B; 19 Q—R5, K—N2; 20 Q—N4 ch, with a strong attack.

17 B×B, Q×B; 18 Q×N, B×P; 19 Q—N4, P—Q4; 20 P—B6, Q—B4 ch; 21 K—R1, P—N3; 22 QR—K1!

Threatening 23 Q—N5, R moves; 24 R—K3.

22. . .R—K1

If 22. . .Q×RP; 23 Q—R4, R—Q1; 24 R×B!, P×R; 25 B×P ch!, K×B; 26 Q×RP ch, K—K3; 27 Q×P, and White wins, e.g. 27. . .N—Q2; 28 P—

B7 dis ch, K—Q4 (or 28. . .K—K2; 29 Q—N4 ch); 29 R—Q1 ch; or 27. . .N—Q4; 28 P—B7 dis ch, K—Q2; 29 Q—B5 ch, K—K2; 30 Q—N5 ch, K—Q2; 31 Q×R ch, K×Q; 32 P—B8(Q) ch, Q×Q; 33 R×Q ch.

23 Q—R4, P—KR4; 24 Q—N5, N—B5; 25 B×N, NP×B

26 R—K3!, Q—KB1

26. . .R—N1 allows 27 R—R3, Q—KB1; 28 R×P, 29 R—R6, and 30 Q—R4.

27 R—QN1!, R—N1; 28 R(K3)—K1

Threatening simply 29 Q×KP.

28. . .R×R

If 28. . .Q—K1?; 29 Q—R6.

29 R×R, B×BP; 30 R—N7

Now Black cannot save his pawn centre.

30. . .B—B4; 31 Q—K3, B—K3; 32 Q×P, Q×P; 33 P—R3, Q—B8 ch; 34 K—R2, P—N4; 35 R—R7, P—R5; 36 R×RP, K—R2; 37 R—R1!, Q—B5 ch

If 37. . .Q×R; 38 Q×NP and mates. And if 37. . .Q—Q7; 38 R—Q1!, with the same idea.

38 Q×Q, P×Q; 39 R—KB1, P—Q5; 40 P×P, K—N3; 41 R×P, B—B4; 42 R—B3, K×P; 43 R—K3!

Cutting off the king.

43. . .K—N4; 44 P—N3!, B—Q6; 45 P—Q5, Resigns

Just in case I have given the reader the impression that Fischer's play in the 1959 Candidates' Tournament was wholly unworthy of praise, I should redress the balance with an example that shows him at his best.

23 FISCHER–BENKÖ
CANDIDATES' TOURNAMENT, BLED 1959

Sicilian Defence

1 P–K4, P–QB4; 2 N–KB3, N–QB3; 3 P–Q4, P×P; 4 N×P, N–B3; 5 N–QB3, P–Q3; 6 B–QB4, Q–N3

This move has regained some popularity during the past three or four years. At the time it had been little played and this game was largely responsible for its remaining unpopular for a decade.

7 N(Q4)–K2

Nowadays 7 N–N3 is the most frequently played move.

7...P–K3; 8 O–O, B–K2; 9 B–N3, O–O; 10 K–R1

Possibly better is 10 B–K3, developing with gain of tempo and obviating the necessity of K–R1 as a preparation for P–B4.

10...N–QR4; 11 B–N5, Q–B4 ?

On this square Black's queen is too exposed in some variations. Correct is 11...Q–B2.

12 P–B4, P–N4; 13 N–N3, P–N5

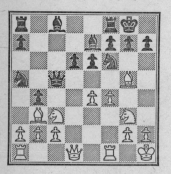

Better is 13...N×B; 14 RP×N, B–N2, controlling important central squares.

14 P–K5 !

Starting an irresistible attack. Black is already lost.

14...P×P

Or 14...P×N; 15 P×N, B×P (or 15...P×P; 16 B–R6); 16 B×B, P×B; 17 N–K4 (that exposed queen), Q–B4; 18 N×QP, Q–N3; 19 R–B3, with decisive threats.

15 B×N, P×B

Or 15...P×N; 16 N–K4, Q–N5; 17 Q–N4, B×B; 18 N×B ch, K–R1; 19 N–R5, P–N3; 20 Q–R4, with a winning attack. On 15...B×B; 16 N(B3)–K4 is very strong, e.g. 16...Q–K2; 17 N–R5, threatening 18 N(K4)×B ch; or 16...Q–B3; 17 N×B ch, P×N; 18 Q–N4 ch, K–R1; 19 Q–R4, B–N2; 20 Q×BP ch, K–N1; 21 Q–N5 ch, K–R1; 22 N–R5, and Black has no defence.

16 N(B3)–K4, Q–Q5; 17 Q–R5, N×B

Or 17...P×P; 18 N–B5 !!, P×N; 19 R×P, and if 19...P×N; 20 R–R4. But perhaps Black could have put up more resistance with 17...B–N2.

18 Q–R6 !, P×P

Or 18...K–R1; 19 N×P, and on 19...B×N; 20 Q×R mate.

19 N–R5, P–B4; 20 QR–Q1, Q–K4; 21 N(K4)–B6 ch, B×N; 22 N×B ch, Q×N; 23 Q×Q, N–B4; 24 Q–N5 ch, K–R1; 25 Q–K7, B–R3; 26 Q×N, B×R; 27 R×B, Resigns

At the end of March 1960 Fischer returned to Argentina to play once again at the millionaires' paradise resort of Mar del Plata. The tournament was a little stronger than that of the previous year and it had an added interest in the presence of the Soviet Union's youngest Grandmaster, Boris Spassky.

From early in his career Spassky had shown such promise that most Soviet experts regarded it only as a matter of time before he would take his place on the ever growing list of Soviet World Champions. And since Fischer was clearly the most likely Western contender for the title, the first battle between these two was eagerly awaited. Their individual encounter came in the second round.

24 SPASSKY–FISCHER
MAR DEL PLATA 1960

King's Gambit Accepted

Notes by Aronin

This was the first meeting of the World's two youngest Grandmasters and both opponents played for a win from the very beginning.

1 P—K4   P—K4
2 P—KB4

Fifty years ago this favourite opening of the chess romantics was classified as not being a very good one and since then the King's Gambit has not been played often in tournaments. Only recently has it started to reappear from time to time. It is interesting that in these recent games White was usually victorious.

Spassky is one of those who have become 'Knights of the King's Gambit', so this choice of opening is very characteristic of the young Leningradian.

2 . . .   P×P
3 N—KB3   P—KN4

This is the so called 'Classical Defence' which, during the last century, was thought to be the only correct one. Only later was it discovered that along with 3...P—KN4, 3...N—KB3 or 3...P—Q4, with an immediate attack on White's centre, also deserved consideration. [A mistake in nomenclature. The name 'Classical Defence' is given to the sequence 1 P—K4, P—K4; 2 P—KB4, B—B4. – DNLL]

4 P—KR4   P—N5
5 N—K5

The Kieseritsky Gambit. The alternative, 5 N—N5, is Algaier's Gambit.

5 . . .   N—KB3
6 P—Q4

If 6 N×NP, N×P; 7 P—Q3, N—N6; 8 B×P, N×R; 9 Q—K2 ch, Q—K2; 10 N—B6 ch, K—Q1; 11 B×P ch, K×B; 12 N—Q5 ch, K—Q1; 13 N×Q, B×N, Black has the better game.

6 . . .   P—Q3
7 N—Q3   N×P
8 B×P   B—N2
9 N—B3

White deviates from 9 P—B3, O—O; 10 N—Q2, which is the continuation recommended by theory. Perhaps Spassky wanted to avoid the well-known continuations but after the text he is forced to follow a sacrificial path.

9 . . .   N×N
10 P×N   P—QB4

Keres recommends, 10...O—O and only then 11...P—QB4. It seems that Fischer was right not to castle first: although, after the check 11 Q—K2, Q—K2 is insufficient because of 12 B×P, Q×Q ch; 13 B×Q, P×P; 14 O—O!, nevertheless 11...B—K3 is quite possible. Now, after 12 P—Q5, B×P ch; 13 B—Q2, B×R; 14 P—B3 (intending to win both bishops) 14... Q—B3!, Black keeps his extra material.

11 B—K2   P×P
12 O—O   N—B3
13 B×NP

On 13 P—B4, Black had the possibility

of defending the KNP by playing 13...
P—KR4. But now Black manages to
complete his development and keep his
material advantage.

13 ...	O—O
14 B×B	R×B
15 Q—N4	P—B4
16 Q—N3	P×P

So Black is two pawns up but his
advantage is not so big as may first
seem. In fact, keeping even a minimal
advantage requires from Fischer very
precise play. Nevertheless, we must
admit that Black has gained the advantage in the opening. So perhaps 9 N—
B3 is not so good for White as 9 P—B3.

17 QR—K1 !

If 17 B×P, then 17...R—B3, followed
by 18...R—N3 with the initiative on the
K side.

17 ...   K—R1

This seems to be a very strong move,
making way for the black rook on KN1.
But as often happens with very clear
plans it is not the best move. Much
stronger for Black is 17...Q—Q2!; 18
B×P, KR—K1. Although White's
pieces are actively placed it is not easy
to show that his position is worth a
pawn. As it is, Spassky ingeniously
creates tactical threats.

18 K—R1   R—KN1

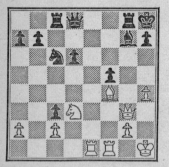

19 B×P !

It would appear that White takes the
pawn at the most inappropriate moment.
But really, what can Black do? After
19...B—Q5; 20 Q—R2, R—N5?; 21

B—K5 ch, N×B; 22 N×N (threatening
23 N—B7 ch), White has defended
against the threat of 22...R×P ch.

19 ...	B—B1
20 B—K5 ch	N×B
21 Q×N ch	R—N2

If 21...B—N2; 22 Q—K7, and Black
has difficulty in keeping the extra pawn.

22 R×P	Q×P ch
23 K—N1	

Although Fischer has kept his material
advantage, Spassky's pieces are placed in
active positions and his losing chances
have diminished. Of course Black is not
worse either, so at this point the position
is equal.

[This note in particular and Aronin's
comments on this game in general are
an excellent example of what Fischer
would call 'typical Iron Curtain objec-
tivity.' As Fischer himself shows in his
notes in *My Sixty Memorable Games*,
Black was better throughout most of
the game – contrary to the impression
gained by reading Aronin's notes – and
Black would have had good winning
chances in this 'equal' position had he
played 23...Q—N6 !—DNLL]

23 ...	Q—KN5
24 R—B2	B—K2
25 R—K4	Q—N4

The best thing for Black here is to
force a draw by playing 25...Q—Q8 ch;
26 R—K1 (if 26 K—R2, R—B3!,
threatening 27...B—Q3 or 27...R—
KR3 ch, and Black forces a draw: 27
Q—N8 ch, R—N1; 28 Q—K5 ch),
26...Q—N5; 27 R—K4, etc. But
Fischer keeps up the pressure.

26 Q—Q4

Again the strongest move. Pinning
the rook at KN7 is unpleasant for Black.
For instance he cannot play 26...B—
B4; 27 N×B, Q×N; 28 R—K8 ch!,
and the draw requires more exact play
from Black. It appears that it was
sufficient to play 26...B—B1 ! and if,
for example, 27 Q×RP, then 27...B—
B4!; 28 N×B, Q×N; 29 R—K8 ch,
R—N1.

Instead Fischer makes a serious
mistake.

26 . . .	R—B1	play 27...B—B3, but then 28 Q—Q6!.
27 R—K5 !		27 . . .	R—Q1
Now Black cannot rescue the piece.		28 Q—K4	Q—R5
Perhaps he had expected to be able to		29 R—B4	Resigns

Apart from this loss Fischer only dropped one other half-point at Mar del Plata (to Bronstein), winning thirteen games! He and Spassky tied for first, two points clear of Bronstein.

Although trained as a journalist, Spassky rarely contributes to the Soviet chess literature. But on his return from Argentina Spassky wrote a tournament report for Shakhmaty v SSSR (Chess in the USSR), in which he devoted almost three pages to comments on Fischer; his first impressions of the young man who was to become his fiercest opponent.

'Robert is capable of playing chess at any time of the day or night. He was often seen playing blitz games after a tiring evening adjournment. The champion of the USA plays blitz with pleasure and daring. The only thing in the sphere of chess that he does not do with pleasure is losing. When he loses he straightaway puts the pieces back on the board for a revenge game. If he doesn't manage to get his revenge he is very nervous. [A word used by East Europeans to mean upset or angry – DNLL.] He hastens with comments and tries to comfort himself saying that he had a won position.

'Fischer has a great knowledge of chess literature, especially the Soviet literature. Once, while he was in our hotel room, he noticed a copy of the bulletins on the latest Soviet championship. He borrowed it and vanished from the room. Fischer is one of the most diligent readers of our chess magazines, and he is concerned about which of his games are published in our press.

'Fischer's favourite player is Capablanca.

'I shall now give some examples of Fischer's creativity. The following position is from the game Fischer v Gadia.

21 R—R1 ! This unobvious move shows very simply the hopelessness of Black's position. [The game concluded 21...P—B3; 22 P—QR4, R—N1 ??;

23 N×B ch, Resigns – DNLL.] Soon after the game had finished, Bronstein asked Fischer how come he had thought of that rook move. Fischer answered "Tal moves his rooks back and forth, why can't I do the same?"

'Fischer is an excellent tactician. But he can subdue his tactical inclination in favour of the main strategic aim in a position. Here is a position from the game Saadi–Fischer.

Black has difficulty in developing his Q side. It is interesting to see how the young Grandmaster solves this problem of the mobilization of his forces. 8...N—KN5; 9 P—K3, P—Q3!; 10 N×N. Better is 10 P—N3. If 10 B×N, P×B; 11 N×P, then 11...Q—Q2; 12 N—Q5, R—K1, with a good game for the sacrificed pawn. 10...P×N; 11 B×P, R—N1. Black has an excellent position. It is interesting to see the continuation: 12 B—B3, N—K4; 13 B—K2, B—QR3; 14 P—N3, N×P; 15 Q—B2, Q—R4; 16 N—Q5, Q×N; 17 P×N, Q—N2 !, and Black wins. This example shows how Fischer bravely sacrifices a pawn in order to take over the initiative or to steer the game into a tactical battle. In this respect his game against Foguelman (who was White) was also interesting.

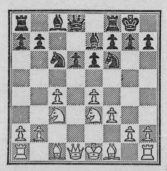

Black did not start this Sicilian Defence very successfully. It seems that he cannot show any initiative. But a surprising move, 9...P—Q4 !?, made Foguelman solve new problems. The correctness of this pawn sacrifice can only be determined by thorough analysis. But from a practical point of view Fischer's idea was reasonable. The game continued: **10 BP×P, P×P; 11 P×P, N—K4; 12 Q—N3, B—QB4; 13 B—Q2, R—K1; 14 B—K2, N—N3; 15 N—B2, N—R5,** and Black had a beautiful attacking position.

'When Fischer *has* to defend himself he does so cold-bloodedly, not taking any chances by counter-attacking. In his game against Bazan he gaily accepted the sacrifice of a pawn and with characteristic optimism defended a very dangerous position.

Bazan continued: **16 P—K4.** After the game Bronstein suggested 16 N—K5, followed by 17 Q—R5 and 18 P—B4 as giving White good chances. **16. . . B—K3; 17 B—B7, Q×B; 18 P×P, P—N5!; 19 N—Q2, N×P; 20 Q—K4, Q—B5!; 21 R×P, Q×Q; 22 N×Q, N—K7 ch; 23 K—R1, B—Q2; 24 R—K1, K—B1; 25 N—B6, B—N4; 26 R—N4, B—R3; 27 N—Q7 ch, K— K2; 28 N—B5, KR—K1!; 29 N×B, K—Q3; 30 R×QNP, N—N6 ch,** and Black wins.

'Sometimes Fischer gets carried away, leaving his opponent dangerous tactical possibilities. This is what happened in his game against Incutto.

In reply to Fischer's last move, 35 Q—N5, instead of 35. . .B—KB3 as happened in the game, Incutto could have played 35. . .N—B6 ch and the complications would have been on his side.

'Although attracted by the tactical battle, the young American can manoeuvre very well, squeezing and besieging his opponent.

'Fischer has good experience of playing in mixed tournaments. [By this Spassky means tournaments in which, as well as Grandmasters and strong International Masters, there are a number of much weaker players against whom Fischer normally scores very heavily – DNLL.] In such competitions he is especially dangerous. Playing against him, the weaker competitors have continually to solve tactical problems. In this respect he is similar to Tal.'

A fine example of the ease with which Fischer disposed of the non-Grandmasters at Mar del Plata is his game against the Chilean International Master Rene Letelier.

25 LETELIER–FISCHER
MAR DEL PLATA 1960

Queen's Pawn

1 P—Q4, N—KB3; 2 B—N5 !?, P—B4; 3 P—QB3, Q—N3; 4 Q—N3

Better is 4 Q—B1.

4...P×P; 5 Q×Q, P×Q; 6 B×N, NP×B; 7 P×P, N—B3

Already Black is winning a pawn (if you can call it a pawn).

8 N—KB3, N—N5; 9 K—Q2, R×P; 10 R×R, N×R; 11 N—R3, P—Q4; 12 P—K3, P—K3; 13 N—B2

More active is 13 B—N5 ch.

13...N—N5; 14 N×N, B×N ch; 15 K—B2, B—Q2; 16 K—N3, B—Q3; 17 B—Q3, K—K2; 18 R—R1, R—QB1; 19 R—R7, B—B3; 20 P—N3, P—R3; 21 R—R1, K—Q2; 22 R—R7, K—B2; 23 R—R1, P—N4; 24 R—QB1, K—N3; 25 R—QR1, B—Q2; 26 N—R4 ?

Now White makes a grave error – he starts to do something. Correct was 26 N—K1, R—B3; 27 N—B2, K—B2 (intending ...R—R3); 28 N—N4, and Black has nothing, e.g. 28...B×N; 29

K×B, R—R3; 30 R×R, P×R; 31 K—B5.

26...R—B3 !; 27 R—R8 ?

Following Bronstein's rule that if a player makes a weak move it is usually the prelude to an even weaker one. 27 N—B3 was correct; at all costs the black rook should be kept out of White's position.

27...R—B8 !; 28 R—R8, P—N5; 29 R×P ?

Putting his rook completely out of play. Obviously Letelier had no inkling of what was about to happen to his king. 29 R—Q8, K—B2; 30 R—QR8 was indicated.

29...K—R4 !

Simple and devastating. White is in a mating net.

30 K—R2, P—N6 ch!; 31 K×P, B—R5 ch; 32 K—R2, K—N5; 33 P—N3, B×QNP ch; 34 K—N2, R—Q8; 35 B—N1, R—Q7 ch; 36 K—R1, K—B6; 37 Resigns

Because of 37...B—R6 and ...B—N7 mate.

Two months after the Mar del Plata tournament, Fischer was again in South America. This time he was competing in a tournament of outstanding calibre that was being held in Buenos Aires to mark the 150th anniversary of the establishment of the Republic of Brazil.

Of the twenty players in Buenos Aires, 15 were Grandmasters. But if rumours are to be believed it was not the strength of the tournament that accounted for his disastrous result (he tied for thirteenth to sixteenth) but the distractions of a local Senorita.

One of Fischer's most interesting games from Buenos Aires is his draw with Ivkov. Instead of playing his favourite Two Knights Variation against the Caro-Kann, Fischer showed that he at last had come to realize the foolishness of being so stubborn. He chose the Panov Attack, surprising his opponent from the outset and causing him not a few practical problems. The effect of this switch in his repertoire can be judged from Ivkov's own notes to the game.

---

26 FISCHER–IVKOV
BUENOS AIRES 1960

Caro-Kann Defence

Notes by Ivkov

1 P—K4	P—QB3
2 P—Q4	

In the 1959 Candidates' Tournament Fischer consistently employed the modern system, developing his knights to QB3 and KB3 without playing the move P—Q4. Petrosian and Keres played this defence (games 20 and 21) and when I was considering what best to play, for 'psychological' reasons I came to the conclusion that it should be the Caro-Kann. But there I was mistaken because I had played this defence only once before, ten years earlier, and I had lost. On the other hand Bobby had played against the Caro-Kann in many games and he had an excellent knowledge of all types of position that arise out of this opening.

Contrary to my expectations, Bobby fought against my Caro-Kann very precisely and with excellent judgement. After the first few moves it was I who had to fight a psychological battle, and not my young opponent. Expecting a modern variation about which I knew a little, I was faced with the Panov, about which I could not even dream.

2 . . .	P—Q4
3 P×P	P×P
4 P—QB4	N—KB3
5 N—QB3	P—K3

Playing this position for the first time in my life I did not know about the interesting idea of sacrificing a pawn: 5 . . . P—KN3; 6 B—N5, B—N2; 7 B× N, B×B; 8 N×P, B—N2, and I cannot see how White can keep the pawn because of . . . N—B3; N—KB3, B—N5.

6 N—B3	B—K2

6 . . . P×P would transpose to a classical Queen's Gambit.

7 P—B5	

Well, one unpleasant surprise is over.

7 . . .	O—O
8 P—QN4	

More precise would have been 8 B—Q3 first so that 8 . . . N—K5 is not now possible.

| 8 . . . | P—QN3 |
| 9 B—Q3 | P×P ? |

I had thought about this position for a long time and I was distressed by what I had played. It was clear to me that the text leads to an inferior position. Later I remembered the game Botvinnik–Golombek (to which Fischer referred in our post-mortem), which illustrates the strength of the move 9...P—QR4.

After 9...P—QR4 White can play 10 N—QR4 when, according to Pachman, Black can reply 10...KN—Q2 or 10...QN—Q2. Bobby said that after 10...KN—Q2, according to Botvinnik 11 P—N5, P×P; 12 P×P, is good for White.

In the meantime something else occurred to me. After 10 N—QR4, KN—Q2; 11 Q—B2, the play becomes very complicated. [An obscure comment. Is Ivkov trying to say that he had considered the continuation 9...P—QR4; 10 N—QR4, KN—Q2; 11 Q—B2, but rejected it because he was afraid of entering a complicated line against Fischer? – DNLL.]

10 NP×P	N—B3
11 O—O	B—Q2
12 P—KR3	

I thought for a long time over this position. Eventually I played . . .

| 12 . . . | N—K1 |

. . . in order to prepare to put pressure on White's QP.

| 13 B—KB4 | B—B3 |
| 14 B—QN5 | N—B2 |

15 B—K2 ?

After the correct 15 B—R4 ! Black's position is very difficult. Now Black makes use of a tactical opportunity which at the first glance looks very dubious but is actually correct.

| 15 . . . | N×P ! |

A very sharp move.

16 N×N	P—K4
17 P—B6	B—K1
18 B—N3	P×N
19 B×N	Q×B
20 N×P	Q—Q3

I didn't have very much time to think when I played this very tempting move. I could have sacrificed my queen by 20...Q×P; 21 B—B3, R—Q1; 22 N—K7 ch, B×N; 23 B×Q, B×B, and it was this continuation of which Fischer was most afraid. Because I was short of time, or perhaps because of White's QRP, I did not go in for this adventure.

21 N×B ch	Q×N
22 P—B7	R—B1
23 R—B1	B—B3

After the skirmish in the centre Black is again in the unknown. The dangerous developments on the QB file aggravated my time trouble, and I was now left with only five minutes.

| 24 R—B4 | R×P |
| 25 B—Q3 | |

Fischer didn't want a draw, even though he, too, was in time trouble. If 25 R×P, the game would have certainly ended in a draw. If 25 Q—B2, then 25...R—K2 ! is a very good reply, and if 25 Q—B1, Q—N3; 26 P—B3, B—N4; 27 R×R, B×B; 28 R—KB2, P—Q6, with compensation for the exchange.

But Bobby chose a complicated line hoping that I would make some mistakes in time trouble.

| 25 . . . | R—Q2 |
| 26 Q—B2 | |

White is still complicating the game, hoping that Black would play 26...B—N4. But although I managed to assess that after 27 B×P ch, K—   ; 28 R—B5, B×R; 29 R—KR5, P—N3, has the better chances, I avoided this line on the principle 'Don't go into complications if you are in time trouble.'

26 . . .	B—Q4
27 R—R4	P—N3
28 Q—B5	KR—Q1
29 B—N5	R—Q3

Although in horrible time trouble I still saw that I was losing my QRP but I thought that it didn't matter because I had a good reply waiting.

30 R—Q1	B—K3
31 P—Q3	R—Q4
32 Q×RP	B×P!

After playing very quickly, Fischer seemingly becomes more content to draw.

33 B—K4	R(4)—Q2
34 Q—R6	Q×Q
35 R×Q	B—K3
36 P—QR4	P—Q6
37 R—Q2	R—Q5

Black must play actively because of White's well placed bishop and his dangerous QRP.

38 P—B3	B—Q4
39 B×B	R(1)×B
40 K—B2	R—QB5

At last the time scramble is over – on both clocks the flags were hanging.

41 P—R5	R—QR5

Still playing quickly through inertia. 41...R—B6 would have been stronger, but it would still have led to a draw.

42 R—QB6!	

Activating his passive rook. If 42... R(R)×P; 43 R—B3 or 42...R(Q)×P; 43 R—Q6.

42 . . .	R—R6
43 R—B1	P—B4

Or 43...R(Q)×P; 44 R—B8 ch and 45 R—Q8.

44 R(1)—Q1	K—N2
45 P—R6	Draw Agreed

That Fischer's theoretical stubbornness had at last given way to his results (so far as the Two Knights Variation of the Caro-Kann was concerned at least), was a sign that he was maturing as a player. He had come to realize that his original assessment of the variation was optimistic. He saw the need for surprising his opponents in the opening; not a profound conception but one that was completely contrary to his earlier philosophy of repeating the same lines time and again.

After the Buenos Aires fiasco Fischer's play took on a new dimension of dynamism. His next important event was the Olympiad in Leipzig in which he scored 71 % on top board for the USA, a brilliant result which pulled his team into second place (the USSR took the gold medals, as is the tradition at Olympiads). In the key match between the USA and the USSR, Fischer had the white pieces against Tal. The new World Champion played a risky line of the Winawer Variation and he came closer than ever before to being beaten by Bobby.

27 FISCHER–TAL
OLYMPIAD, LEIPZIG 1960

French Defence

1 P—K4	P—K3
2 P—Q4	P—Q4
3 N—QB3	B—N5
4 P—K5	P—QB4
5 P—QR3	B—R4 ?!

The only real merit of this inferior move is that it leads to complex positions that are well suited to Tal's style. Besides, after the hiding that he gave Botvinnik in the first game of their match it is hardly surprising that Tal refrained from the normal 5...B× N ch; 6 P×B, Q—B2, which was Botvinnik's choice.

| 6 P—QN4 ! | P×QP |

6...P×NP; 7 N—N5, P×P dis ch; 8 P—B3, followed by B×P, is well known to give White more than enough attacking chances to compensate for the pawn.

| 7 Q—N4 | N—K2 |
| 8 P×B | |

Also good for White is 8 N—N5, B—B2; 9 Q×NP, R—N1; 10 Q×RP.

8 ...	P×N
9 Q×NP	R—N1
10 Q×RP	QN—B3 !

An improvement on the ninth game of the 1954 Smyslov–Botvinnik match which went 10...N—Q2; 11 N—B3, N—B1; 12 Q—Q3, Q×P; 13 P—KR4, with advantage to White.

11 N—B3

Fischer refrained from 11 P—B4 because it restricts the activity of his QB and creates some dark-squared weaknesses, but it seems that after 11 P—B4, Q×P; 12 N—B3, B—Q2; 13 N—N5, White has an excellent game, e.g. 13... R—KB1; 14 B—K2 ! (threatening 15 N×BP), or 13...R×N; 14 P×R, O—O—O, when Black's compensation is inadequate.

| 11 ... | Q—B2 |

If 11...Q×P, then 12 N—N5, R—B1; 13 P—B4, with the same idea as in the previous note (14 B—K2 and 15 N×BP).

12 B—QN5 !

The most active move. If now 12... R×P ?, then 13 K—B1, R—KN1; 14 R—KN1, R×R ch; 15 K×R, and after a timely back rank check to keep Black's king in the centre, White will simply advance his KRP without hindrance.

| 12 ... | B—Q2 |
| 13 O—O | O—O—O |

Some of the kibitzers suggested 13... N×KP, but Tal had seen the refutation 14 N×N, Q×N; 15 B×B ch, K×B; 16 Q—Q3, when White is still clearly better, e.g. 16...Q—K5 ?; 17 Q×Q, P×Q; 18 P—B3, winning a pawn – Fischer.

14 B—N5 ?

The dynamo fails. In *My Sixty Memorable Games* Fischer analyses 14 B×N ! as leading to a win for White, e.g. 14...B×B (after 14...N×B; 15 R—K1, followed by B—N5 and P—KR4, Black has no counterplay); 15 Q×P, P—Q5; 16 Q×P ch, B—Q2; 17

Q×N, R×P ch; 18 K×R, B—R6 ch;
19 K×B, Q×Q; 20 B—N5, with a
winning material advantage.

14 . . .   N×KP !

Under pressure from all sides, Tal
finds a neat tactical solution.

15 N×N

Fischer had originally intended 15
B×B ch, R×B; 16 N×N (or 16 B×N ?,
N×N ch; 17 K—R1, Q×P ch!; 18
Q×Q, N×Q, with a won ending),
16...Q×N; 17 B×N, but then 17...
R—R1; 18 QR—K1, R×Q; 19 R×Q,
R×B, gives Black the better ending
because of his central pawn mass and
White's shaky Q-side pawn structure.

15 . . .   B×B !

The crowd had expected 15...Q×N,
but as Tal points out this would have
been a mistake: 16 B×N, R—R1 (not
16...B×B ?; 17 B×R); 17 KR—K1 !
(17 QR—K1 ?, Q—N1 !, and the KB1
rook is trapped), 17...Q×R ch; 18
R×Q, R×Q; 19 B×R, K×B; 20
B×B, K×B; 21 R—Q3, P—Q5; 22
R—K4, and White wins a pawn.

16 N×P   B×R
17 N×R   R×B
18 N×KP   R×P ch!

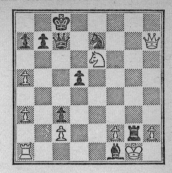

19 K—R1 !

Not 19 K×B ??, R×RP, and suddenly White is lost.

19 . . .   Q—K4

19...Q—QB5; 20 Q×N, R—N1; 21
N—B4 !, P—Q5; 22 Q—K4, should win
for White.

20 R×B   Q×N

After 20...R—N3; 21 Q×N, R×N;
22 Q—B8 ch, R—K1; 23 Q—B3, White
has the better endgame chances because
of his passed K-side pawns.

21 K×R   Q—N5 ch
Draw Agreed

As with all four of his losses to Tal in the Candidates' Tournament, this
game shows that Fischer's play loses some of its incisiveness whenever his
opponent has attacking possibilities or dynamic counter-chances. I have
used the Sicilian Dragon before as an example of this facet of Fischer's style,
and so it seems natural to include his sensational loss to Cesar Munoz, top
board of the team from Ecuador.

28 FISCHER–MUNOZ
OLYMPIAD, LEIPZIG 1960

Sicilian Defence

1 P—K4, P—QB4; 2 N—KB3, P—Q3;
3 P—Q4, P×P; 4 N×P, N—KB3; 5
N—QB3, P—KN3; 6 B—K3, B—N2; 7

P—B3, O—O; 8 Q—Q2, N—B3; 9
B—QB4, P—QR3

This is too slow. 9...B—Q2 is correct.

10 B—N3, Q—R4; 11 O—O—O, B—
Q2; 12 K—N1, QR—B1; 13 P—N4,

N—K4; 14 B—R6?
14 P—KR4 is natural and good.
14...N—B5; 15 B×N, R×B; 16
N—N3, Q—K4!
Now Black has a very good game.
17 P—KR4
If 17 B—B4, Q—K3; 18 N—Q4, N×
KP!; 19 N×Q, N×Q ch; 20 B×N,
B×N, and Black has won a pawn.
17...KR—B1; 18 B—B4, Q—K3; 19
P—R5, P—QN4; 20 P×P, BP×P;

21 B—R6, B—R1; 22 P—K5, P—
N5!; 23 P×N, P×N; 24 Q—R2,
Q×P; 25 B—N5, Q—B2
White's attack is over. Now his Q side
crumbles.
26 Q—K2, P×P; 27 Q×P, Q×Q; 28
B×Q, R×BP; 29 R×QP, B—R5; 30
B—N5, R—B7; 31 B—K3, R×P; 32
B—Q4, B×N; 33 P×B, B×B; 34
R×B, R×P; 35 R—Q2, R—N1; 36
R—Q7, R—QR6!; 37 Resigns

As a last example of Fischer's play at Leipzig, here is his attractive positional
win over Unzicker. A typical case of Fischer's masterly handling of the
white side of the Closed Ruy Lopez.

29 FISCHER–UNZICKER
OLYMPIAD, LEIPZIG 1960

Ruy Lopez

1 P—K4, P—K4; 2 N—KB3, N—QB3;
3 B—N5, P—QR3; 4 B—R4, N—B3; 5
O—O, B—K2; 6 R—K1, P—QN4; 7
B—N3, P—Q3; 8 P—B3, O—O; 9 P—
KR3, N—QR4; 10 B—B2, P—B4; 11
P—Q4, BP×P; 12 P×P, B—N2
12...Q—B2 is more flexible.
13 QN—Q2, N—B3
Better than 13...R—B1; 14 N—B1, P—
Q4; 15 QP×P, N×P; 16 N(B1)—Q2!,
N—B5; 17 N×N(B4), R×N; 18 B—
N3, with a slight edge for White.
Aronin–Saigin, Moscow 1960.
14 P—Q5, N—QN5; 15 B—N1, P—
QR4; 16 N—B1, N—R3; 17 N—N3,
B—B1; 18 B—Q3, B—Q2; 19 B—K3,
Q—N1
Black is contorting himself in an effort
to get his rooks into play. If 19...R—
B1; 20 P—QR4!, N—QN5; 21 P×P,
and Black has nothing to show for the
pawn.
20 R—QB1, B—Q1?
It is more important for Black to relieve
the pressure along the QB file by
exchanging rooks. After 20...R—B1;
21 R×R ch, Q×R; 22 Q—K2, Q—N2;
23 R—QB1, N—QN5; 24 B—N1, R—
QB1, Black has achieved equality.
21 Q—K2, Q—N2
White was threatening 22 P—QN4.
22 N—R2, N—QN5; 23 B—N1, B—
N3; 24 B—N5
Forcing the bishop to return to Q1,
since the KN cannot move (24...N—
K1??; 25 B—K7).
24...B—Q1; 25 Q—B3, N—K1; 26
B—K3, B—N3; 27 B—Q2, N—KB3

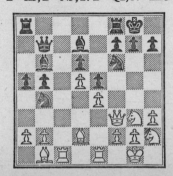

Black has nothing better. White could now gain another tempo by 28 B—N5 (cf. moves 24 to 27), but Fischer decides that the time is right to get on with the attack.

28 N—N4, N×N; 29 P×N, QR—B1; 30 N—B5, B×N; 31 Q×B

31 NP×B is also good in as much as the threat of 32 P—B6 forces Black to weaken himself by 31...P—B3. But the text has the advantage of hindering the exchange of both pairs of rooks and thereby maintains the tension in the QB file.

31...B—Q5; 32 P—R3, N—R3; 33 P—N4, P×P

33...B—N7; 34 R×R, R×R; 35 Q—B3 (threatening 36 P×P) leaves Black with little option but to transpose to the game continuation by 35...P×P.

34 P×P, B—N7; 35 R×R, R×R; 36 Q—B3, Q—N3; 37 R—Q1, B—Q5; 38 P—N3, R—B5; 39 B—Q3, R—B2; 40 K—N2, B—B6; 41 B—K3, Q—N1

Not 41...B—Q5 ?; 42 B×B, P×B; 43 P—K5!, and White's attack breaks through, e.g. 43...P×P; 44 P—Q6!, R—Q2; 45 Q—B5.

42 R—KR1, Q—QB1; 43 B×P, N× P; 44 Q—Q1

Preventing the knight from entering the game via QB7. The text also threatens 45 Q—R4 (which threatens both 46 R— QB1 and 46 R—QN1).

44...B—Q5; 45 B×B, P×B; 46 P— N5

Threat 47 Q—R5.

46...Q—N1; 47 Q—R5

Fischer ignores the threat to his bishop. Black's king is hounded to the centre, and the game is over.

47...Q×B; 48 Q×RP ch, K—B1; 49 Q—R8 ch, K—K2; 50 Q×P

Now the main threat is 51 Q—B6 ch, K—Q2; 52 R—R8, with threats of mate at Q8 and KB7. If 50...Q—K1, White wins by 51 R—R8, and so Black must return his extra piece.

50...N×P; 51 Q×QP, N—B6

The rook ending after 51...R—B5; 52 Q×N, Q×Q; 53 P×Q, is also quite hopeless for Black.

52 Q—B6 ch, K—Q2; 53 P—N6, N×P

Or 53...P×P; 54 R—R7 ch, K—B1; 55 R×R ch, K×R; 56 Q×N ch, and the queen ending is an easy win.

54 Q×BP ch, K—B1; 55 P—N7, Resigns

5

ANOTHER TRY

By the end of 1960 there was little point in Fischer playing in the US Championship. He had already showed that he was in a different class from all his countrymen and so the championship tournaments lacked much of their competitive interest. Up to 1967 Fischer played in eight US Champion-ships scoring sixty-one wins, twenty-six draws, and only three losses. With the destiny of the $2,000 first prize never in doubt, the tournaments seemed to serve as no more than a vehicle for Fischer to exhibit his ever increasing creative talent.

But every three years the US Championship is also a Zonal tournament

and so Fischer's participation was an essential rung on the ladder to the
World Championship. The 1960/61 US Championship was the Zonal
preliminary to the 1962 Interzonal that was to be held in Stockholm.
Fischer won this particular championship by a two point margin, the best
result that he had so far achieved in the event. But although his overall
superiority was overwhelming and he was undefeated in eleven rounds,
Fischer had some nasty moments. The following spot of bother, from the
first round, shows that even in the hands of a relatively weak player the
Winawer Variation could be a dangerous weapon against Fischer.

30 FISCHER–WEINSTEIN

US CHAMPIONSHIP 1960/61

French Defence

Notes by Vukovic

1 P—K4	P—K3
2 P—Q4	P—Q4
3 N—QB3	B—N5
4 P—K5	N—K2
5 P—QR3	B×N ch
6 P×B	P—QB4
7 P—QR4	

[7 Q—N4 was more fashionable at the
time—DNLL.]

7 . . .	QN—B3
8 N—B3	Q—R4
9 Q—Q2	B—Q2
10 B—Q3	P—B5
11 B—K2	O—O—O
12 B—R3	P—B3
13 O—O	N—B4

This move was played by Botvinnik
against Rabinovitch in 1939, after which
White continued 14 P—N4, N(B4)—
K2; 15 KR—N1, when, instead of
15...Q—R3, 15...QR—B1 is stronger.

On 13...P—R4, which Botvinnik
considered to offer equal chances, White
continues 14 P×P, P×P; 15 N—R4,
and if 15...QR—N1; 16 P—B4, or
15...P—K4, 16 P×P, P×P; 17 B×N,
N×B; 18 Q—N5. In his book Keres also
has an alternative in 13...B—K1, and
I should add that 13...QR—N1 must

also be taken into consideration.

14 KR—K1 ?

This move shows that Bobby doesn't
really study chess books as hard as a lot
of people think. 14 P—N4 was necessary
because now Black can get a good game
by playing 14...P—R4 !

14 . . .   B—K1 ?

But young Weinstein fails to take
advantage of his opportunity and plays
a move which loses two tempi! Maybe it
is just as a result of too much theory or
maybe he was thinking of the moves
...N—B4 and ...B—K1 which Keres
gives as alternatives at move thirteen
(and which, by the way, don't have very
much sense to them).

15 P—N4	N(B4)—K2
16 B—KB1	B—Q2

Admitting his mistake and the fact
that his position requires the loss of
another tempo. 16...B—B2 wouldn't
be any better; according to Keres that
square should be occupied by a black
rook.

17 B—R3	P—KR3
18 B—Q6	QR—B1
19 QR—N1	R—B2
20 P×P	P×P
21 B—N3	N—N3
22 R—N5	Q—R3

If 22...Q×RP; 23 R(5)—N1, Q—

R4; 24 R—R1, Q—Q1; 25 R—R2, and White has a dangerous attack along the QR and QN files.

23 KR—N1	P—N3
24 Q—B1?	

Correct is 24 N—R4. After White's weak move Black recovers and has a level position.

24 ...	Q×RP
25 R(5)—N2	Q—R6 !
26 Q—K3	K—N2
27 N—R4	N×N
28 B×N	

28 ...   P—K4?

Black should consolidate his extra pawn by 28...K—R1, and not open up the position (especially in time trouble).

29 P×P	P×P?

This new mistake makes Black's position entirely hopeless. Had Black played 29...P—Q5 ! he might have survived, although 30 Q—B4 would have left White with the advantage.

30 R×P ch!   K—R1

He cannot capture the rook because of 31 Q×NP ch, and to 30...K—B1 White would play 31 R×N ch and 32 Q×KP.

31 R(6)—N5	B—K3
32 B—N3	P—K5?
33 Q×KRP !	Resigns

If 33...R—K1; 34 Q×B.

[A fine display by Fischer after Black had failed to take advantage of his opening inaccuracy. It is interesting that Fischer's choice, 7 P—QR4, came back into fashion a year or two after this game was played, and that 7 Q—N4 is rarely seen nowadays in Master chess – DNLL.

The Reshevsky Match

Although this book is intended primarily to be a study of the development of Fischer's style, I feel that the farce created out of his match with Reshevsky deserves to be put in its correct perspective. Many uninformed chess players and the vast majority of the non-chess playing public do not understand why it was that Fischer was compelled to withdraw from this match. As a result, Fischer received a lot of unfavourable publicity. In the eyes of many, Fischer's premature termination of the Reshevsky match (coupled with his walkout at Sousse which was almost equally justifiable in my opinion) made him into the game's anti-hero. This in turn helped to augment the growing hostility that existed between him and the race known as tournament organizers who frequently seem to inhabit a world in which the wishes of the players have no place. The end result of this accumulating mutual animosity was Fischer's sixteen-month hibernation at the end of 1968 and his determination, on his return, to show the world that the needs of the best players *must* be respected.

It was clear to everyone, by the beginning of 1961, that Fischer was undoubtedly the best tournament player in the USA. He had won the national championship for four years in succession without loss of a single game. But there were those who thought that in match play he might still be unable to outclass Samuel Reshevsky, who for two decades had dominated the US chess scene.

I think it highly probable that even in 1961 Fischer was a better match player than Reshevsky. The fifty-year-old Grandmaster was certainly more experienced than Fischer in the endgame and in many types of quiet middle game positions. But in tactics and dynamism Fischer was the better, and in the openings Fischer's advantage was very marked. One amusing example of Reshevsky's failure to keep up to date with theory was their game from the 1958/59 US Championship. Fischer was White:

1 P—K4, P—QB4; 2 N—KB3, N—QB3; 3 P—Q4, P×P; 4 N×P, P—KN3; 5 N—QB3, B—N2; 6 B—K3, N—B3; 7 B—QB4, O—O; 8 B—N3, N—QR4 ??. Only months earlier this move had been refuted in the Soviet magazine Shakhmaty v SSSR by 9 P—K5!, N—K1?. Relatively best (but still losing) is 9...N×B; 10 P×KN, N×R; 11 P×B. 10 B×P ch!, K×B; 11 N—K6 !, when Black must lose his queen or be mated. Reshevsky had not seen this published refutation and had not worked it out for himself (even though the Accelerated Dragon was one of his favourite defences). But of course Fischer did know about 9 P—K5!, and he managed to win with the extra queen.

Another example of an important void in Reshevsky's theoretical knowledge can be found in Fischer's notes to the second game of this match (also an Accelerated Dragon), in *My Sixty Memorable Games*.

The Fischer–Reshevsky match was sponsored by the American Chess Foundation and the Herman Steiner Chess Club in Los Angeles (of which Jacqueline Piatigorsky was a patron). The first four games were to take place in New York, the next eight in Los Angeles and the last four in New York again. The match proceeded without too many incidents until the score was level at five and a half points each, Fischer having thrown away two half points by inexact endgame play.

The twelfth game had originally been arranged for the evening of Saturday August 12th, starting at 9.00 p.m. so as to avoid Reshevsky's sabbath. But since this made it likely that the players would still be battling at 2.00 a.m. the next day, the match committee rearranged the game for Sunday afternoon at 1.30. Oh, but on Sunday afternoon Mrs Piatigorsky wants to hear her husband play the cello, so can't we please change the game to an earlier hour, say 11.00 a.m.? After all, surely Mrs Piatigorsky's concert is more important than the wishes of the players.

And so, without consulting Fischer, the twelfth game was rearranged in accordance with Mrs Piatigorsky's wishes. Fischer first learned of this decision on August 10th and immediately issued a protest. (It was while this protest was being considered that Fischer had to play out the adjourned eleventh game – one of the two in which a winning endgame was allowed to slip into a draw. Had the rumpus not started until the eleventh game was over, Fischer would almost certainly have been leading at the time the match was interrupted.)

Fischer's reason for the protest, a perfectly natural one, was that in common with many other Grandmasters he likes to spend most (or all) of the morning in bed. For a Grandmaster to change his internal clock is a traumatic experience far worse than missing hearing one's husband play the cello. But when Fischer's protest was turned down his determination remained. He failed to appear for the twelfth game and was declared to have lost it by default.

Naturally the matter did not end there. Fischer protested against the decision to default him and was told that his appeal would be considered by the match committee and their decision announced before the conclusion of the match. But there was one snag – Fischer would have to continue with the thirteenth game *while his appeal was being considered*.

With such impossible conditions being imposed on Fischer and threats to sue being issued on both sides, the match was clearly destined to be carried no further. After various statements, telephone calls, telegrams and threats, Reshevsky was awarded the match and the winner's prize. The whole, unsavoury matter was debated in the chess press with the overwhelming majority of the opinion being on Fischer's side. But at least Mrs Piatigorsky got to hear her husband play the cello!

The Bled tournament of 1961 was an exceptionally strong event, commemorating the famous tournament that had been held there thirty years earlier. Seventeen of the twenty players at Bled were Grandmasters, four of them from the Soviet Union. There was no doubt that the fight for first place would be between Tal and Fischer, with Tal the hot favourite. In the final analysis the pundits were proved correct – Tal won the tournament by a full point, with Fischer second, a point ahead of Geller, Gligoric, and Keres. Naturally Fischer wouldn't have been satisfied with his result, but his tally of eight wins and eleven draws incorporated two very important psychological triumphs: he had scored three and a half points from his four games against the Soviet players and, more important still, he had finally beaten Mikhail Tal.

---

31 FISCHER–TAL
BLED 1961

Sicilian Defence

Notes by Tal

1 P—K4	P—QB4
2 N—KB3	N—QB3
3 P—Q4	P×P
4 N×P	P—K3

This system has become very popular because of Taimanov. In this game the American chooses a solid system instead of keeping the game open.

5 N—QB3	Q—B2
6 P—KN3	

I must confess that this combination surprised me. The most recent vogue in this variation is 6 B—K3, P—QR3; 7 P—QR3. Now, after the natural 6. . .P—QR3; 7 B—N2, N—B3; 8 O—O, Black can either play 8...B—K2, 8...P—Q3, transposing into a Scheveningen system, or 8...N×N; 9 Q×N, B—B4.

6 ...   N—B3 ??

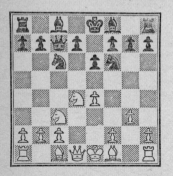

I made this move, stood up and went for a walk round the podium, waiting for my opponent to move. And when, on the demonstration board, the white knight appeared on QN5, I was surprised. 'A piece sacrifice' I thought to myself. And when I came to the board I was shocked to see, instead of the normal 6...P—QR3, I had played the move 6...N—B3.

7 N(Q4)—N5

After this reply Black's position is probably lost.

7 ...   Q—N1
8 B—KB4   N—K4

After 8...P—K4; 9 B—N5, P—QR3; 10 B×N, P×B (or 10...P×N; 11 B—N5), it is difficult for Black to find a good move.

9 B—K2 !

The straightforward 9 B×N, Q×B; 10 P—B4, Q—N1; 11 P—K5, P—QR3, gives Black chances for counter-play.

With the text White covers his KB3 square in preparation for Q—Q4.

9 ...   B—B4

I spent a lot of time on this move. Of course 9...P—QR3; 10 Q—Q4, P—Q3; 11 R—Q1, P×N; 12 B×N, was no good. Neither was 9...P—Q3; 10 Q—Q4, because of the threat of R—Q1, e.g. 10...N—B3; 11 N×QP ch (or 11 Q×QP, with the better ending), 11...K—

Q2; 12 B—QN5, B×N; 13 O—O—O.

9...B—N5 was possible: 10 Q—Q4, N—B3 !?; 11 B×Q, N×Q; 12 N—B7 ch, K—K2; 13 N×R, N×P ch, and if 14 K—Q2, then 14...N×R; 15 R×N, N×P ch; 16 K—B2, N×N; 17 P×N, B—B4, with quite a good game. But I renounced this continuation because of 14 K—Q1, N×R; 15 P—K5, B×N; 16 B—Q6 ch, K—Q1; 17 P×B, N—K5; 18 R—KB1, N×QBP ch; 19 K—Q2, N×B; 20 K×N, N—B7; 21 K—Q3, which wins a piece. Even so this line would have given better chances than the text; but the battle would have been very sharp.

Objectively, possibly the best move would have been 9...N—N1 ?!!, but Black missed it.

10 B×N

With the black bishop on QB4 this move is good.

10 ...   Q×B
11 P—B4   Q—N1
12 P—K5   P—QR3

12...N—N1; 13 N—K4 (and 14 N—Q6 ch) is equally hopeless.

13 P×N   P×N
14 P×P

In this position, the way to realize White's advantage is a matter of taste. A tactical chess player would have preferred 14 N—K4, B—B1; 15 Q—Q4, which forces ...P—KN3. Instead Fischer decided to take the pawn.

14 ...   R—N1
15 N—K4   B—K2
16 Q—Q4   R—R5

In practice, 16...Q—R2; 17 N—B6 ch, B×N; 18 Q×B, Q—K6, gives more chances, though after 19 K—B1 White would still be able to win. But I wanted to bring one of my active pieces into the game.

17 N—B6 ch   B×N
18 Q×B   Q—B2

If Black could have got his queen to Q5, he would have had a better chance in the ending even though a pawn down. Unfortunately 18...Q—R2 was not possible because of 19 B—R5. Black tries to avoid this manoeuvre and to make use of the weakness of White's king, but with his reply Fischer puts an end to my illusions.

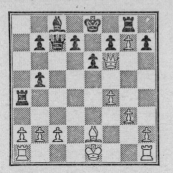

19 O—O—O !
Excellent. He is not afraid of losing his QRP.

| 19 . . . | R × RP |
| 20 K—N1 | R—R3 |

If 20...Q—R4; 21 P—N3, and neither of Black's major pieces can come to the aid of his king.

21 B × P   **R—N3**

If 21...R—R4, not 22 Q—R6?, R × B; 23 Q × RP, R × QNP ch!; 24 K × R, Q—N3 ch; 25 K—B1, Q—K6 ch; 26 R—Q2, Q—R6 ch; 27 K—Q1, Q—KB6 ch!, but 22 P—B4.

22 B—Q3   **P—K4**

If 22...Q—N1; 23 Q—R6, P—B4; 24 Q—R5 ch, K—K2; 25 P—KN4.

| 23 P × P ! | R × Q |
| 24 P × R | Q—B4 |

In this way Black manages to get rid of the pawns at KN7 and KB6 but at what a price!

25 B × P	Q—KN4
26 B × R	Q × BP
27 KR—B1	Q × KNP

28 B × P ch   **K—Q1**
The position is clear. White has two rooks and two passed pawns for the queen.

29 B—K6
After 29 B—Q5 Black would have had no chance, but Fischer wants to simplify the game and prevents me from developing my bishop.

29 . . .	Q—R3
30 B × P	B × B
31 R—B7	Q × P
32 R(1) × B ch	K—K1
33 R(Q)—K7 ch	K—Q1
34 R—Q7 ch	

White could have played 34 R × P, Q—R8 ch; 35 K—R2, Q—Q4 ch; 36 P—N3, Q—QR4 ch; 37 K—N2, Q—K4 ch; 38 P—B3, Q—K7 ch; 39 K—R3, Q—R3 ch; 40 K—N4, Q—Q3 ch; 41 K—N5, Q—Q6 ch; 42 K—N6, Q—K6 ch; 43 K—R6, Q—K3 ch; 44 K—R7.

34 . . .	K—B1
35 R—B7 ch	K—Q1
36 R(KB7)—Q7 ch	K—K1
37 R—Q1	P—N4

It is obvious that Black's position is completely lost. Besides, I was in very bad time trouble.

38 R—QN7   **Q—R4**
One way or another. 38...Q × NP is also bad.

39 P—KN4 !   **Q—R6**
If 39...Q × P; 40 R—R1.

40 P—N5	Q—KB6
41 R—K1 ch	K—B1
42 R × P	K—N2
43 R—N6	Q—KN6
44 R—Q1	Q—B2
45 R—Q6	Q—B1
46 P—N3	K—R2
47 R—QR6	Resigns

Stockholm

When Bobby arrived in Stockholm for the 1962 Interzonal he had no doubts about who was going to win the tournament. He had shown at Bled that he could now take care of any Soviet players who were put in his path, and from outside the Soviet Union there was no one who could challenge him. Tal had lost the return World Championship match to Botvinnik in 1961, but along with Keres (who was second in the 1959 Candidates' Tournament) he was exempted from the Interzonal stage of the qualifying cycle. With Tal out of the way the stage was set for Fischer to score the most remarkable tournament success of his career.

The Stockholm Interzonal was only slightly weaker than the previous year's tournament at Bled, and so Fischer's winning margin of two and a half points caused a sensation. As at Bled he was undefeated, winning thirteen games and drawing nine. To the new dynamism that was noticed in his play at the Leipzig Olympiad, Fischer had added a terrible new psychological weapon: he was no longer content to draw as Black against strong players.

For this reason he had made a slight change in his opening repertoire. While continuing to play the Najdorf Variation he no longer replied to 6 B—KN5, P—K3; 7 P—B4, with 7...B—K2 but chose instead the ultra-sharp move 7...Q—N3!?. This, the so called 'Poisoned Pawn' Variation, remained Fischer's favourite defence to 1 P—K4 right up to the time that he was playing Spassky in Iceland. Black grabs a pawn and then hangs on for dear life, hoping to survive White's attack and emerge with a decisive material advantage. The Russians later criticized Fischer's materialistic attitude to the game, claiming that he equated pawns with dollars and would grab hold of both with equal avarice.

32 BILEK–FISCHER
INTERZONAL TOURNAMENT, STOCKHOLM 1962

Sicilian Defence

1 P—K4, P—QB4; 2 N—KB3, P—Q3; 3 P—Q4, P×P; 4 N×P, N—KB3; 5 N—QB3, P—QR3; 6 B—KN5, P—K3; 7 P—B4, Q—N3; 8 Q—Q2, Q×P; 9 R—QN1, Q—R6; 10 P—K5

The first time that Fischer employed this variation (against Parma at Bled 1961), White chose 10 B×N, P×B; 11 B—K2, N—B3; 12 N—N3, and the game was eventually drawn. The text is considerably stronger.

10...P×P; 11 P×P, KN—Q2; 12 B—QB4, B—K2?

It was later discovered that 12...Q—R4! is correct. Fischer's move should have lost the game.

13 B×KP!

This move had been known since the game Duckstein–Euwe, Clare Benedict Tournament 1958, in which White's attack was quickly decisive after 13... O—O; 14 O—O, P×B; 15 N×P, N—QB3; 16 N—Q5!.

13...O—O; 14 O—O, B×B

This move represents Fischer's attempt to rehabilitate the whole variation.

15 Q×B, P—R3!

The only move. If 15...Q×N?; 16 N—B5, Q×KP; 17 QR—K1, Q—N7; 18 N—R6 ch, K—R1; 19 N×P ch, R×N; 20 Q—Q8 ch.

16 Q—R4?

16 Q—R5 has been shown by deep and complex analysis to give White a winning attack, e.g. 16...Q×N; 17 R×P!, Q×N ch; 18 K—R1, K—R1; 19 QR—KB1, with a terrific attack. One can sympathize with Bilek for losing his way in

the complications. After all, the variation was still in its infancy.

16...Q×N; 17 R×BP, R×R; 18 Q—Q8 ch, N—B1; 19 B×R ch, K×B; 20 R—KB1 ch, K—N3; 21 R×N No better is 21 Q—K8 ch, K—R2; 22 R×N, Q—K8 ch!; 23 R—B1, Q—K6 ch; 24 K—R1, Q×N; 25 Q×B, Q—Q2, and White can resign.

21...B—Q2 !; 22 N—B3, Q—K6 ch; 23 K—R1, Q—B8 ch; 24 N—N1, Q×P; 25 R—N8 Or 25 Q—K7, Q×RP; 26 R×N, R×R; 27 Q—Q6 ch, K—R2; 28 Q×R, B—B3.

25...Q—B7; 26 R—B8, Q×RP; 27 R—B3, K—R2, and White lost on time.

One of the things that has always surprised me about Soviet comments on Fischer's style is that it has repeatedly been stated that Fischer likes to avoid complications, that he prefers simple positions. Typical of such comments is the following extract from a report on the Stockholm Interzonal that appeared in Shakhmaty v SSSR in June 1962. The author of this article was Abramov.

'In this tournament Fischer was trying to reach "simple" positions in the middle game, playing them, just as with endgames, very convincingly, creating premises for his opponents' mistakes and making full use of his advantages.'

Such statements, asserting Fischer's desire for simple positions, are ridiculous. How can anyone who revels in the myriad complications of the Poisoned Pawn Variation possibly be accused of having simple tastes?

Fischer played so many good games at Stockholm that it is difficult to be selective. I have chosen the two games that follow because they illustrate the clarity and directness that I like so much in Fischer's play.

33 FISCHER–GERMAN
INTERZONAL TOURNAMENT, STOCKHOLM 1962

Petroff Defence

1 P—K4, P—K4; 2 N—KB3, N—KB3; 3 P—Q4, P×P; 4 P—K5, N—K5; 5 Q—K2
Fischer had made a thorough study of the games and ideas of the leading players from Morphy's time onwards. His interest in the games of the nineteenth century appears to be more than cursory. When asked by *Chess Life* to write a series of articles during the early 1960s he chose to annotate the games of the Steinitz–Dubois match of 1872. This interest in the more historic games and opening ideas occasionally shows itself in his own games. The text, for example, is a move of Steinitz's which has never been popular in master chess. Another example was seen in Fischer's opening in the final game of his 1972 match against Spassky.

5...N—B4
Already an error. The recommended defence is 5...B—N5 ch; 6 K—Q1, P—Q4; 7 P×P, P—KB4 !, with a good game for Black.

6 N×P, N—B3; 7 N×N, NP×N; 8

N—B3, R—QN1; 9 P—B4, B—K2
After 9...N—K3; 10 P—KN3, B—B4
(or 10...B—K2; 11 B—N2); 11 N—K4,
White has a clear advantage. 9...B—
R3; 10 Q—B2, B×B; 11 R×B, N—K3,
is also inadequate: 12 P—B5, B—B4
(if 12...N—B4; 13 B—K3); 13 Q—
N3, N—Q5; 14 Q×P, R—KB1; 15
K—Q1 (also good is 15 B—KN5, B—
K2; 16 P—B6, followed by 17 O—O—O),
15...Q—R5; 16 P—KR3!, and Black
is a pawn down with the worse position.

10 Q—B2!, P—Q4
Not 10...P—Q3; 11 B—K3, R×P?;
12 O—O—O! and White wins a piece.
Now White gains no material advantage
but he does win a tempo.

**11 B—K3!, N—Q2; 12 O—O—O,
O—O; 13 P—KN4!?**
Playing for mate!

**13...B—N5; 14 N—K2, N—N3; 15
N—Q4, Q—K1; 16 P—B3, B—K2;
17 P—B5, P—B4; 18 N—N5, P—
Q5!; 19 B—KB4**
It is too risky to take the pawn: 19 P×P,
P×P; 20 N×QP, Q—R5.

19...P×P?
Overlooking Fischer's 21st move. Correct was 19...B—N2; 20 R—N1, P—

QR3!, when the position is not so clear.
20 N×P(B3), N—R5; 21 B—QN5!

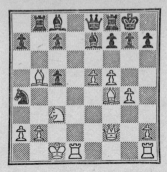

The winning move. With the exchange
of minor pieces Black's attack is destroyed, while White's K-side onslaught
remains intact.

**21...R×B; 22 N×N, R—N5; 23
N—B3, B—N2; 24 KR—K1, K—R1;
25 P—B6!, B—Q1; 26 B—N5**
Threatening 27 R×B, Q×R; 28 P×
P ch, winning the queen.

**26...R—Q5; 27 P×P ch, K×P; 28
B—B6 ch, K—N1; 29 Q—R4, R×
R ch; 30 N×R, Resigns**

---

34 FISCHER–OLAFSSON
INTERZONAL TOURNAMENT, STOCKHOLM 1962

Sicilian Defence

**1 P—K4, P—QB4; 2 N—KB3, P—Q3;
3 P—Q4, P×P; 4 N×P, N—KB3; 5
N—QB3, N—B3; 6 B—QB4, P—K3; 7
B—N3, B—K2; 8 P—B4**
More accurate than 8 O—O, O—O; 9
P—B4, when Black can play 9...P—
Q4, and if 10 P—K5, N×N; 11 Q×N,
N—N5; 12 P—B5, Q—N3!, with a
good game. Estrin–Taimanov, Leningrad 1954. Instead of 9...P—Q4, Black
can play 9...N×N; 10 Q×N, P—
QN3, as in one of the Fischer–Geller

games from the Curaçao Candidates'
Tournament but then White can get the
better game with 11 Q—Q3!, preventing
11...B—R3.
For 8 O—O, O—O; 9 B—K3, see game
4 page 154.

8...O—O
If 8...P—Q4; 9 P—K5, N×N; 10
Q×N, N—N5; 11 P—B5, White already
has a winning positional advantage.

9 B—K3, N×N
If 9...P—Q4; 10 P—K5, N—Q2;
11 O—O, N—B4; 12 Q—R5, with excellent attacking possibilities for White.

Vasyukov–Baranov, Moscow 1955.

   10 B×N, P—QN4; 11 P—K5, P×P; 12 P×P, N—Q2; 13 O—O, P—N5
Now White's attack develops quickly. An interesting defensive try was 13...
B—B4; 14 B×B (not 14 N×P, Q—N3), 14...N×B; 15 Q×Q, R×Q; 16 N×P, B—R3; 17 B—B4 (if 17 N—B7, B×R; 18 N×R, B×P), 17...B×N (Fischer-Geller, Curaçao 1962 went 17...QR—N1; 18 P—QR4, N×P, and now instead of taking the safe, drawing line 19 R×N, B×N; 20 B×B, R×B; 21 R×P, R×P; 22 R(R7)×P, Fischer played 19 N—Q6, and eventually lost): 18 B×B, QR—N1; 19 KR—Q1, R×R ch; 20 R×R, P—N3, and it is difficult to see how White can hold the pawn.

   14 N—K4, B—N2
Not 14...Q—B2; 15 N—B6 ch!, K—R1; 16 Q—R5, with a winning attack.

   15 N—Q6. B×N; 16 P×B, Q—N4; 17 Q—K2, B—Q4
After 17...P—K4; 18 B—K3, White's QN3 bishop is very active.

   18 QR—Q1, B×B; 19 RP×B, P—K4
Apparently the only way to defend against the threat of 20 R—Q3 and 21 R—N3.

   20 Q—N5, P—QR3
Not 20...KR—Q1; 21 Q—Q5, R—KB1; 22 R×P!

   21 Q×N, P×B; 22 Q—B5, Q×Q
After 22...Q—K6 ch; 23 K—R1, the threat of 24 R—Q3, winning the QP, is impossible to meet.

   23 R×Q, KR—Q1; 24 R×QP, QR—B1; 25 R—B2, P—QR4; 26 R(2)—Q2, P—B3; 27 R—QB4, K—B2; 28 R—B7 ch, K—N3
Or 28...R×R; 29 P×R, R—QB1; 30 R—Q7 ch, K—N3; 31 K—B2, wins.

   29 R—K7, P—R4; 30 P—Q7, R—B2; 31 P—B4, K—R2; 32 P—R4, K—N3; 33 R—Q5, Resigns

Curaçao

The site chosen for the 1962 Candidates' Tournament was the island of Curaçao in the Dutch West Indies. As in Yugoslavia three years earlier, there were eight Grandmasters competing in a quadruple round tournament. After his great success at Stockholm, Fischer, and many of his fans, fully expected that he would sweep all the remaining opposition out of the way, and that in 1963 he would be challenging Botvinnik for the world crown. Botvinnik himself was not so sure – he expressed great faith in Tal who, he said, had won every tournament in his life that he had needed to. But the contest on Curaçao was far from the two horse race that had been expected. Tal was unwell almost from the start and had to retire from the tournament before the final quarter could be played. Fischer had no real excuse – he was just in bad form from the very beginning of the tournament. Witness his games from the first two rounds:

35 BENKÖ-FISCHER

CANDIDATES' TOURNAMENT, CURAÇAO 1962

Benkö's Opening

1 P—KN3
Benkö became addicted to this move at Curaçao. He played it eight times scoring three wins, three draws and two losses.
1...N—KB3; 2 B—N2, P—KN3; 3 P—K4, P—Q3; 4 P—Q4, B—N2; 5 N—K2, O—O; 6 O—O, P—K4; 7 QN—B3
Keeping the game in more original channels than 7 P—QB4, which would transpose to the King's Indian Defence.
7...P—B3; 8 P—QR4, QN—Q2; 9 P—R5, P×P?
Conceding ground in the centre. The correct plan was 9...Q—B2, followed by ...R—K1, ...N—B1 and ...N—K3.
10 N×P, N—B4; 11 P—R3, R—K1; 12 R—K1, KN—Q2
Black could have freed his game a little with 12...P—Q4; 13 P×P (13 P—K5, N(B3)—K5), 13...R×R ch; 14 Q×R, N×P; 15 N×N, P×N (not 15...B×N?; 16 N—K7 ch, K—N2; 17 P—R6!, N×P; 18 R×N!, P×R; 19 N×BP, winning) but his position would remain inferior. The line chosen by Fischer leaves him with a cramped position and almost no counterplay.

13 B—K3, Q—B2; 14 P—B4, R—N1; 15 Q—Q2, P—QN4; 16 P×P e.p., P×P?
16...N×NP was essential, even though it left Black with a worse Q-side pawn structure.
17 P—QN4!, N—K3; 18 P—N5!
Winning a pawn.
18...N×N; 19 B×N, B×B ch; 20 Q×B, P—QB4; 21 Q—Q2, B—N2
Black cannot save his QP. If 21...N—B3; 22 QR—Q1, R—K3; 23 P—B5!, P×P; 24 Q—N5 ch, K—B1; 25 P×P, and White wins.
22 QR—Q1, R—K3; 23 P—K5!, B×N; 24 K×B, Q—N2 ch; 25 K—B2, R—Q1; 26 P×P, N—B3; 27 R×R, P×R; 28 Q—K3, K—B2; 29 Q—B3, Q—N1; 30 N—K4!, N×N; 31 Q×N, R—Q2
31...R×P allows 32 Q—K5, R—Q1 (or 32...K—K2; 33 Q—N7 ch); 33 R—Q7 ch!
32 Q—B6, Q—Q1; 33 K—B3, K—N2; 34 P—N4, P—K4
Sacrificing a second pawn in the hope of finding a perpetual check.
35 P×P, R—KB2 ch; 36 K—N2, Q—R5; 37 R—KB1, R×R; 38 K×R, Q×RP ch; 39 Q—N2, Q—K6; 40 Q—K2, Q—KR6 ch, and Black Resigned

36 GELLER-FISCHER

CANDIDATES' TOURNAMENT, CURAÇAO 1962

Sicilian Defence

1 P—K4, P—QB4; 2 N—KB3, P—Q3; 3 P—Q4, P×P; 4 N×P, N—KB3; 5 N—QB3, P—QR3; 6 B—K2, P—K4; 7 N—N3, B—K2; 8 O—O, O—O
The modern approach to the variation is to delay castling by 8...B—K3; 9

P—B4, Q—B2; 10 P—QR4, QN—Q2; 11 K—R1, O—O, although this line also favours White.

9 B—K3, Q—B2; 10 P—QR4, B—K3
An improvement on 10...P—QN3, which Fischer played against the same opponent at Stockholm: 11 Q—Q2, B—N2; 12 P—B3, B—B3 ?; 13 KR—Q1, QN—Q2; 14 Q—K1, P—R3; 15 Q—B1, Q—N2; 16 B—QB4, with a clear advantage to White. Geller later reached a winning position but went astray and only drew.

11 P—R5, QN—Q2; 12 N—Q5
If 12 P—B3, then P—QN4!; 13 P× P e.p., N×NP; 14 B×P, P—Q4, with a complicated position.

12...N×N ?
Correct was 12...B×N; 13 P×B, P—QN4, preventing P—QB4, which puts Black in a vice-like bind on the Q side, e.g. 14 P×P e.p., N×NP; 15 P—QB4, P—QR4 (not 15...N×BP; 16 P—B2!); 16 N×P, N(N3)×QP, with good counter-play for Black.

13 P×N, B—B4; 14 P—QB4, B—N3; 15 R—B1, N—B4 ?
After this move Black is strategically lost. He should have sought counterplay on the K side by 15...P—B4; 16 P—B5, P×P; 17 N×P, N×N; 18 P—QN4, P—B5; 19 B×N, B—Q3.

16 N×N, P×N; 17 P—QN4 !, QR—B1
Not 17...P×P; 18 B—N6 and 19 P—B5, when White completely dominates his left half of the board.

18 Q—N3, B—Q3; 19 KR—Q1, Q—K2; 20 P×P, B×P; 21 B×B, R×B; 22 R—R1 !

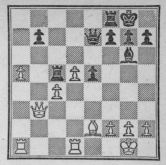

Starting an infiltration along the QN file.
22...R—Q1; 23 R—R4, B—B4; 24 R—N4, B—B1; 25 R—N6, R—Q3
If 25...R×RP; 26 P—Q6, Q—Q2; 27 B—B3, winning the QNP and creating united passed pawns.

26 Q—N4, Q—B2; 27 R×R, Q×R; 28 R—N1, Q—B2; 29 Q—R4 !
Threatening mate, and making way for the entry of the remaining rook at QN6.

29...B—Q2; 30 Q—R3, R×RP; 31 R×P, Q×R; 32 Q×R, P—N3; 33 P—R3, Q—N8 ch; 34 K—R2, B—B4; 35 Q—B3 !
If 35 Q×P, Q—K8.

35...Q—K5; 36 B—B3, Q—Q5; 37 Q×Q, P×Q; 38 P—N4, B—B1; 39 P—B5, P—QR4; 40 P—B6, K—B1; 41 P—Q6
The sealed move. If now 41...K—K1; 42 B—Q1, B—R3; 43 P—N5, B—N4; 44 P—B7, B—Q2; 45 B—R4, or 41... P—R5; 42 P—B7, P—R6; 43 B—B6, P—R7; 44 P—Q7, B×P; 45 B×B, P—R8(Q); 46 P—B8(Q) ch, and so **Black Resigned** without resuming play.

Fischer never recovered from this disastrous start to the tournament. At the halfway stage his score had pulled back to fifty per cent, but by then Petrosian was already two points ahead of him. His play seemed confused. Many of his ideas were shallow. And when he tried something new in the opening his innovation turned out to be a lemon: Fischer–Petrosian (Round 13), French Defence. **1 P—K4, P—K3; 2 P—Q4, P—Q4; 3 N—QB3, N—KB3; 4 B—KN5, B—N5; 5 P—K5, P—KR3; 6 B—Q2, B×N; 7 B×B?!, N—K5; 8 B—R5?.** The 'point' of Fischer's idea – he plans to keep the advantage of the two bishops. **8...O—O; 9 B—Q3, N—QB3; 10 B—B3,**

N×B; 11 P×N, P—B3!; 12 P—KB4, P×P; 13 BP×P, N—K2; 14 N—B3, P—B4 Black already has the advantage. White has a Winawer pawn structure without the compensating advantage of the bishop pair. Petrosian won in forty-three moves.

One of the principle ingredients of Fischer's play that was lacking at Curaçao was the clear attacking style that had been so prevalent in his games at Stockholm. He rarely managed to steer the openings towards positions that gave scope to his attacking instincts. And when he did get into a variation that offered him attacking prospects he misplayed it horribly.

37 FISCHER–KORCHNOY
CANDIDATES' TOURNAMENT, CURAÇAO 1962

Pirc Defence

1 P—K4, P—Q3; 2 P—Q4, N—KB3; 3 N—QB3, P—KN3; 4 P—B4, B—N2; 5 N—B3, O—O; 6 B—K2
After this game the text move rapidly disappeared from favour, and 6 B—Q3 came into vogue, e.g. Fischer–Benkö, US Championship 1963/64: 6 B—Q3, B—N5?; 7 P—KR3, B×N; 8 Q×B, N—B3; 9 B—K3, P—K4; 10 QP×P, P×P; 11 P—B5, P×P; 12 Q×P, N—Q5; 13 Q—B2, N—K1; 14 O—O, N—Q3; 15 Q—N3!, K—R1; 16 Q—N4 P—QB3 (better 16...P—QB4); 17 Q—R5!, Q—K1? (17...N—K3 was the only move); 18 B×N, P×B; 19 R—B6!!, K—N1 (if 19...P×N; 20 P—K5, P—KR3; 21 R×P ch, wins); 20 P—K5, P—KR3; 21 N—K2!, Resigns (because of the threat 22 R×N).

6...P—B4; 7 P×P, Q—R4; 8 O—O, Q×BP ch; 9 K—R1, N—B3
9...N—N5; 10 N—Q5, N—B7 ch; 11 R×N, Q×R; 12 B—K3 is a well known trap.

10 N—Q2
10 Q—K1 is a perfectly playable alternative,.

10...P—QR4!
Typical Sicilian strategy, preparing to drive away White's knight if it goes to QN3.

11 N—N3?
An incredibly weak move from a player of Fischer's calibre, walking into the full force of Black's Q-side counterplay. Best is 11 N—B4, B—N5!; 12 B—K3, Q—R4; 13 B—B3, P—QN4; though Black is still better.

11...Q—N3; 12 P—QR4
Not 12 N—Q5, N×N; 13 P×N, P—R5; 14 P×N, P×N; 15 P(B6)×P, R×P!; 16 P×B(Q), R×Q, and Black wins, e.g. 17 R—QN1?, P×P, or 17 B—Q2, B×P; 18 R—B1, B×R, and 19...P—N7.

12...N—QN5; 13 P—N4?
Overlooking the force of the ensuing combination. Correct was 13 B—B3, when Black's advantage is not all that great.

13...B×P!; 14 B×B, N×B; 15 Q×N, N×P; 16 N—N5
On 16 Q—Q1, Q×N; 17 R—R3, Q—B5, Black keeps his two pawn advantage.
16...N×R; 17 N×N, Q—B3!; 18 P—B5
Since 18 Q—B3, P—B4!; 19 P×P, R×P, leaves White's BP ripe to fall in the ending, and 18 Q—N2, Q—B5; 19 P—N3, Q—Q6, gives Black as much play as in the actual game but without White having any attacking chances.
18...Q—B5; 19 Q—B3, Q×RP; 20 N—B7, Q×N; 21 N—Q5
The last swindling chance was 21 N×R, R×N; 22 P—K5 (if 22 P×P, BP×P; 23 Q—B7 ch, K—R1; 24 Q×KP, Q—R5!; 25 Q×NP, R—K1, winning),

e.g. 22...QP×P? (22...B×P? comes to the same sort of thing); 23 P×P, BP×P; 24 Q—B7 ch, K—R1; 25 B—R6, Q×R ch; 26 Q×Q. But after 22 P—K5 Black simply moves his queen off the exposed QR8 square (22...Q—R5!), and White is lost.
21...QR—K1; 22 B—N5, Q×P; 23 B×P, B—K4!
Threatening mate in one, and thereby enabling his queen to come back to the defence of his K side.
24 R—B2, Q—B8 ch; 25 R—B1, Q—R3; 26 P—R3, P×P; 27 B×R, R×B; 28 N—K7 ch, K—R1; 29 N×P, Q—K3; 30 R—KN1, P—R5; 31 R—N4, Q—N6; 32 Q—B1, P—R6; 33 Resigns

When Fischer returned home from Curaçao he furiously attacked the Soviet contingent for playing as a team. 'There was open collusion between the Russian players. They agreed ahead of time to draw the games they played against each other. Every time they drew they gave each other half a point... They consulted during the game. If I was playing a Russian opponent, the other Russians watched my games and commented on my moves in my hearing.'

He also alleged that during the second half of the tournament Korchnoy deliberately lost games to Petrosian, Keres and Geller just to make sure that one of them would win the tournament.

There was definitely more than an ounce of truth in Fischer's accusations. The fact that so many games between the top Soviet players had been drawn in very short order, indicated that they were quite content to agree quick draws with each other so that they would be fresh when they came to play the other competitors. Fischer, on the other hand, would fight hard in every game and would therefore be far more subject to the strain imposed by a twenty-eight round event.

As to the question of Soviet players advising each other during the games, although I know of one instance (see page 139) when Fischer's non-Soviet opponent was given advice by Soviet players, I would be reluctant to assert that anything of the kind happened at Curaçao unless I had some corroborating evidence to add to Fischer's own accusation.

The third part of Fischer's claim, that Korchnoy deliberately threw games to his compatriots, seems by far the most unlikely of the three. As Keres asked in his widely published rebuttal of Fischer's article: 'Why should Korchnoy offer himself up suddenly as a sacrifice (as Fischer claimed), when he himself still had good chances of finishing first?'

The real reason for Bobby's failure at Curaçao can be detected from the three games given above: he was simply in bad form. It is quite possible that his poor score was affected by the worry that his opponents were conspiring against him, but even so, it was very unfortunate that his accusation should come at a time when it could only be construed as a case of 'Sour Grapes'.

After so much criticism of Fischer's play at Curaçao it would be unfair of me not to give an example of one of his better games. In this lively encounter against Tal, Fischer employs an old line of the Ruy Lopez which he had used a few times during 1960. Since most of Fischer's theoretical preferences were quickly adopted by a multitude of players of all strengths (the Sozin Sicilian, 6 B—QB4 against the Najdorf, the Poisoned Pawn Variation, and later the Exchange Variation of the Lopez), it is a little mysterious why this obscure byway of the Lopez did not also have a spate of popularity.

One also wonders why Fischer never again used this defence after this game. (Probably he considered that it was only good for a draw and therefore inadequate!)

---

38 TAL–FISCHER
CANDIDATES' TOURNAMENT, CURAÇAO 1962

Ruy Lopez

1 P—K4, P—K4; 2 N—KB3, N—QB3; 3 B—N5, B—B4; 4 P—B3
Evans–Fischer, Buenos Aires 1960 went 4 O—O, KN—K2; 5 P—B3, B—N3; 6 P—Q4, P×P; 7 P×P, P—Q4; 8 P×P, KN×P; 9 R—K1 ch, B—K3, and the game was a short draw.
4...KN—K2
4...N—B3; 5 P—Q4, P×P (5...B—N3; 6 O—O, O—O; 7 R—K1, P×P; 8 P×P, P—Q4; 9 P—K5, N—K5, also led to a short draw in Unzicker–Fischer, Leipzig Olympiad 1960); 6 P—K5, N—K5!; 7 O—O (or 7 P×P, B—N5 ch; 8 B—Q2, N×B; 9 QN×N, O—O; 10 O—O, P—QR3; 11 B—R4, P—Q3 with an equal game. Jimenez–Fischer, Leipzig Olympiad 1960), 7...P—Q4!; 8 N×P, O—O; 9 P—B3, N—N4; 10 B×N(B6), P×B, Gligoric–Fischer, Buenos Aires 1960, was yet another short draw.
5 P—Q4, P×P; 6 P×P, B—N5 ch;

7 B—Q2, B×B ch; 8 Q×B, P—QR3; 9 B—R4, P—Q4; 10 P×P, Q×P; 11 N—B3, Q—K3 ch; 12 K—B1, Q—B5 ch; 13 K—N1, O—O; 14 P—Q5, N—R2
Improving on the game Alekhine–Bogolyubov, St. Petersburg 1914 which went 14...R—Q1?; 15 Q—K1!, B—N5; 16 B—N3, Q—B5; 17 P×N, B×N; 18 Q×N, B×BP, and now, with Alekhine's suggestion of 19 N—K2 followed by N—N3, White would have remained a piece ahead with an easy win.
15 R—K1, N—B4
The knight later becomes a target on this square (21 P—N4), and hence 15...N—N3 would probably have been better. Against 15...N—N3 Tal had intended 16 P—R4.
16 P—KR3, N—N4; 17 N×N, P×N; 18 B—N3, Q—B4; 19 R—QB1, Q—Q3; 20 Q—B3, B—Q2!
Now the QBP is indirectly defended because of the reply 21 Q×BP, R—B1.

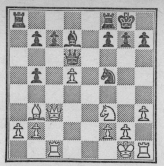

21 P—N4, N—N6!; 22 P×N, Q×
NP ch; 23 K—B1, P—KB4; 24 P—N5,
P—B5; 25 P—Q6 dis ch, K—R1; 26
P×P
If 26 N—K5, P—B6.

26...QR—K1
Not 26...B—B3; 27 R—KN1!, but
stronger than the text is 26...P—N5;
26 Q—Q3, and then 26...QR—K1, the
difference being that with White's queen
driven away from the QB file the pro-
motion of his QBP is not such a useful
tactical resource.
27 B—Q5, B×P ch
Black can also force a draw by 27...R—
K6; 28 P—B8(Q), B×Q; 29 Q×B, R×
N ch, etc. But if Black had played the
variation given in the last note, 27...R—
K6 would win, so White would have had
to find a defence to replace 27 B—Q5.
28 R×B, Q×R ch; 29 K—B2!
Not 29 K—N1?, R—K7, when the
game also ends immediately but with a
slightly different result. **Draw Agreed**

Fischer's furore over the Russian's 'cheating' at Curaçao led him to announce
that he would never again play in the Candidates' Tournament unless the
system was changed. He wanted the last eight players to be forced to play
a series of knockout matches: the quarter-finals and semi-finals to be for the
best of ten games and the final for the best of twelve. In this way, Fischer
argued (correctly), if two players from the same country drew all their
games they wouldn't be harming anyone else. If the score in a match was
level a few more games would be played and if it was still level then the
winner of that match would be decided by the drawing of lots.

Fischer's suggestion was sensible. It reduced the organizational problems
of the Candidates' stage, because whereas most countries cannot afford to
host an event so grand as a twenty-eight round tournament, many are able
to arrange for one or more of the eliminating matches.

This new scheme was discussed at the FIDE Congress in 1963, and, after
meeting with general approval, was put into operation for the next World
Championship cycle.

Convinced that he had been cheated at Curaçao, Bobby was in no doubt
that it was he who was the strongest player in the world and not Botvinnik
or Petrosian. When he arrived at Varna for the 1962 Olympiad he amused
the Russians no end by announcing that he wanted to play the Lady World
Champion, Nona Gaprindashvili, a match at knight odds for a stake of
$3,000. Of course the Russians treated the whole suggestion as a great joke
and the match was never arranged. (There is no doubt that Fischer would
have lost. As Tal put it: 'Fischer is Fischer, but a knight is a knight.')

Fischer's self-confidence at Varna was unbounded. The night before he
was due to play Najdorf, Bobby announced to the rest of his team that he
would win the game in twenty-five moves. Najdorf played the Najdorf
Variation and lost – in twenty-four!

39 FISCHER–NAJDORF
OLYMPIAD, VARNA 1962

Sicilian Defence

Notes by Euwe

1 P—K4	P—QB4
2 N—KB3	P—Q3
3 P—Q4	P×P
4 N×P	N—KB3
5 N—QB3	P—QR3
6 P—KR3	

Obviously directed against 6...P—QN4 as is played in this game. If 6...P—K4; 7 N(Q4)—K2, B—K2; 8 P—KN4!, with advantage to White.

For 6...P—KN3, see Fischer–Reshevsky (game 41).

6 ...   P—QN4

Good or bad? As this game shows, it is, at the very least, a risky move.

7 N—Q5!

An important theoretical innovation.

7 ...   B—N2?

A dubious continuation. On 7...N×P, 8 Q—B3! is very strong: 8...N—B4; 9 N—B6 ch, NP×N; 10 Q×R, B—N2; 11 Q—R7, P—K4; 12 P—QN4!. [According to Fischer, this line is good for Black if he plays 11...Q—B2 instead of 11...P—K4. White should play 9 P—QN4 with equal chances in the complications—DNLL.]

8 N×N ch	NP×N
9 P—QB4	P×P?

Contradicting all principles of opening play. Although Black wins a pawn, this move just helps White to develop his forces. Preferable is 9...P—N5.

10 B×P   B×P

Even if Black hadn't taken this pawn he would still have had a lost position.

11 O—O   P—Q4

After the game Najdorf said that 11...P—K4 would have been better, although it is obvious that Black is still in difficulties.

12 R—K1   P—K4

The best defence was 12...B×P, even though after 13 K×B, P×B; 14 B—K3, one can hardly doubt White's advantage.

13 Q—R4 ch   N—Q2

Of course not 13...Q—Q2 because of 14 B—QN5.

14 R×B!

An exceptionally unusual position. With the help of this positional sacrifice White will keep the initiative for a long time.

14 ...   P×R

15 N—B5!

The aggressing knight soon leads to Black's downfall. After the game Najdorf said that this knight had the power of a queen and a rook.

15 ...   B—B4

If the bishop had stayed 'at home' the attack on the Q file would have been decisive, e.g. 15...R—KN1; 16 B—K3, Q—B2; 17 R—Q1 (threatening 18 B—QN5), 17...R—Q1; 18 B×RP, R—QR1; 19 R—QB1, Q—Q1; 20 Q—B6, etc.

16 N—N7 ch!

Naturally this was not played with the idea of forcing a draw but to prevent Black from castling.

16 ...   K—K2

17 N—B5 ch   K—K1
18 B—K3
Exchanging Black's only active piece.
18 . . .   B×B
19 P×B   Q—N3
If 19...Q—B2; 20 R—QB1, K—B1; 21 Q—Q1, R—B1 (to prevent 22 B—Q5); 22 Q—R5, is decisive; and if 19...R—R2, then 20 Q—N4! threatening 21 N—N7 mate.
20 R—Q1

Also possible was 20 B×BP ch, K—Q1; 21 R—Q1, or 20...K×B; 21 Q×N ch, K—N3; 22 Q—N7 ch, K×N; 23 Q—N4 mate.
But Black's position is so hopeless that White can win in many ways.
20 . . .   R—R2
21 R—Q6   Q—Q1
22 Q—N3   Q—B2
23 B×BP ch   K—Q1
24 B—K6   Resigns

The key game at Varna, as at the previous Olympiad in Leipzig, was Fischer's encounter with the World Champion, this time Botvinnik.

40 BOTVINNIK–FISCHER
OLYMPIAD, VARNA 1962

Grünfeld Defence

Notes by Botvinnik

1 P—QB4   P—KN3
2 P—Q4   N—KB3
3 N—QB3   P—Q4
Fischer plays the Grünfeld very rarely. [This game was actually the first occasion that Fischer had used the Grünfield apart from his game with Donald Byrne in 1956 in which the defence was reached by transposition – DNLL.]
4 N—B3   B—N2
5 Q—N3
Ragozin's system is one of the strongest answers to the Grünfeld Defence.
5 . . .   P×P
6 Q×BP   O—O
7 P—K4   B—N5
And this is Smyslov's system, one of the best methods of defence.
8 B—K3   KN—Q2
9 B—K2
This modest move is not very popular. More energetic here is 9 O—O—O.
9 . . .   N—QB3

More precise would have been 9... N—N3, not yet committing the QN. That variation was played against me by Smyslov in the fourth game of our return match in 1958.
10 R—Q1   N—N3
11 Q—B5   Q—Q3
12 P—KR3   B×N
13 P×B   KR—Q1
A little careless. The correct move was pointed out by Furman: 13...P—K3!, and Black equalizes. But now White can start a dangerous attack with his pawns.
14 P—Q5   N—K4
15 N—N5
On 15 P—B4, Black can play 15... N(K4)—B5.
15 . . .   Q—KB3
16 P—B4   N(K4)—Q2
17 P—K5
Preparing for the 1958 match with Smyslov I analysed the Grünfeld Defence and the diagrammed position in particular! I thought that it didn't matter whether the black queen goes to KR5 or KB4 – the position would still be dangerous for Black, e.g. 17...Q—B4; 18 Q—N4, P—QR4; 19 Q—Q4, P—B4;

20 P×P e.p., P×P; 21 B—N4, P—B4;
22 Q×N; or 17...Q—R5; 18 Q—R3,
P—N4; 19 R—Q4!

Alas my opponent found a third
continuation.

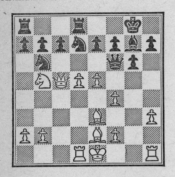

17 ...   Q×BP!

A very unpleasant surprise! For
White the game has just started (up to
now I had been following my earlier
analysis). Now it was quite difficult. I
vaguely remembered that I could
perhaps trap the black queen on the K
side – that was how I reconstructed the
variation in my memory. But when at
last everything seemed to be in order and
I had a familiar position on the board, I
realized that in the position which I had
analysed so much, I had missed something which Fischer found without
difficulty. Now the reader can guess at
the state of my morale!

But when we assess the move 17...
Q×BP from an objective point of view
we can see that it is the best solution to
Black's problems, even though his
position is still not easy.

[What Botvinnik has been trying to
avoid saying is that Fischer found a
strong, one move deep combination
which he, Botvinnik, had overlooked
despite having studied the position for
hours – DNLL.]

18 B×Q   N×Q
19 N×BP   QR—B1
20 P—Q6   P×P
21 P×P   B×P

Black has won a pawn but White's
knight at QB7 and the pawn at Q6 limit
the scope of Black's rooks. Besides,
White has the two bishops.

First White must complete his
development.

22 O—O   N(N3)—Q2

A serious blunder; Black obviously
overestimated his chances. Natural and
better was 22...N(B4)—Q2, preparing
to transfer his bishop to K4. After 23
B—B3, B—K4; 24 B×B, N×B; 25
B×P, R—N1, White's advantage is very
slight.

But now White controls the important
squares Q5 and K5 and he has a considerable advantage in space.

23 R—Q5   P—N3
24 B—B3

Hopeless. Until this moment White
had played quite consistently, and by
continuing 24 B—B4, threatening R—
K1—K7, he would have increased his
activity as much as possible. But the
bishop on KB3 is not doing anything
and it just becomes an object of attack.

Now Black frees himself while White
is a pawn down and in a critical position.

24 ...   N—K3!

Seemingly forcing the exchange of the
knight at QB7, since 25 B—R2, N—Q5;
26 B—N2, N—KB3, is quite bad for
White. But in fact, by playing 26 R×N!
(suggested by Geller), 26...B×R; 27
R—K1, White has a good chance to
come out 'dry from the water.'

Now White makes a second mistake
which renders his position quite hopeless.

25 N×N   P×N
26 R—Q3   N—B4
27 R—K3   P—K4

This is the simplest. If 27...B—Q5;
28 R—R3, P—K4; 29 B—N5, R×P; 30
B—K7, R—Q2; 31 B—N4, and Black
loses the exchange.

28 B×P   B×B
29 R×B   R×P
30 R—K7   R—Q2
31 R×R   N×R
32 B—N4

Futile, because White cannot go into
the (lost) rook ending. I should have

played the immediate 32 R—K1, K—B1; 33 R—K3 (or 33 B—Q5), and Black would have had some technical difficulties.

32 . . .	R—B2
33 R—K1	K—B2
34 K—N2	

Better was 34 B—K6 ch. The bishop isn't well placed on KN4.

34 . . .	N—B4
35 R—K3	R—K2
36 R—KB3 ch	

White's best chance lay in exchanging rooks and creating a position with his king on Q4 (or K3), bishop on K2, and pawn on KB4. But now this is impossible because if 36 K—B3, then P—KR4!, and White loses his bishop.

36 . . .	K—N2
37 R—B3	R—K5
38 B—Q1	R—Q5

Until this moment I thought the game was lost but the text made me think a bit. Why did my opponent allow my bishop to reach the only good square QB2? By playing 38...R—K8 ! (39 B—B2, R—QB8), Fischer would have completely destroyed White's defence.

| 39 B—B2 | K—B3 |
| 40 K—B3 | K—N4 |

Generally speaking the king belongs on Q3, when Black's knight on QB4 no longer needs the protection of the QNP. Black can then win by advancing his QRP and QNP.

But the text manoeuvre is not bad either.

41 K—N3

White is now almost in zugzwang. If he moves his king, Black plays ...K—R5 and ...N—K3—B5(×RP); on B—N1, R—Q8 wins; and if the white rook moves then ...R—K5 is decisive. So after 41...R—N5; 42 P—R3, R—Q5; 43 P—B3, P—QR4, White would not have had a satisfactory move.

41 . . .   N—K5 ch

This could have led to an immediate draw even in the moment when Black was quite near realizing his aim.

Psychologically it is obvious why Black wanted to play a rook ending: because earlier (look at White's 33rd move), White refused to do so. But the difference between these rook endings is vital – Black's king position on KN4 is not so appropriate.

| 42 B×N | R×B |
| 43 R—R3 | |

Natural and bad. Now White again has the wish to lose. 43 R—B7! was necessary, when White reaches a drawn position as in the game; the position of the QRP, on R2 instead of R4, is not important.

43 . . .   R—K2

It seems that 43...P—QR4! would have been better. If 44 R—N3, then R—N5, and Black has either a won rook ending or, after 45 R×R, P×R; 46 P—B4 ch, K—B4; 47 K—B3, K—K3; 48 K—K4 (48 K—N4, P—R3), 48...K—Q3; 49 K—Q4, P—QN4; 50 K—Q3, K—Q4, probably a won pawn ending.

44 R—KB3   R—QB2

The last chance to win was in the manoeuvre ...K—R3—N2, improving the position of the king.

45 P—QR4

Here Black sealed the move. White's threat was 46 P—R5 (e.g. 45...R—B5; 46 P—R5, P×P, - or 46...P—N4; 47 R—B7, - 47 R—B7, P—QR3; 48 P—R4 ch, K—R3; 49 R—Q7), to exchange a few pawns on the Q side thus guaranteeing him the draw because of Black's weak KRP and badly placed king.

The most cunning move was 45...K—R3, but even then, after 46 R—Q3 !, R—

B4; 47 P—R4, R—QR4; 48 R—Q4, Black does not achieve much.

What happened in the game should probably also lead to a draw.

45 . . .	R—B4
46 R—B7	R—R4
47 R×KRP !!	

An excellent idea, found by Geller during the night's analysis. Because of the bad position of Black's king the connected passed pawns are not so mobile.

| 47 . . . | R×P |
| 48 P—R4 ch | K—B4 |

Or 48...K—B3; 49 R—QN7!, R—R4; 50 K—N4, P—QN4; 51 P—B4, P—R3; 52 R—N6 ch, K—B2; 53 R—N7 ch, and White is out of danger.

| 49 R—KB7 ch | K—K4 |
| 50 R—KN7 | |

The weakness of Black's KNP and QRP give White enough counterplay.

| 50 . . . | R—R8 |
| 51 K—B3 | P—QN4 |

Black cannot win by 51...K—Q4 or 51...K—Q5, e.g., 51...K—Q5; 52 R×NP, P—N4; 53 P—R5, P—N5; 54 P—R6, R—R8 (or 54...P—N6; 55 R—N4 ch!, K—B4 – 55...K—Q6; 56 R—N4, K—B7; 57 R—QB4 ch – 56 R—N5 ch, K—N5;* 57 R—N4 ch, K—R6; 58 R—KR4!, P—N7; 59 P—R7, P—N8(Q); 60 P—R8(Q), and Black cannot win because his rook on QR8 is blocked by his own king); 55 K—N2, R—R4; 56 R—R6, P—N6; 57 R×P, R×P; 58 R—QN7, K—B5; 59 K—B3, R—QB3; 60 K—K3, K—B6; 61 P—B4, R—B4; 62 K—B3, P—N7 (62...R—B5; 63 P—B5, P—N7; 64 P—B6, R—B3; 65 P—B7, R—B3 ch; 66 K—K3); 63 R×P, K×R; 64 K—K4, and White is saved by his KBP.

| 52 P—R5 ! | |

Now Black is left with two RPs and the position is a theoretical draw.

52 . . .	R—R6 ch
53 K—N2	P×P
54 R—N5 ch	K—Q3
55 R×NP	P—R5
56 P—B4	K—B3
57 R—N8	P—R6 ch
58 K—R2	P—R4
59 P—B5	K—B2
60 R—N5	K—Q3
61 P—B6	

Generally speaking, even without White's KBP, the ending is drawn, as can be discovered from any textbook.

61 . . .	K—K3
62 R—N6 ch	K—B2
63 R—R6	K—N3
64 R—B6	P—R5
65 R—R6	K—B2
66 R—B6	R—Q6
67 R—R6	P—R6
68 K—N1	
	Draw Agreed

* In *My Sixty Memorable Games* Fischer analyses a win from this position starting with 56...K—B3! – DNLL.

6

FISCHER THE MAGICIAN

In the opening a chess master should play like a book; in the middle game like a magician and in the endgame like a machine. SPIELMANN

After the disappointment of the Curaçao Candidates' Tournament Fischer's internal dynamo seemed to wind itself down over a two-year period. Apart from the Varna Olympiad he did not compete again in the international arena until the Capablanca Memorial Tournament in August 1965. During 1963 however, he was not entirely dormant. At the beginning of the year he won the US Championship for the fifth time; on this occasion he lost one game, to Mednis, on the white side of the Winawer Variation.

The tournament was a race between Fischer and Reshevsky. The two had not met since their abortive match had ended sixteen months earlier, and their individual encounter was to decide first place.

---

41 FISCHER–RESHEVSKY
US CHAMPIONSHIP 1962/63

Sicilian Defence

Notes by Tal

This game was, no doubt, the centre of attraction at the US Championship. From the moment when the realm of chess first heard the name Fischer, there has been a constant battle between him and Reshevsky for the title of Chess King of the New World. Many people remember their sensational game from the championship of their country in 1958/59 when Reshevsky was in a hopeless position on the tenth move (see page 64). A number of tournament meetings between them have finished in a draw but the wunderkind usually had

the initiative. This time, though, the initiative was in Reshevsky's hands.

Fischer's impressive victories in the USA Championships (four times in succession!) and particularly his jump up the graph of stronger players, has created for the young Grandmaster the reputation of 'American player number one.' Reshevsky could not reconcile himself to this fact and at the big international tournament in Buenos Aires (1960) declared to a journalist that his main aim was to finish ahead of 'that young upstart.' And there he succeeded: playing very well Reshevsky scored one of the biggest successes of his career, sharing the first place with Korchnoy.

Meanwhile Fischer had one of his worst tournaments; he did not score even fifty per cent. So again it was not clear who was the number one American chess-player.

In 1961 they played a match which did not determine anything. It was interrupted with the score standing at +2 —2 =7. Again it was not decided who was the strongest player.

The year 1962 started very well for Fischer. He won the Stockholm Inter-zonal Tournament brilliantly, and then he had a good result in the Candidates' Tournament but was dissatisfied with his performance because he thought of himself as being the unrecognized World Champion. Whose fault was Fischer's failure at Curaçao? It appears that the 'fault' lies in the system, (why are the scores from the Interzonal not taken into consideration?); and in the winners of the tournament, the Soviet Grand-masters to whom Fischer lost, for agreeing draws amongst each other; and in Botvinnik, who refused to play a match with Fischer who was challenging the World Champion's title. Fischer uttered declarations like these after the tournament in Curaçao.

And in the meantime? Fischer played very unsuccessfully in the XVth Olympiad. [Fischer's score at Varna was eight wins, six draws, and three losses –DNLL.]

In 1962 Reshevsky did not take part in serious competitions. Perhaps he was preparing for the next USA Championship. The first round of the tournament brought a surprise when Fischer lost to Mednis. The tournament was only eleven rounds long so the interest was then quite high. And then, in the middle of the tournament, came the meeting of these two old opponents.

1	P—K4	P—QB4
2	N—KB3	P—Q3
3	P—Q4	P×P
4	N×P	N—KB3
5	N—QB3	P—QR3
6	P—KR3	

Until recently, the variation adopted by Reshevsky was almost the only one possible against Fischer's 1 P—K4. It is not easy to refute one's own favourite opening; that is why Fischer, who is consistent in his opening tastes, has tried various continuations 6 B—QB4, 6 B—K2, and 6 P—KR3. The text move became infamous after the game Gereben–Geller, Budapest 1952, but was fully rehabilitated by Fischer's convinc-ing victories over Bolbochan (Stockholm Interzonal 1962) and Najdorf (Varna Olympiad 1962 – page 78). It is not such a bad move as one might think after the first of these games, but it is not so strong either. White's idea is not at all to attack Black's king with his K-side pawn advance, but to play for control of the square Q5!

[The first sentence of this note is completely contrary to what I have been saying. It is also wrong. Fischer's score against the Najdorf Variation in master tournaments up to the time that this game was played was 66.7% compared with a 55% record against the Winawer Variation and 58.3% against the Caro-Kann. Tal's comment was probably corrupted by his own experiences against Fischer, which included a score of two out of two with the Najdorf – DNLL.]

6 . . .   P—KN3

I think that the easiest way to stress the harmlessness of White's plan is to play 6. . .P—K3, going into the Scheven-ingen Variation, in which the move P—KR3 usually turns out to be useless. But even the scheme chosen by Reshevsky gave Black a good game.

7	P—KN4	B—N2
8	P—N5	N—R4!

Very strong. Black is going to put his knight on White's weakened KB4 square.

9	B—K2	P—K4
10	N—N3	N—B5
11	N—Q5	N×N

Why? Black devalues his preceding manoeuvre. Was he really afraid of White taking on KB4? More logical would have been 11...O—O (a similar idea to the King's Indian Defence!), followed by 12 P—KR4, N—Q2 (12...

P—B4!? is interesting); 13 B—N4, P—B4; 14 P×P e.p., N×BP, which leads to a sharp position that is not bad for Black.

  12 Q×N   N—B3

Allowing a manoeuvre which gives White a positional advantage. The correct counter-attack was 12...B—K3; 13 Q×NP, N—Q2, when the disadvantages of the early march of the KNP are quite obvious.

13 B—N4!

It is obvious here that the exchange of light-squared bishops is better for White, because the black pawns on Q3 and K4 obstruct the bishop at KN2. Black's QB is one of the defenders of his Q4 square, and it is good for White to destroy it.

  13 . . .   B×B

Reshevsky under-estimated White's position after the recapture. Otherwise it is difficult to explain why he adds to White's positional advantage by half-opening the KR file. This new advantage is decisive, because Black is now tied down to defend the weak pawn at KR2. Here he should probably have considered the counter-attack 13...P—B4; 14 P× P e.p. (14 KP×P, N—K2; 15 Q—Q3, P×P), 14...Q×P; 15 B×B, R×B; 16 P—QB3, R—B2.

  14 P×B   Q—B1
  15 Q—Q1!

The only (but adequate) defence of both the QBP and the forward KNP.

  15 . . .   N—Q5

Black's play in this game is very passive. After the exchange of knights, White gains another half-open line and Black just has to defend himself without having much of a future – the difference in scope between the bishops is far too big.

After 15...Q—K3; 16 B—K3, O—O—O, Black would have had a tenable position, but now it is probably hopeless. It is true that in order to win White must possess an exceptional technique. This, Fischer now demonstrates with full strength.

  16 P—QB3   N×N
  17 P×N   Q—K3
  18 R—R5!

White's control of the Q5 square is overwhelming. Black tries to activate his pieces but meets a neat tactical refutation.

  18 . . .   P—B3
  19 Q—Q5!   Q×Q

19...Q×NP; 20 Q×NP, O—O, is not possible because after 21 P×P the game will be decided along the KR file.

  20 R×Q   K—Q2
  21 P×P   B×P
  22 P—N5   B—K2
  23 K—K2

Taking into account the fact that Black must wait patiently for the situation to develop, White does not hurry. He improves the position of all his pieces!

  23 . . .   QR—KB1
  24 B—K3   R—B1
  25 P—N4

Playing to weaken Black's Q-side pawns.

  25 . . .   P—N4

Preventing 25 P—N5; but now something even worse happens. Since the QR file belongs to White, the weak pawn at QR3 is more important than that at QN2 (after 26 P—N5, P×P; 27 R× NP).

  26 R(Q5)—Q1!

This second retreat from Q5 to Q1 (cf. White's fifteenth move) is the best continuation. White can afford to switch the pressure from the Q file since Black's rooks, tied down to the defence of the RPs, will not be available for action.

26 . . .   K—K3
27 R—R1   R—B3
28 R—KR3   B—B1

There is no other way of defending the KRP.

29 R(R1)—R1   R—B2

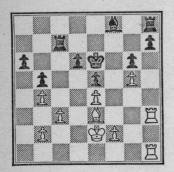

30 R—R4!

White does not prevent . . .P—Q4 but encourages it. Black cannot move anything else without losing either the KRP or the QRP (e.g. 30...R—Q2; 31 R—R1). If 30...R—B5, instead of 31 R×P, R×R; 32 R×R, R—B2; 33 R—R7, more consistent would be 31 P—B3, R—B2; 32 R(4)—R3.

30 . . .   P—Q4

Now Black has one weakness less, but White gains an open file, which is more important.

31 R—R1   R—B3

32 P×P ch   K×P
33 R—Q1 ch   K—K3
34 R—Q8

It is obvious that White is winning. It is just a matter of method, and here Fischer finds a very subtle one.

34 . . .   K—B4
35 R—R8   R—K3
36 R—R3   B—N2

Forced, since 36...K—N5 is impossible because of 37 R—N3 ch, K—R4; 38 R—B3, B—N2; 39 R×R, B×R; 40 R—B8, B—N2; 41 R—B7.

37 R×R   B×R
38 R×P   R—K1
39 R—KB7 ch

White's rook is very impressive.

39 . . .   K—N5

After 39...K—K5, White wins without much effort by 40 B—B5.

40 P—B3 ch   K—N6
41 K—Q3

It is a matter of taste. 41 K—B1, threatening mate, was not bad, but the move in the game is more consistent.

41 . . .   P—K5 ch

Preventing 42 K—K4. The rest is simple.

42 P×P, R—Q1 ch; 43 B—Q4, K—N5; 44 R—B1, B—K4; 45 K—K3, B—B2; 46 R—KN1 ch, K—R5; 47 K—B3, R—Q2; 48 P—K5, R—B2 ch; 49 K—K4, R—B4; 50 P—K6, B—Q1; 51 B—B6, B×B; 52 P×B, R×P; 53 K—Q5, R—B7; 54 R—K1, Resigns

After the 1962/63 US Championship, Fischer virtually withdrew from competitive chess for a year. He played in two Swiss system tournaments, conceding only one draw between them. When Gregor and Jacqueline Piatigorsky sent out invitations for the first 'Piatigorsky Cup' tournament, Fischer must dearly have wanted to accept. Here was an opportunity to play in a tournament in which only two of the aspirants were from the Soviet Union (so no 'cheating'), and one of them was the World Champion, Tigran Petrosian. For Fischer to win a tournament ahead of Petrosian would have added credibility to his claim that Curaçao did not provide a just result. But because of the ill feeling that was left over from the abortive match with Reshevsky, Fischer decided not to play in the Piatigorsky Cup. His next proper tournament was the US Championship that began at the end of 1963.

I have already remarked that in the USA most of Fischer's opponents seemed like children in comparison. In the following game, for example, we see how a strong master, when presented with an excellent opportunity in the opening, can turn a really fine position into a losing one within the space of two or three moves.

42 ADDISON–FISCHER
US CHAMPIONSHIP 1963/64

Ruy Lopez

1 P—K4, P—K4; 2 N—KB3, N—QB3; 3 B—N5, P—QR3; 4 B—R4, P—QN4; 5 B—N3, N—R4

This system of Taimanov's has never been popular in top class chess for a good reason – it is very bad for Black. Fischer's choice of it here as a surprise weapon probably owes something to the great self confidence that he feels when playing against opponents who are below Grandmaster calibre. Against Addison, Fischer had a particularly good reason to feel confident. He had already demonstrated that he could give the master pawn and move at five-minute chess, play blindfold and still make an even score!

6 P—Q4, P×P; 7 Q×P, N—K2; 8 P—B3, N×B; 9 P×N, B—N2

White has an excellent position from the opening but after his next move his advantage disappears. Now you see it . . .

10 B—B4?

Overlooking Fischer's sharp reply. Best was 10 O—O, and if 10. . .P—Q4, then 11 P×P, N×P?; 12 R—K1 ch. Also good was 10 P—QN4 e.g. 10. . .P—Q4; 11 P—K5!.

10. . .P—Q4!

. . . now you don't! Black has snatched the initiative.

11 P—K5

On 11 P×P, N×P, Black has the advantage because of the two bishops.

11. . .P—QB4!; 12 Q—Q3

Not 12 Q×BP ??, N—B4, winning the queen.

12. . .N—N3; 13 B—N3

If 13 B—N5, Q—B2; 14 O—O, P—R3, followed by . . .B—K2, . . .O—O and White's KP is in trouble.

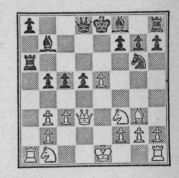

13. . .B—K2

From an inferior opening Fischer has reached a clearly superior position. He has the bishop pair, a spatial advantage on the Q side and the more active piece development.

14 QN—Q2, N—B1; 15 O—O, N—K3; 16 QR—Q1, P—N4!; 17 P—R3, P—KR4: 18 KR—K1, Q—N3; 19 N—B1

Threatening 20 N—K3 and 21 N—B5, with some counterplay.

19 . . .P—Q5!

Counterplay overruled.

20 N(B3)—Q2

Naturally White cannot capture twice on Q4 because of the pin on the Q file.

20. . .P—KN5

Threatening 21. . .P—R5; 22 B—R2, P—N6; 23 P×NP, P—B5, followed by . . .QP×P dis ch.

21 P—R4, Q—B3; 22 Q—K4

If 22 N—K4 ?, then P—B5!; 23 NP× P ?, N—B4!

22. . .O—O—O; 23 Q×Q ch, B×Q

The exchange of queens has eradicated White's fears of a mating attack, but Black's positional advantage is overwhelming. White's KRP is weak and his KP is artificially isolated. Black on the other hand has a passed QP.

24 P—QB4, K—Q2!; 25 R—R1, R— R1; 26 N—K4, B×N!; 27 R×B, N— N2!

The KRP dies.

28 N—Q2, N—B4; 29 R—B4, K— K3; 30 N—K4, P×P; 31 P×P, KR— QN1; 32 R—R2, R—N5; 33 N—Q2, N×P

Threatening 34. . .B—N4.

34 B×N, B×B; 35 R—K4, B—N4; 36 P—B4, P×P e.p.; 37 N×P, B— K6 ch; 38 K—R2, R×BP; 39 Resigns

The almost pure simplicity with which Fischer annihilated his master opponent from a substantially inferior position is somewhat embarrassing.

The 1963/64 Championship is the best known of all Fischer's tournament results because that was the year that he scored 100%. Making a clean sweep in a tournament as strong as the US Championship is an incredible feat even for a Fischer. Once a player has started a tournament with a string of wins it becomes the obligation of each successive opponent to stop the run. That none of Fischer's eleven opponents, even those endowed with the advantage of the white pieces, could manage to hold him to a draw, is an outstanding ovation to the magical qualities that had crept into his play. Part of his success in this tournament is probably due to the overbearing psychological pressure that was placed on every one of Fischer's opponents: each of them could, as an individual, be expected to have great difficulty in beating the champion or even holding him to a draw. But collectively? – The odds against an 11–0 shutout must be enormous.

As in the Addison game, Fischer's magical powers occasionally needed the help of an assistant – his opponent. His game against Reshevsky was a prime example.

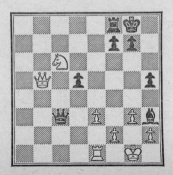

Reshevsky, in time trouble as usual, continued with **34 R—N1 ?. 34 R—Q1** would pick up the QP, e.g. 34...R—K1; 35 Q×P, R×P, and now not 36 N—K7 ch?, R×N; 37 Q—Q8 ch, K—R2; 38 Q×R, because of 38...Q—B6, but simply 36 P×R, Q×P ch; 37 K—R1. **34...Q—B7; 35 N—K7 ch?.** Another error. 35 R—K1 was correct, and if 35...Q—K5; 36 Q×P !, or 35...Q—Q7; 36 Q—N4 (36...Q—Q6 ?; 37 N—K7 ch, K—R1; 38 N—N6 ch). **35...K—R1; 36 N×P, R—B1; 37 N—B3 ?.** Yet another lemon. I wish I had £1 for every mistake that Reshevsky has made in time trouble. White must play 37 Q—N4 so that 37...Q—B8 ch can be met by 38 Q—K1.

37...R×N; 38 Q×P ch, K—N1; 39 N—N8 ch, R—B1; 40 R×R ch, B×R. So Reshevsky has made the time control but in the process his position has disappeared. Now he plays a few more moves through inertia. **41 K—B1, B—R3 ch; 42 K—K1, Q—B6 ch; 43 K—Q1, Q—Q6 ch; 44 K—B1, Q—B6 ch; 45 K—Q1, B—B5; 46 Q—B3, B—N6 ch; 47 K—K2, Q—B5 ch; 48 Resigns.**

But Fischer did not need to resort to luck in every game. Against Robert Byrne he produced what is probably the greatest creative masterpiece of his career.

---

43 R. BYRNE–FISCHER
US CHAMPIONSHIP 1963/64

Grünfeld/Slav Defence

1	P—Q4	N—KB3
2	P—QB4	P—KN3
3	P—KN3	P—B3
4	B—N2	

Weak is 4 P—Q5, P×P; 5 P×P, P—Q3; 6 B—N2, B—N2; 7 N—QB3, O—O; 8 N—B3 (thus far Euwe–Stahlberg, Zurich 1953), 8...B—N5; 9 N—Q4, Q—B1 !, with a good game for Black.

4	...	P—Q4
5	P×P	

The clearest continuation, eliminating the possibility of ...P×P which, in some variations, wins a pawn for Black, e.g. 5 N—KB3, B—N2; 6 O—O, O—O; 7 N—B3, P×P, and now 8 P—K4, QN—Q2; 9 Q—K2, N—N3; 10 R—Q1, P—KR3 (Colle–Grünfeld, Meran 1926), and 8 N—K5, B—K3; 9 P—K4, QN—Q2;

10 P—B4, Q—N3 (Bogoljubov–Alekhine, match 1929), are both favourable to Black.

5	...	P×P
6	N—QB3	B—N2
7	P—K3	

A more active continuation is 7 N—R3 (aiming for KB4), B×N; 8 B×B, N—B3; 9 B—N2, P—K3; 10 P—K3, O—O; 11 B—Q2, R—B1; 12 O—O. Botvinnik–Bronstein, match 1951. Also 7 N—B3, followed by O—O and N—K5 is more logical than the text. Byrne's system of development gives his opponent too much leeway in the centre.

7	...	O—O
8	KN—K2	N—B3
9	O—O	P—N3
10	P—N3 ?!	

10 N—B4 would have been more consistent.

10 . . .   B—QR3

In contrast to White's quiet intentions, Fischer is keen to seize the initiative. Just watch White's Q3 square.

11 B—QR3   R—K1
12 Q—Q2   P—K4 !

Byrne probably underestimated this move, thinking that he could take advantage of Black's isolated QP. But the dynamic features of the position are more important.

13 P×P ?!   N×P
14 KR—Q1 ?

A fatal error, leaving the KBP without sufficient protection. After 14 QR—Q1, Black must play carefully to avoid losing a pawn, e.g. 14...N—K5; 15 N×N, P×N; 16 B×P, Q×Q; 17 R×Q, B× N; 22 R—Q7, and White wins. Analysis by Averbakh.

After 14 QR—Q1, Black must play 14...Q—B1 ! (not discovered by Fischer until months after the game), when the QP is taboo: 15 N×P (best is 15 B— N2, when 15...Q—KB4 keeps the initiative), 15...N×N; 16 B×N, R— Q1; 17 P—B4, R×B!; 18 Q×R, B— N2!; 19 Q—Q8 ch, Q×Q; 20 R× Q ch, R×R; 21 P×N, B×P, with the better ending for Black. Analysis by Fischer.

14 . . .   N—Q6
15 Q—B2

If 15 N—B4, N—K5; 16 N×N, P× N (not 16...B×R; 17 N—Q6!); 17 QR—N1, R—QB1!; 18 N×N, B— B6!; 19 Q—K2, B×N, with an overwhelming position.

15 . . .   N×P !!

The logical culmination of Fischer's strategy – White's king is blasted open and immediately becomes the victim of a beastly attack. When making this move Fischer must have calculated to the end of the game and seen what Rossolimo and Sherwin missed seven moves later.

16 K×N   N—N5 ch
17 K—N1   N×KP
18 Q—Q2   N×B !

Exposing White's king still further. If instead 18...N×R ?, then 19 R×N, and White picks up the QP for free.

19 K×N   P—Q5 !

Opening the long white diagonal.

20 N×P   B—N2 ch
21 K—B1

If 21 K—N1, B×N ch; 22 Q×B, R— K8 ch!; 23 K—B2, Q×Q ch; 24 R×Q, R×R, and Black wins; or 21 K—B2, Q—Q2; 22 B—N2, Q—R6; 23 N—B3, B—KR3; 24 Q—Q3, B—K6 ch; 25 Q×B, R×Q; 26 K×R, R—K1 ch; 27 K—B2, Q—B4.

21 . . .   Q—Q2 !

Threatening 22...Q—R6 ch.

The enormity of Fischer's conception may be judged from the fact that more than one titled player thought that Byrne had a won game: 'The kibitzers (in a separate room with demonstration boards) had predicted all of Fischer's moves, after 12...P—K4, but could not see how he won after 22 Q—KB2. In

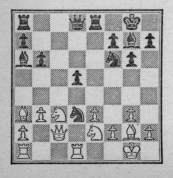

fact Rossolimo had started saying Fischer, having no winning line, might even be lost! Byrne kept on thinking and ... eventually he did resign. Rossolimo said this was insanity. Then Byrne came in and showed us 22 Q—KB2, Q—R6 ch; 23 K—N1, R—K8 ch. Sherwin was also very ashamed of not seeing this simple win.' – Stewart Reuben in *Chess*.

Winning the US Championship with a 100% score brought Fischer more fame than any other chess player has ever known – he was profiled in *Life* magazine. Since the 1963/64 Championship was also a zonal tournament Fischer had qualified for a place in the Amsterdam Interzonal. But although FIDE had, after Fischer's complaints following the Curaçao tournament, changed the form of the Candidates' stage to a series of eliminating matches (as Fischer had suggested), he still abstained from Amsterdam. He complained that the prize money (first was about 500 dollars), was totally inadequate for the work involved in a twenty-two round tournament. His only chess in 1964 was a nationwide exhibition tour.

In 1965 Fischer received an invitation to play in the Capablanca Memorial Tournament, a very strong event that is held annually in Cuba, usually in Havana. Because of the strained relations that have existed for some time between the Governments of the USA and Cuba, Fischer was refused permission to play by the US State Department. Fidel Castro was particularly anxious that Fischer should participate. A keen chess player himself, Castro would sometimes go along to watch the play in the Capablanca Memorial. The only way that it was possible for Fischer to take part was for him to communicate with Havana by telephone or telex, in that way he could play from New York.

Even when all the other players had just arrived in Havana no decision had been reached on Fischer's participation. A players' meeting was held to discuss the situation. For five hours they argued and argued – the Russians wanted him excluded, the others were anxious to have him play. Eventually the Soviet players made the concession that Fischer could play provided that all the other competitors signed a petition against the US State Department, but Donner and Lehmann refused. In an attempt to break the deadlock, Senor Barreras, the President of the Cuban Chess Federation, produced a tray of cocktails. Then he produced another tray of cocktails; and another, and ... But still there was no agreement. After ten or so Daiquiris, Smyslov stood on the table and most emphatically insisted that Fischer should not be allowed to play. But that was not really what Barreras, or his federation, or the other players wanted. So with more diplomacy than democracy Senor Barreras made the decision himself. He notified Fischer that he would be allowed to play by telex.

Due to the delays involved in transmitting moves Fischer's games lasted for about seven hours rather than five. The extra strain imposed on him was enormous yet he managed to finish in a tie for second place (with Geller and Ivkov) behind Smyslov. Had he been playing his games in the Havana Libre Hotel (formally a Hilton, but donated to the Revolutionary Government in

1959) instead of the Marshall Chess Club, I am sure that Fischer would have won the tournament by the same sort of margin as at Stockholm.

From 1962 to 1965 Fischer had made no changes in his opening repertoire. But at the same time one of his favourite systems, the Poisoned Pawn Variation, was being extensively analysed and repeatedly played in the international arena. New ideas were being found all the time, but when he came up against one of them Fischer showed that reams of theoretical analysis can be made useless by one really strong move. Witness the following dramatic climax.

44 TRINGOV–FISCHER
HAVANA 1965

Sicilian Defence

1 P—K4, P—QB4; 2 N—KB3, P—Q3; 3 P—Q4, P×P; 4 N×P, N—KB3; 5 N—QB3, P—QR3; 6 B—KN5, P—K3; 7 P—B4, Q—N3; 8 Q—Q2, Q×P; 9 R—QN1, Q—R6; 10 P—K5, P×P; 11 P×P, KN—Q2; 12 B—QB4, B—N5; 13 R—N3, Q—R4; 14 O—O, O—O; 15 N×P, P×N; 16 B×KP ch, K—R1; 17 R×R ch, B×R; 18 Q—B4

Thus far the game has followed an analysis which appeared in Archives a few months earlier. The analysis continued 18...Q×KP, and at the end of the complications White was on top.

But now comes an improvement which enables Fischer to wipe out his Grandmaster opponent in only four more moves!

18...N—QB3 !

As it says in the beginner's books, develop your pieces.

19 Q—B7, Q—B4 ch; 20 K—R1, N—B3 !

Preventing the mate and intending 21... B×B.

21 B×B, N×P; 22 Q—K6, N(K4)—N5 !; 23 Resigns

Black threatens 23...R×B as well as 23...N—B7 ch; 24 K—N1, N—R6 dbl ch; 25 K—R1, Q—N8 mate.

Although he did not win the Havana tournament I feel that Fischer's result represented an improvement on his previous playing strength. As I said in the first chapter, Fischer's three periods of hibernation were each marked by stronger play on his return. Had he been present in Havana to play at his best his score there would have been sufficiently better to have added even more weight to my argument. As it is, I shall illustrate this particular advance in Fischer's ability by listing his results for the next three years.

Year	Tournament	Place	Won	Drew	Lost
1965/66	US Championship	1st	8	1	2
1966	Piatigorsky Cup	2nd	7	8	3
1966	Havana Olympiad		14	2	1
1966/67	US Championship	1st	8	3	0
1967	Monaco	1st	6	2	1
1967	Skopje	1st	12	3	2
1967	Sousse Interzonal	withdrew when leading	7	3	0
1968	Natanya	1st	10	3	0
1968	Vinkovci	1st	9	4	0

From these nine events Fischer scored a total of 81 wins, 29 draws and 9 losses – just over 80%. At the Havana Olympiad he could have taken the gold medal awarded for the best performance on top board had he agreed to a draw in his last round game with Gheorghiu, but when the Rumanian Grandmaster offered the draw Fischer, in an inferior position, replied 'Of course not' and lost.

The Piatigorsky Cup tournament started very badly for Fischer, who was wasting too much of his nervous energy in a search for an absolutely silent hotel room. Each time he changed rooms he soon discovered another source of noise and wanted to be moved again. By the halfway stage (when he was in last place with Ivkov), Fischer had made himself a social outcast, searching endlessly for a silent room instead of fraternizing with the other players. Then Spassky asked him why he was wasting himself instead of relaxing with his friends during his free time, and almost at once Fischer gave up his search, became more socially amenable and improved his score so much that when he met Spassky for the second time, in the penultimate round, he could have won the tournament had he defeated him.

Probably the most important of Fischer's games in this tournament was his encounter with Spassky from the first half. It is an excellent example of how, even at this mature stage of Fischer's career, he fails to play exactly when his opponent has attacking chances. In this case the error comes as early as move twelve.

45 SPASSKY–FISCHER
PIATIGORSKY CUP, SANTA MONICA 1966

Grünfeld Defence

Notes by Panov

The twenty-three year old Robert Fischer, eight times Champion of the USA [Panov cannot count; at the time it was only seven – DNLL] is the strongest player of the Western Hemisphere. Boris Spassky has just fought for the World Championship title. It is unnecessary to say that this game was watched by millions of people all over the world.

1 P—Q4	N—KB3
2 P—QB4	P—KN3
3 N—QB3	P—Q4

Grünfeld's Defence. Was it not a mistake for Fischer to choose this particular opening and variation in which his opponent has such good theoretical and practical experience? And especially if we take into account the psychological situation in the tournament before the game. It was played in the eighth round. In the first five rounds both Grandmasters had scored three points. In the following two rounds Spassky scored 1½ points and Fischer, trying to overtake him, lost to Larsen and Najdorf. In such a discouraging situation and against such a dangerous opponent as Spassky, Fischer should, perhaps, have aimed at a draw and chosen a variation which is not so 'obliging'.

4 P×P	N×P
5 P—K4	N×N
6 P×N	B—N2
7 B—QB4	P—QB4
8 N—K2	N—B3
9 B—K3	O—O
10 O—O	Q—B2

The fashionable continuation which has superceded both 10...N—R4; 11 B—Q3, P—N3; 12 P×P, P×P; 13 B×P, Q—B2 (which leads to the regaining of the pawn with an active game), and also the classical variation 8...P×P; 9 P×P, N—B3; 10 B—K3, O—O; 11 O—O, B—N5.

11 R—B1	R—Q1
12 Q—K1	

In 1958 Spassky played the straightforward 12 P—B4, N—R4; 13 B—Q3, against Korchnoy to which Black should have answered 13...P—B4! (now 14 P—N4 loses a pawn), and not 13...P—B5; 14 B—N1, P—B4; 15 P—N4!, P×P; 16 N—N3, as in the game.

For 12 P—KR3 see game 62.

12 . . .	P—K3

The pawn on Q5 is untouchable because of the check on KB2. But a better answer to White's plan would have been 12...Q—R4, threatening 13...P×P.

13 P—B4 !	N—R4

But now 13...P×P; 14 P×P, B×P; 15 N×B, N×N, is no good for Black because of 16 B×P!

14 B—Q3	P—B4
15 R—Q1 !	

It seems illogical to remove the rook from QB1 where it was indirectly threatening Black's queen, but it is important for White to maintain the pressure in the centre and free the square QB1 for the bishop in case of 15...P×KP; 16 B×P, N—B5.

15 . . .	P—N3
16 Q—B2	P×QP

The offer of the QBP is now no good: 16...P—B5; 17 B—N1, and White has a powerful pawn centre.

17 B×P	B×B

Changing the pawn structure in this way is bad. The weak white QBP and the possibility of a counter-attack on the Q and QB files gave Black more defensive chances. It would have been more precise to play 17...B—N2, and if 18

B×B, then 18...Q×B; 19 N—Q4, Q—
KB2, with better chances than in the
game.

| 18 P×B | B—N2 |
| 19 N—N3 | Q—B2 |

After 19...P×P; 20 B×P, B×B; 21
N×B, Black would have difficulty in
defending his weakened K side and the
pawn at K3. But better would be 19...
Q—N2.

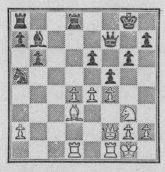

20 P—Q5!

An effective and well calculated
breakthrough after which it appears
that the black king is not very well
defended.

| 20 ... | P×KP |
| 21 P×KP | Q×KP |

If 21...Q—B3; 22 N×P, Q×KP; 23
N—N5, with a very strong attack.

| 22 P—B5! | Q—B2 |

22...P×P loses immediately, because
of 23 N×BP, P×B; 24 Q—N3 ch, Q—
N3; 25 N—K7 ch, or 24...K—B1; 25
N—N7 dis ch.

| 23 B×P | R×R |

Distracting the rook from the KB file.
If, for example, 23...B×B; 24 N×B,
Q×BP, then 25 R×R ch, R×R; 26
Q—R4, and White wins.

| 24 R×R | R—KB1! |

In a difficult position Fischer finds the
best possible defence. The exchange
24...B×B; 25 N×B loses quickly, e.g.
25...P×P; 26 R—Q7, Q—N3; 27 R—
Q6, Q—N2; 28 N—B6 ch, K—R1; 29
Q×BP, and there is no defence against
the threat of 30 R—Q7. If 29...R—

KB1, then 30 R—Q7!, R×N (or 30...
R—B2); 31 R—Q8 ch, and on 29...
Q—N3 comes 30 Q×Q, P×Q; 31 R—
Q7, with unavoidable mate.

25 B—N1!

Both bishops are aimed at the
opposing K sides, but White's is the
stronger.

| 25 ... | Q—B3 |
| 26 Q—K2 | K—R1 |

26...P×P; 27 N×P, is too dangerous
for Black.

27 P×P	P×P
28 Q—Q2	K—N2
29 R—KB1!	Q—K2

On other moves White wins a pawn
by 30 R×R, K×R; 31 Q—R6 ch.

| 30 Q—Q4 ch | R—B3 |

Of course 30...K—R2? is bad
because of 31 R×R, Q×R; 32 P—
KR4!, N—B3; 33 Q—K4, and Black
cannot defend himself against P—R5.

30...K—R3 comes into consideration, and if 31 R×R, Q×R; 32 Q—
KR4 ch, K—N2; 33 Q—N5, then 33...
Q—QB4 ch; 34 Q×Q, P×Q, with the
worse, but not necessarily lost endgame
for Black. If 31 N—K4, B×N; 32 Q×B,
Q—Q3, Black has some defensive
chances.

| 31 N—K4 | B×N |
| 32 B×B | Q—B4 |

Forced, because after 32...K—B2
comes 33 B—Q5 ch, followed by 34 P—
N4, and Black's position is hopeless.

| 33 Q×Q | R×R ch? |

A mistake. More precise was 33...
P×Q; 34 R×R, K×R. If now 35 P—
KR4, then 35...N—B5; 36 K—B2,
N—Q3, with good drawing chances.

| 34 K×R | P×Q |

A textbook endgame, with White
having the advantage of bishop for
knight and a majority of pawns on the
K side. With his next move White fixes
Black's weak KNP on a square of the
same colour as his bishop. Black's
passed pawn is weak and is easily kept
under control. In contrast to a knight, a
bishop can work on both sides of the
board simultaneously. The winning plan
is clear – threaten to create a passed

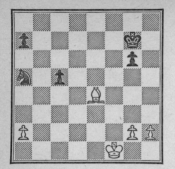

pawn on the K side, and march to the Q side with the king.

35 P—KR4 !

After 35 B—Q5, K—B3; 36 P—KR4, K—K4, sacrificing the bishop with 37 P—N4 ? does not work.

35 . . .	N—B5
36 K—K2	N—K4
37 K—K3	K—B3
38 K—B4	

38 B—B2 could have been played immediately, making room for the king on the K4 square.

| 38 . . . | N—B2 |
| 39 K—K3 | P—N4 |

Black wants to free his king from the defence of the KNP and leave his knight to defend the K side, but now White emerges with a dangerous passed pawn.

Even by passive defence the game could not have been saved, e.g. 39... N—K4; 40 B—B2!, P—R3; 41 K—K4, K—K3; 42 K—B4, K—B3; 43 P—N4.

Now White's passed pawn is too far away from Black's king.

40 P—R5	N—R3
41 K—Q3	K—K4
42 B—R8	K—Q3
43 K—B4	P—N5
44 P—R4	N—N1
45 P—R5	N—R3

Black cannot do much. If 45...N—B3, then 46 P—KR6 and 47 B—K4.

| 46 B—K4 | P—N6 |

On 46...N—N1, White would have played 47 P—N3, N—R3; 48 B—Q3, N—N1; 49 B—B2, N—R3; 50 K—N5 ZUGZWANG. 46...K—K4 does not change much because of 47 B—Q3.

47 K—N5	N—N1
48 B—N1	N—R3
49 K—R6	K—B3
50 B—R2 !	

Sweeping away Black's last chance for a draw: 50 K×P, P—B5; 51 P—R6 ?, K—B2, drawing. But instead of 51 P—R6 ? if White plays 51 B—K4 ch, Black still doesn't have much.

| 50 . . . | Resigns |

At the Havana Olympiad Fischer showed that he had added to his theoretical armoury a deceptively innocuous looking weapon that was capable of causing severe problems to even the strongest of Grandmasters.

46 FISCHER–GLIGORIC
OLYMPIAD, HAVANA 1966

Ruy Lopez

1 P—K4	P—K4
2 N—KB3	N—QB3
3 B—N5	P—QR3
4 B×N	

'This is a drawing variation but I once had some trouble with it' – Gligoric.

It is quite refreshing to see an old variation renovated from time to time. Were it not possible, opening theory would become rather stale. Fischer's support of the Exchange Variation in modern master play and his occasional use of the King's Gambit reflect his colossal appetite for work at the game. His study of the old chess literature as well as the recent, and his work on some of the almost forgotten variations have served him more than once.

4 . . .   QP×B
5 O—O

This move gives White a more lasting initiative than 5 P—Q4.

5 . . .   P—B3

Since this game there has been much theoretical controversy as to the relative merits of Black's various possibilities in this position. So far (July 1973), no definite conclusion has been reached but the text is still the most popular move.

6 P—Q4   B—KN5

Fischer–Portisch from an earlier round at Havana went 6...P×P; 7 N×P, P—QB4 (better is 7...N—K2; 8 B—K3, N—N3; 9 N—Q2, B—Q3; 10 N—B4, O—O; 11 Q—Q3, N—K4; 12 N×N, B×N; 13 P—KB4, B—Q3; 14 P—B5, when White's advantage is very small. Fischer–Unzicker, Siegen Olympiad 1970); 8 N—N3, Q×Q; 9 R×Q, B—Q3; 10 N—R5!, P—QN4; 11 P—QB4!, with a lasting initiative for White.

7 P—B3!

A move suggested by Gligoric himself a few months prior to this game.

After the Havana Olympiad Fischer gave up this move for 7 P×P, Q×Q; 8 R×Q, e.g. (i) 8...P×P ?; 9 R—Q3, B×N; 10 R×B, N—B3; 11 N—B3, B—N5; 12 B—N5, B×N; 13 P×B, R—KB1; 14 B×N, R×B; 15 R×R, P×R; 16 R—Q1, with a clear advantage in the endgame. Fischer–Smyslov, Monaco 1967; or (ii) 8...B×N; 9 P×B, P×P; 10 B—K3, B—Q3; 11 N—Q2, N—K2; 12 N—B4, O—O; 13 R—Q3, P—QN4; 14 N—R5, with advantage to White. Fischer–Rubinetti, Buenos Aires 1970.

7 . . .   P×P

The alternative plan is to over-protect the KP by 7...B—Q3, and then to continue with ...N—K2 and ...N—N3.

8 P×P   Q—Q2

If Black grabs the QP his queen becomes embarrassed and White gets a decisive lead in development: 8...B× N ?; 9 Q×B, Q×P; 10 R—Q1, Q—B5; 11 B—B4.

9 P—KR3   B—K3

In the last round at Havana the Cuban top board, Elezar Jimenez, improved with 9...B—R4; 10 N—K5, B×Q; 11 N×Q, K×N; 12 R×B, R—K1 when, although White still had the better endgame prospects, Black should be able to draw (Jimenez didn't).

10 N—B3   O—O—O
11 B—B4

It is evident that White has an opening advantage because of his well placed minor pieces, his strong central pawn duo and his Q-side attacking chances.

11 . . .   N—K2?

Fischer recommends 11...B—Q3!; 12 B×B, Q×B.

12 R—B1   N—N3
13 B—N3   B—Q3
14 N—QR4!

Threatening 15 P—Q5, P×P; 16 N— N6 ch, winning the queen.

14 . . .   B×B?

Conceding the QB5 square to White's QN with catastrophic results. Necessary was 14...K—N1.

15 P×B   K—N1
16 N—B5!

Already Black's position is hopeless. He has no way to repel the attack.

16 . . .   Q—Q3
17 Q—R4

Threatening to win a pawn by 18
Q—N4.

17 . . .   K—R2 ?

Losing by force. The only hope was
17...B—B1 when 18 R—B3, followed
by R—R3 would have kept up strong
pressure.

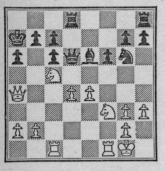

18 N×RP !   B×KRP
After 18...P×N; 19 R×P, Black

must give up his queen to prevent the
mate.

19 P—K5   N×P

Or 19...P×P; 20 N—B5 dis ch, K—
N1; 21 P×P, N×P; 22 P×B, and White
is a piece ahead.

20 P×N   P×P
21 N—B5 dis ch   K—N1
22 P×B

At this moment various Grandmasters
who had not been watching the whole
game were of the opinion that Gligoric
had some drawing possibilities! They
had glanced quickly at the board, saw
that Fischer had two minor pieces to
Gligoric's none and didn't bother to
count the rooks, assuming Fischer to
have one rook less (i.e. that he had won
two minor pieces for a rook). Perhaps
Gligoric was suffering from the same
misconception. If so, it didn't last for
long.

22 . . .   P—K5
23 N×KP   Q—K2
24 R—B3   P—QN4
25 Q—B2   Resigns

And the Black side of Fischer's theoretical armoury had also been enriched.

---

47 POMAR–FISCHER
OLYMPIAD, HAVANA 1966

Modern Benoni

1 P—Q4   N—KB3
2 P—QB4   P—B4
3 P—Q5   P—K3

Having tried various defences to 1 P—
Q4 throughout his career, Fischer now
switches to one of the very sharpest.
Since 1966 he has used the Modern
Benoni on a number of occasions against
strong players and although his score
with the defence is enormous (over 88%)
some of the positions that he has had

from it have been very dubious, even
downright bad.

Although this was the first occasion
on which Fischer employed the (normal)
text move order this was not his first
Modern Benoni – he had played the
defence by transposition against Larsen
at the Piatigorsky Cup.

4 N—QB3   P×P
5 P×P   P—KN3(?)

This move order is thought, by some
authorities, to be seriously inaccurate,
as White can now get a very good game

by sacrificing a pawn 6 P—Q6 !, Q—N3;
7 B—N5, N—R4; 8 N—B3, P—B3; 9
B—K3, B×P; 10 N—Q5, Q—Q1; 11
Q—N3.

    6 P—K4(?)   **P—Q3**
    7 B—K2   **B—N2**
    8 P—B4

A few rounds later Najdorf played
8 N—B3 against Fischer (with a slightly
different move order), and had a good
position which he destroyed with one
weak move:

    8 N—B3, O—O; 9 O—O, R—K1; 10
N—Q2, N—R3 (not 10...QN—Q2; 11
P—QR4, N—K4; 12 Q—B2, P—KN4;
13 N—B3, N×N ch; 14 B×N, P—
KR3 ?; 15 B—Q2, P—R3; 16 B—K2,
Q—K2; 17 QR—K1, with an excellent
game for White. Gligoric–Fischer, Palma
Interzonal 1970); 11 P—B3, N—B2; 12
P—QR4, P—N3; 13 K—R1 (after 13
N—B4, N—Q2; 14 N—K3, N—K4; 15
R—K1, R—N1; 16 P—B4, N—Q2; 17
N—B4, N—B3; 18 B—B3, White also
has the advantage.

This was the system chosen by the
strong Israeli International Master Yair
Kraidman against Fischer at Netanya
1968. Kraidman built up a winning
position, but Fischer was somehow
allowed to survive), 13...N—Q2; 14
N—B4, N—K4; 15 N—K3, P—B4; 16
P—B4, N—B2; 17 P×P, P×P; 18 B—
Q3, Q—B3; 19 N—K2, N—KR3; 20
N—N3, Q—N3; 21 Q—B2, R—B1; 22
B—Q2, B—Q2, and now 23 R—B3 !,
threatening N—K2 followed by R—N3,
would have left White with a clear plus.
Instead, Najdorf played 23 QR—K1 ?,
and after 23...QR—K1; 24 B—K2 ?
(24 B—B3, R—K2; 25 B×B, R×B; 26
P—N4, offers chances to both sides),
24...R—K2; 25 B—Q3, B—Q5, Black
had by far the more active game.

    8 . . .   **O—O**
    9 N—B3   **R—K1**

Many complications arise out of
9...P—QN4 !?; 10 P—K5, P×P; 11
P×P, N—N5; 12 B—KB4, which was
played in the final game of the 1965
Keres–Spassky match. Fischer's move
is more solid.

    10 N—Q2   **P—B5 !?**

An interesting innovation. Fischer's
idea is to vacate the QB4 square for
occupation by a knight, and also to
create play along his QR2—KN8
diagonal. The disadvantage of the text
is that it puts the QBP on an extremely
vulnerable square and it relinquishes
Black's control of his Q5.

The normal move is 10...N—N5,
with an unclear position.

    11 B—B3

In a later round of the Olympiad the
game Padevsky–Ciocaltea went 11 P—
QR4, QN—Q2; 12 O—O, N—B4; 13
B—B3, B—R3; 14 Q—B2, N—Q6; 15
N×P, N×B; 16 Q×N, B—Q2; 17 P—
QN3, Q—B2; 18 Q—K3, P—R3; 19
Q—N6, with advantage to White.

    11 . . .   **QN—Q2**
    12 O—O

Naturally not 12 N×P ?, N×KP,
completely destroying White's centre.

    12 . . .   **P—QN4 !**
    13 K—R1   **P—QR3**
    14 P—QR4   **R—N1**
    15 P×P   **P×P**

    16 P—K5

A dangerous sacrifice, but it was the
only way in which White can play for an
active game.

    16 . . .   **P×P**
    17 N(2)—K4   **N×N**
    18 N×N   **N—B3**
    19 P—Q6

This advanced passed pawn is White's
trump card.

19 . . .	B—K3
20 N—B5	

Naturally not 20 P×P ?, N×N; 21
B×N, B×P, and the QP falls.

20 . . .	P—K5 !

Returning the pawn so as to keep the
more active position.

21 N×P	N×N
22 B×N	Q—N3

Threatening 23. . .QR—Q1.

23 P—B5	

The only way to keep the QP.

23 . . .	P×P
24 B—B2	Q—Q5
25 Q—R5	

Exchanging queens would give White
a lost ending – the QP would soon fall.

25 . . .	Q—N5

Not 25. . .Q×QP; 26 B—B4, B—K4;
27 B×B, Q×B; 28 B×P, with a good
game for White.

26 Q×Q	P×Q
27 B—N5	

With the threat of 28 QR—Q1 . . .

27 . . .	B×P !

. . . which Fischer ignores. In return
for the exchange Black has more than
ample compensation in his passed Q-side
pawns.

28 QR—Q1	P—N5

Not 28. . .B—Q2 ?; 29 B×P ch.

29 P—Q7	KR—Q1
30 B—QR4	P—QN6

So long as Black plays accurately his
advancing pawns must conclude the
issue.

31 KR—K1	K—N2

Not 31. . .P—B6; 32 B×R, P—B7;
33 B—B7, winning.

32 B×R	R×B
33 R—Q6	B—B3
34 R(K1)—Q1	B—N4

After 34. . .P—B6; 35 R×B, P×R;
36 B×P, the game is a dead draw.

35 R—N6 ?	

Short of time Pomar finds a move that
makes the win easy. But there was no
satisfactory defence against the threat
of 35. . .R—QR1, e.g. 35 R—R6, R—
QN1.

35 . . .	P—R3
36 R—B6	R—QR1
37 B—N5	B×P
38 P—R4	B×R
39 B×B	P—B6
40 P×B	P—B7
41 P×P ch	K—R1
42 Resigns	

A fine example of Fischer's lucid style
and a practical vindication of his
decision to adopt another double-edged
defence.

In some ways the Modern Benoni is an ideal defence for Fischer. As with
the Poisoned Pawn Variation of the Najdorf, Black creates sharp positions
from which he will often be able to snatch the initiative especially if White
does not find the most accurate move at every point. The big disadvantage
is that White, by precise play in the opening, can deprive his opponent of
counterplay, as in the examples contained in the note to Pomar's eighth
move.

Also, White frequently gets attacking chances in the centre as well as play
on the K side. Here, for example, is another of Fischer's Havana wins. His
opponent steers away from the main line by delaying P—QB4, and Fischer
tries for too much on the Q side, leaving himself vulnerable in the centre.

48 JOHANNESSEN–FISCHER
OLYMPIAD, HAVANA 1966

Benkö Gambit Declined

(by transposition)

1 P—Q4, N—KB3; 2 N—KB3, P—B4; 3 P—Q5, P—QN4 ?!; 4 P—B4, B—N2; 5 P—KN3
Also good for White is 5 QN—Q2, e.g. 5...P×P; 6 P—K4, P—K3; 7 P×P, BP×P; 8 P—K5!, and 9 N×P.

5...P—N3; 6 B—N2, P×P; 7 N—B3, B—N2; 8 O—O, O—O; 9 N—K5, P—Q3; 10 N×QBP, QN—Q2; 11 R—K1, B—QR3
Now that Black has completed his development he prepares for action on the QN file.

12 Q—R4, Q—B1
Black can also play 12...B×N; 13 Q×B, R—N1, with some initiative, but Fischer has other ideas – he has already calculated the consequences of White's sixteenth move.

13 N—R5, N—N3; 14 Q—R4, R—K1; 15 B—N5
Intending to intensify his pressure against K7.

15...Q—B2; 16 N—B6, B—N2; 17 P—K4, N(N3)—Q2
Not 17...B×N; 18 P×B, Q×P?; 19 P—K5, N(B3)—Q4; 20 N×N, N×N; 21 P—K6!, and Black's Q4 knight will soon be lost.

18 P—B4, K—R1
A dual purpose move, vacating KN1 as a retreat square for his KN, and ensuring that if White ever plays N×KP (or N—K7) it will not be with check.

19 P—K5!
Otherwise comes 19...N—KN1, when White's QB is doing nothing.

19...P×P; 20 P×P ?
After 20 N×P(K5)! White still has some advantage, e.g. 20...K—N1; 21 N—B6!, or 20...N×N; 21 P×N, N—

Q2; 22 P—K6, P×P; 23 R×P, B—KB3; 24 QR—K1. Probably Fischer missed 20 N×P when analysing his twelfth move. Now the game ends in a hurricane.

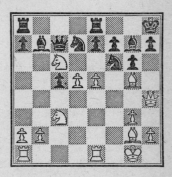

20...N×QP!; 21 N×N
No better is 21 B×N, B×N; 22 B×BP, N×P; 23 R×N, Q×R; 24 B×NP, Q—Q5 ch.

21...Q×N
Now we see why it is important for Black's king to be away from KN1.

22 P—K6, N—K4!
If 22...P×P; 23 N—B4, threatening 24 N×NP ch.

23 R×N
After 23 P×P, R—KB1; 24 B×P, R×P, Black has a tremendous game.

23...B×R; 24 P×P, R—KB1
Threatening 25...B—Q5 ch; 26 K—R1, Q×N!

25 P—KR3, R×P; 26 N—B4, R×N!; 27 Resigns
Since 27 B×Q, R×Q; 28 B×B, R×P; 29 B×R, R×P ch, leaves Black three pawns ahead in the endgame, and 27...B—Q5 ch; 28 K—N2, R—B7 ch; 29 K—N1, B×B, is also not without its points.

In 1967 Fischer lost three games (out of thirty-six), two of them to Geller. He had also lost to Geller on their previous meeting (the 1965 Capablanca Memorial Tournament) and up to the time of writing Geller leads in their individual contest by five wins to three with two draws. Probably the trouble was stylistic – Geller too, likes to play positions where his opponent has little or no counterplay. But part of the problem was certainly psychological.

49 FISCHER–GELLER
MONACO 1967

Sicilian Defence

1 P—K4, P—QB4; 2 N—KB3, P—Q3; 3 P—Q4, P×P; 4 N×P, N—KB3; 5 N—QB3, P—QR3; 6 B—KN5, P—K3; 7 P—B4, Q—N3!

That's not fair, that's my line.

8 Q—Q2, Q×P; 9 R—QN1, Q—R6; 10 P—B5

Avoiding the critical lines starting with 10 P—K5. Some commentators claimed that this was because Fischer was already assured of first place and didn't want to give away any free information. But I cannot believe that anyone who is so devoted to the game would wilfully play what he considered to be an inferior move.

10...N—B3; 11 P×P, P×P; 12 N×N, P×N; 13 P—K5, N—Q4?

At the time this game was played it was thought that 13...P×P; 14 B×N, P×B; 15 N—K4, was crushing for White, but Fischer reversed this opinion a few months later in his game with Kavalek from the Sousse Interzonal (page 106).

14 N×N, BP×N; 15 B—K2!, P×P; 16 O—O, B—B4 ch; 17 K—R1, R—B1; 18 P—B4, R×R ch; 19 R×R, B—N2

Probably stronger is 19...P—R3! so that after 20 B—R4 Black can play 20...P—N4 to kill White's play on the dark squares. After 19...P—R3, the game might continue 20 B—R5 ch, K—Q2; 21 P×P, P×B; 22 P×P dbl ch,

K—B2; 23 Q—Q5, R—R2; 24 B—B3 R—N2, and White's attack soon peters out.

20 B—N4?

This natural move loses almost immediately. After the game Fischer maintained that 20 Q—B2 would have won and indeed Tal employed this move in a brilliancy a few months later: (20 Q—B2), P—K5 (better is 20...P—N3; 21 B—N4, B—QB1, and if 22 Q—Q2, Q—N5; or 22 Q—Q1, B—K2. According to O'Kelly the best defence is 20... B—K2; 21 Q×P, B×B; 22 Q—R5 ch, K—Q2; 23 Q×B, K—Q3; 24 Q×NP, R—QN1); 21 B—N4, B—K2; 22 Q—B2, O—O—O; 23 B—B4!, B—Q3; 24 B×P ch, K—N1; 25 Q—N6!, B×B; 26 Q×R ch, K—R2; 27 R—QN1, Q—Q3; 28 B×P!, B×B; 29 Q×Q, B×Q; 30 P×B, Resigns. Tal–Bogdanovic,

Budva 1967. 20 B—Q1 would also be better than Fischer's move. A lengthy analysis by Matsukevitch indicates that it leads to a level position.

    20...P×P!; 21 B×P, Q—Q6; 22 Q—K1, B—K5; 23 B—N4, R—N1; 24 B—Q1, K—Q2; 25 R—B7 ch, K—K3; 26 Resigns

Black is two pawns up with an overwhelming attack.

50 FISCHER–GELLER
SKOPJE 1967

Sicilian Defence

Notes by Murei

1 P—K4	P—QB4
2 N—KB3	P—Q3
3 P—Q4	P×P
4 N×P	N—KB3
5 N—QB3	N—B3
6 B—QB4	

This system was worked out by the Soviet master V. Sozin and has been employed by Fischer for a long time.

6 . . .	P—K3
7 B—K3	B—K2
8 B—N3	O—O
9 Q—K2	Q—R4

This is a new continuation specially prepared by Geller. But in this game Black goes through a lot of unpleasantness.

10 O—O—O	N×N
11 B×N	B—Q2
12 K—N1	

Now, after exchanging on KB6, White threatens to take the QP.

12 . . .	B—B3

Fischer–Sofrevsky, from the same tournament, went: 12...QR—Q1; 13 Q—K3!, P—QN3 (if 13...B—B3; 14 B×RP, N—Q2; 14 B×P, N—Q2; 15 B—Q4, P—K4; 16 N—Q5!; or 13.. N—N5; 14 Q—N3); 14 B×N!, P×B; 15 N—Q5!!, KR—K1 (15...P×N; 16 R×P, Q—R3; 17 R—R5, forces mate); 16 N×B ch, R×N; 17 R×P, R—QB1; 18 Q—Q4, B—K1; 19 Q×BP, Resigns.

    13 P—B4

This move is possible because Black's bishop has moved away from Q2: After 13...P—K4; 14 P×P, P×P; 15 B—B2, Black cannot play 15...B—N5.

    13 . . .   QR—Q1

Defending the QP and preparing for the advance...P—Q4.

    14 KR—B1

In reply to 14 P—K5, P×P; 15 P×P, Black does not play 15...N—Q4 because of 16 N—K4, with good attacking chances for White. Instead he should play 15...N—Q2 so that the weakness of White's KP prevents him from comfortably regrouping his pieces.

14 P—N4 was a possible alternative.

14 . . .   P—QN4

The essence of Black's plan, achieved without the necessity of . . .P—QR3. But in my opinion this difference is not really significant, because even with the extra tempo Black cannot achieve anything in the centre: 14. . .P—Q4 is bad because of 15 P—K5, followed by P—B5; or 14. . .P—K4; 15 N—Q5, B×N; 16 B—B3!, Q—B2; 17 P×B, and Black's queen is too far away to come to the defence of his king.

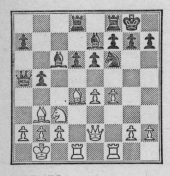

15 P—B5

Better than 15 P—K5, P×P; 16 P× P, N—Q2 (16. . .N—Q4; 17 N—K4); 17 R×P, R×R; 18 B×P, N—B1; 19 B—N3 (threatening 20 R—KB1), B— Q2!; 20 P—K6, B×P; 21 B×B, N× B; 22 Q×N, R—Q3, and Black is perfectly well defended.

15 . . .   P—N5
16 P×P   P×N
17 P×P ch?

Missing the promising move 17 R× N!, after which Black's defence would have become extremely difficult, e.g. 17. . .P×R; 18 P×P ch, K—R1 (or 18. . .R×P; 19 B×R ch, K×B; 20 Q— B4 ch); 19 Q—N4. Now White threatens 20 Q—K6, 20 R—KB1 and 20 Q—R4. Black can guard against all three threats only by playing 19. . .R—QN1 (if 19. . . P—KR3; 20 P—KR4, followed by Q— N6 winning; or 19. . .B—Q2; 20 Q— R4, K—N2; 21 R—Q3, R×P; 22 R—

N3 ch, K—B1; 23 Q×P!, with an unavoidable mate).

After 20 Q—K6, Q—Q1; 21 R— KB1, R—N5!; 22 B×BP (22 P×P, B—Q2; 23 Q—Q5, R—N4), 22. . .R× KP; 23 R×P, R—K8 ch!; 24 Q×R, B×R; 25 Q—N3, P—Q4, Black has an extra rook. But after 20 B×BP, Q— Q1; 21 B—K6!, Black is badly off despite his material advantage In this case the rook on QN1 cannot leave the back rank because of R×P, and to defend against the threat R—Q3— N3 is possible only by playing 21. . . B—Q2; 22 B×B, R×P, when White still has excellent winning chances.

Black's best defence is (17 R×N), B×R; 18 B×B, P×B; 19 P—K7, Q— K4 (19. . .R—Q2; 20 R—Q5!); 20 P×R(Q8)=Q, R×Q; 21 Q—B4, B— K1 (or 21. . .B×P; 22 Q×KBP ch, K— R1; 23 P×P); 22 Q×QBP.

17 . . .   K—R1
18 R—B5

Now the sacrifice on KB6 is no longer effective – Black can take the rook with the bishop. 18 B×BP would have given White three pawns for the piece, but after 18. . .Q—N4; 19 B—B4, Q—N2 his prospects would be poor.

18 . . .   Q—N5!
19 Q—B1

19 R×N, B×R; 20 B×B, P×B; 21 Q—B3, loses to 21. . .R×P, and 19 P×P to 19. . .Q—N2, and 19 B×BP to 19. . .Q×P.

19 . . .   N×P
20 P—QR3

[Fischer claims that 20 Q—KB4 would have won – DNLL.]

20 . . .   Q—N2
21 Q—KB4   B—QR5!
22 Q—N4

22 Q—R6, B—KB3; 23 R×B, B×B, doesn't change the situation: if the rook moves from KB6 24. . .B—R7 ch!! is decisive, while on 24 P×B comes 24. . . Q×NP; 25 R—B2, Q×R ch; 26 K— R2, Q×B.

22 . . .   B—KB3
23 R×B   B×B
24 Resigns

Some time after this game was played Geller wrote that it was his policy when playing Fischer to steer the game into complicated channels whenever possible.

The Sousse Interzonal

The tragedy of Fischer's withdrawal from the Sousse Interzonal is all the greater when one realizes how powerful was his play there. From the ten games that he played at Sousse, Fischer won seven and drew three. I would like to give all ten games in this volume but alas, space is limited.

From even before the tournament began the signs were ominous for a Fischer v Organizers dispute. While he was still in Yugoslavia (following the Skopje tournament) Fischer telephoned Colonel Edmondson, the executive director of the USCF, to tell him that the organizing committee had not yet understood his religious holidays and that some rescheduling of the games was going to be required. When this happened there was very little time before the start of the tournament so Edmondson told Fischer to deal with the matter himself when he arrived in Tunisia. (Having observed the successful efforts of Colonel Edmondson in arranging Fischer's participation in and smooth passage through the 1970/71 series of qualifying events, I am reasonably certain that had Edmondson been present in Sousse Fischer would have finished the tournament.)

Four of the twenty-three rounds were to have been played on days that were religiously impossible for Fischer and Reshevsky, and so these two were allowed to play those four games on days that would otherwise have been free. The first game that Fischer played was his round three encounter with the Mongolian International Master Miagmasuren. This was played on the day before round one.

51 FISCHER–MIAGMASUREN
INTERZONAL TOURNAMENT, SOUSSE 1967

King's Indian Attack

1 P—K4, P—K3; 2 P—Q3, P—Q4; 3 N—Q2, N—KB3; 4 P—KN3, P—B4; 5 B—N2, N—B3; 6 KN—B3, B—K2; 7 O—O, O—O; 8 P—K5, N—Q2; 9 R—K1, P—QN4; 10 N—B1, P—N5; 11 P—KR4, P—QR4; 12 B—B4, P—R5; 13 P—R3 !!
A completely new idea in a very well known type of position. White blocks the Q-side attack before Black can complete his undermining of the dark

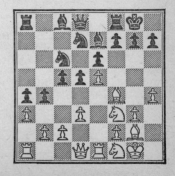

squares with the move...P—R6. The result of Fischer's innovation is to render Black's Q-side counterplay quite ineffective.

13...P×P; 14 P×P, N—R4; 15 N—K3, B—R3; 16 B—R3

Preventing...P—B3.

16...P—Q5; 17 N—B1, N—N3; 18 N—N5, N—Q4; 19 B—Q2, B×N; 20 B×B, Q—Q2; 21 Q—R5, R(B1)—B1; 22 N—Q2, N—B6 23 B—B6 !

As usual the attack comes on the dark squares, but here Fischer has refrained from P—R5—R6 so that his pieces have more squares available near Black's king.

23...Q—K1

If 23...P×B; 24 P×P, K—R1; 25 N—B3, R—KN1; 26 N—K5!, winning.

24 N—K4, P—N3; 25 Q—N5!, N×N; 26 R×N, P—B5; 27 P—R5!, BP×P; 28 R—R4, R—R2

If 28...QP×P; 29 P×P, BP×P; 30 R×P, winning.

29 B—N2, QP×P

Essential otherwise White would play 30 B—K4 followed by a sacrifice on KN6.

30 Q—R6, Q—B1; 31 Q×RP ch!, Resigns

Because of 31...K×Q; 32 P×P dbl ch, K×P; 33 B—K4 mate.

From the first five rounds Fischer scored four and a half points. In round six he faced Kavalek with the black pieces, and since the Czech Grandmaster is a very sharp player with a thorough theoretical knowledge it was natural that Fischer should be compelled to defend the Poisoned Pawn Variation.

52 KAVALEK–FISCHER
INTERZONAL TOURNAMENT, SOUSSE 1967

Sicilian Defence

1 P—K4, P—QB4; 2 N—KB3, P—Q3; 3 P—Q4, P×P; 4 N×P, N—KB3; 5 N—QB3, P—QR3; 6 B—KN5, P—K3; 7 P—B4, Q—N3; 8 Q—Q2, Q×P; 9 R—QN1, Q—R6; 10 P—B5, N—B3; 11 P×P, P×P; 12 N×N, P×N; 13 P—K5, P×P

In the Fischer–Geller game (page 102) the Soviet Grandmaster had played the inferior 13...N—Q4.

14 B×N, P×B; 15 N—K4, B—K2; 16 B—K2, P—KR4; 17 P—B4, P—KB4; 18 R—N3, Q—R5; 19 O—O

'In spite of the two pawns I would not like to be Black after 19 N—Q6 ch, but Fischer probably knows a defence' – Larsen.

19...P×N; 20 Q—B3, Q×RP!; 21 B—Q1

After 21 Q×P, Q×R; 22 Q×R ch, K—Q2, Black's king escapes.

21...R—B1

Not 21...B—B4 ch; 22 K—R1, B—Q5, because of 23 Q—N3, B—Q2; 24 Q—N5. – Larsen.

22 B×P ch, K—Q1; 23 R—Q1 ch, B—Q2; 24 Q—K3, Q—R4; 25 R—N7, B—B4; 26 R(Q1)×B ch, K—B1; 27 R(Q7)—B7 ch, K—Q1; 28 R—Q7 ch, Drawn

The next round Fischer produced what, in my opinion, is one of his greatest masterpieces.

53

FISCHER–STEIN

INTERZONAL TOURNAMENT, SOUSSE 1967

Ruy Lopez

1 P—K4	P—K4
2 N—KB3	N—QB3
3 B—N5	P—QR3
4 B—R4	N—B3
5 O—O	B—K2
6 R—K1	P—QN4
7 B—N3	P—Q3
8 P—B3	O—O
9 P—KR3	B—N2

Unusual. Stein is trying to steer the game away from well-known channels.

10 P—Q4	N—QR4

10...P×P; 11 P×P, P—Q4; 12 P—K5, N—K5; 13 N—B3, is also considered to favour White.

11 B—B2	N—B5
12 P—QN3	N—N3
13 QN—Q2	

If 13 P×P, P×P; 14 Q×Q, QR×Q; 15 N×P, Black can simply regain the pawn by 15...N×P; 16 B×N, B×B.

13 ...	N(N3)—Q2

Black has made too many moves with this knight. Fischer prefers 13...P×P; 14 P×P, P—B4, while another interesting possibility is 13...N(B3)—Q2; 14 N—B1, P—QB4; 15 N—N3, P—N5!

14 P—QN4!	

Reaching a position in which Black's knight manoeuvrings have left him a tempo behind a line of the Breyer Defence (9...N—N1; 10 P—Q4, QN—Q2; 11 QN—Q2, B—N2; 12 B—B2, R—K1 – the missing tempo – 13 P—QN4).

14 ...	P×P?

Black should maintain his control over K4 and try to create play by 14...P—QR4; 15 N—N3, RP×P; 16 BP×P, P—Q4!?, with terrific complications – Wade.

15 P×P	P—QR4!

Still best.

16 P×P	P—B4
17 P—K5!	

Opening lines in preparation for an attack against the black king. In particular, White's QN now has a potential outpost at K4.

17 ...	QP×P
18 P×KP	N—Q4
19 N—K4	N—N5!

Black has no time for ...R—K1, followed by ...N—B1: 19...R—K1; 20 P—QR4, R×P; 21 R—N1, P—N5; 22 B—N5, B×B; 23 N—Q6!

20 B—N1	R×P
21 Q—K2	

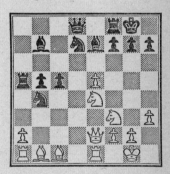

21 ...	N—N3?

Fischer suggests that this move is possibly directly responsible for Black's defeat. 21...R—K1, followed by ...N—B1 was a more solid alternative. Stein's difficulties in this position were hampered by his being short of time.

22 N(B3)—N5

Threatening 23 N×RP, K×N; 24 Q—R5 ch and 25 N—N5 mating.

22 . . .   B(N2)×N

Not 22...P—R3; 23 N—R7!, R—K1; 24 N(R7)—B6 ch!

23 Q×B   P—N3
24 Q—R4   P—R4
25 Q—N3!

Threatening both 26 P—K6 and 26 N—K6.

25 . . .   N—B5

25...Q—Q5 allows 26 N×P, R×N; 27 Q×P ch, R—N2; 28 Q—K8 ch, B—B1; 29 Q—K6 ch, K—R1; 30 B—R6.

26 N—B3!

This is better than winning the exchange by 26 P—K6, P—B4; 27 N—B7, R×N; 28 P×R ch, K×P, because now White remains with a strong attack.

26 . . .   K—N2
27 Q—B4   R—KR1
28 P—K6   P—B4

If 28...B—B3 (28...P—B3; 29 N—R4!); 29 N—N5!, N—Q4 (29...B×N allows mate in two); 30 Q—N3, B×R; 31 P×P!, Q—B3; 32 R—K6, winning – Wade.

29 B×P!!   Q—KB1

If 29...P×B; 30 Q—N3 ch, and now: (i) 30...K—R2; 31 N—N5 ch, B×N; 32 B×B followed by 33 QR—Q1 and R—Q7; or (ii) 30...K—B1; 31 Q—N6, Q—K1; 32 B—R6 ch, R×B; 33 Q×R ch, K—N1; 34 N—N5, B×N; 35 Q×B ch and 36 QR—Q1, with a

decisive penetration. Analysis by Wade.

30 B—K4?

John Littlewood writing in *Chess* shows that 30 N—R4! is the correct way of keeping up the attack, e.g. (i) 30...B×N; 31 Q×B, P×B (or 31... Q×B; 32 Q—K7 ch, K—N1; 33 Q—Q8 ch, K—N2; 34 Q—B7 ch, K—N1; 35 P—K7); 32 Q—N5 ch, K—R2; 33 P—K7!; (ii) 30...P×B; 31 Q—N3 ch mating; (iii) 30...B—Q3; 31 Q—N5, Q—B3; 32 N×P!, Q×Q; 33 B×Q, R—K1; 34 P—K7!, R—R2; 35 QR—Q1, N×P; 36 R—K6!.

30 . . .   Q×Q
31 B×Q   R—K1?

During the post-mortem Stein claimed that 31...R—QR3 would lead to a draw, but Larsen pointed out the strong move 32 P—R3!, e.g. 32...N×P; 33 N—K5!, or 32...R×RP; 33 R×R, N×R; 34 B—K5 ch, B—B3; 35 B—Q6.

The correct line, given by Fischer in *My Sixty Memorable Games* is 31... R×P; 32 R×R, N×R; 33 N—K5, P—N4; 34 B—N3, when White still has the initiative but Black may be able to draw.

32 QR—Q1!   R—R3
33 R—Q7   R×KP
34 N—N5   R—KB3
35 B—B3!   R×B
36 N—K6 ch   K—B3
37 N×R   N—K4
38 R—N7   B—Q3
39 K—B1   N—B7
40 R—K4   N—Q5

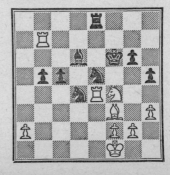

The time control. White still has a few technical problems to solve but his exchange advantage is decisive.

41 R—N6	R—Q1
42 N—Q5 ch	K—B4
43 N—K3 ch	

The sealed move. Black could well have resigned.

| 43 ... | K—K3 |
| 44 B—K2 | |

Threatening 45 P—B4.

| 44 ... | K—Q2 |
| 45 B×P ch | N×B |

If 45...K—B2; 46 N—Q5 ch.

46 R×N	K—B3
47 P—QR4	B—B2
48 K—K2	P—N4
49 P—N3	R—QR1
50 R—N2	R—KB1
51 P—B4	P×P
52 P×P	N—B2
53 R—K6 ch	N—Q3

Or 53...B—Q3; 54 R—B6 threatening 55 N—B4.

54 P—B5	R—QR1
55 R—Q2	R×P
56 P—B6	Resigns

If 56...R—KB5; 57 N—Q5.

It was after the seventh round that things began to go haywire. Fischer's eighth round game against Korchnoy had been postponed on religious grounds until five days later than scheduled. His ninth round game was also postponed (unnecessarily, according to Fischer). Suddenly Fischer decided that due to the rescheduling he was faced with five difficult games on successive days. (In fact he had forgotten that he had the bye in this sequence. He thus only had to meet four opponents on successive days.) Accordingly he asked the tournament committee to rearrange his schedule again, because he considered the run of difficult games to be unfair on him. (At this stage he was half a point behind the tournament leader, Larsen, but with two games in hand.)

When the committee refused to agree to any more changes in the playing schedule, Fischer immediately announced his withdrawal from the tournament. His clock was started at the beginning of the tenth round and after one hour he was forfeited (his opponent was Gipslis). Fischer went from Sousse to Tunis from where he intended to take a 'plane back to the USA, but on the morning of the eleventh round he was visited by Monsieur Belkadi, President of the organizing committee, who persuaded him to return to Sousse and play his eleventh round game. Fischer rushed back to the tournament hall and arrived with only three minutes left before he would forfeit against Reshevsky. Naturally enough Reshevsky had been confidently striding around the playing arena, fully expecting the point to be his. When Fischer arrived the veteran Grandmaster was so upset that he played weakly, blundering on the twenty-fourth move. According to Wade's lucid description of this whole farce which appeared in his excellent account of the tournament 'Sousse 1967', Reshevsky was so irate that he very nearly withdrew from the tournament as well.

The next day Fischer played his postponed game against Korchnoy and drew. This brought him level on points with Larsen but he still had a game in hand against Geller. The following day was to be his last game in the tournament. His fellow countryman Robert Byrne used Fischer's favourite variation of the Najdorf against him and was soundly thrashed.

54 R. BYRNE–FISCHER
INTERZONAL TOURNAMENT, SOUSSE 1967

Sicilian Defence

1 P—K4, P—QB4; **2** N—KB3, P—Q3; **3** P—Q4, P×P; **4** N×P, N—KB3; **5** N—QB3, P—QR3; **6** B—QB4, P—K3; **7** B—N3, P—QN4; **8** P—B4, B—N2

For 8...P—N5 see the famous Fischer–Tal game (page 42).

9 P—B5, P—K4; **10** N(Q4)—K2, QN—Q2

10...N×P? is bad because of 11 B—Q5!, and now: (i) 11...N—B4; 12 P—QN4, Q—R5 ch; 13 P—N3, Q×QNP; 14 B×B, N×B; 15 Q—Q5, R—R2; 16 B—K3, N—B4; 17 R—QN1, Q—R6; 18 R—N3, Q—R4; 19 B×N, winning; or (ii) 11...N×N; 12 N×N, B×B; 13 N×B, N—Q2; 14 O—O, B—K2 (if 14...N—N3; 15 P—B6!); 15 Q—N4, B—B3; 16 B—K3, O—O; 17 R—B3, with a strong attack.

11 B—N5

The key to White's strategy. The idea is to exchange off both black knights (one for the QB and the other by means of the manoeuvre N—N3—R5), when Black is left with a bad dark-squared bishop and a gaping hole at Q4.

11...B—K2; 12 N—N3, R—QB1

If 12...P—KR4; 13 B×N, N×B; 14 Q—Q3, overprotecting the KP and preventing the exchange sacrifice ...R×N, followed by ...N×P.

13 O—O?

White has two better moves: (i) 13 N—R5, N×N; 14 Q×N, O—O; 15 B×B, Q×B; 16 Q—K2, with roughly equal chances; and (ii) 13 B×N, N×B; 14 N—R5, N×N (unclear is 14...R×N!?; 15 P×R, B×P; 16 N×P ch, K—B1); 15 Q×N, O—O; 16 Q—K2, again with approximate equality. After the text White is strategically lost.

13...P—KR4!

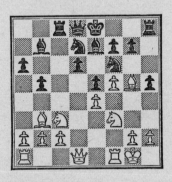

14 P—KR4

How else to meet the threat of 14...P—R5, winning the KP? If 14 B×N, N×B; 15 Q—Q3 (15 B—Q5, P—R5!), 15...R×N; 16 Q×R, P—R5; 17 N—K2, N×P; 18 Q—K1, Q—N3 ch; 19 K—R1, P—R6.

14...P—N5; 15 B×N, B×B!

Stronger than 15...N×B; 16 N—Q5, N×N; 17 P×N, B×RP; 18 N—K4.

16 N—Q5, B×P; **17** N×RP, Q—N4; **18** P—B6, P—N3!

Not 18...Q×N?; 19 P×P, nor 18...R×N; 19 R—B5. Now White's knight becomes incarcerated.

19 N—N7 ch, K—Q1; **20** R—B3, B—N6; **21** Q—Q3, B—R7 ch; **22** K—B1, N—B4; **23** R—R3!?

The last swindling try. If now 23...N×Q; 24 R×R ch, K—Q2; 25 B—R4 ch, with some chance of saving the game.

23...R—R5!; 24 Q—KB3, N×B; **25** RP×N, R×R; **26** Q×R, B×N; **27** P×B, Q×BP ch; **28** K—K1, Q—B5; **29** Resigns

White is playing with one piece less.

In the thirteenth round Fischer had the bye (the odd number of players was caused by Bolbochan's failure to get a visa before trying to reach Tunisia – had he merely flown to Tunis the Argentine master would have been issued with a visa on the spot).

Fischer's return to Sousse at the start of round eleven had only been achieved by promising him that the question of his game with Gipslis should be referred to the president of FIDE, Folke Rogard. Fischer still hoped that he would be allowed to play the game that he had already forfeited. Rogard, instead of making a decision on the matter, referred the problem back to Jaroslav Sajtar who was the chief arbiter. Sajtar decided against Fischer and before the hour had run out on White's clock in the Fischer–Hort game from round fourteen, Fischer was once again on his way to Tunis. Despite some efforts to make it possible for him to re-enter the tournament, no more was seen of him and his score was cancelled. Thus, for the second time, Fischer had opted out of the qualifying system that had been changed exactly in accordance with his wishes.

For the next eight months Fischer played no competitive chess. Then he took part in the traditional tournament at Netanya, Israel. By now Fischer's appearance fees were already beyond the budgets of many tournament committees but the Israeli Federation was lucky: the financial persuasion came from the world's most travelled chess kibitzer, I. S. Turover of Washington D.C. Fischer finished three and a half points ahead of an undistinguished field.

Shortly after the Netanya tournament Fischer turned up in Athens where the Yugoslav Grandmaster Trifunovic was helping to get the Greek Chess Federation properly organized and their top players trained. Trifunovic lost little time in arranging for Fischer to give a clock exhibition against five of the strongest Greek players.

Under normal circumstances I would not consume valuable space with a game from an exhibition played against a player whose name was unknown outside his own country. But Fischer's game against Anastasopoulos was not a normal circumstance – the Greek player seemed to refute Fischer's pet Exchange Variation of the Ruy Lopez.

55 FISCHER–ANASTASOPOULOS
CLOCK EXHIBITION, ATHENS 1968

Ruy Lopez

1 P—K4, P—K4; 2 N—KB3, N—QB3; 3 B—N5, P—QR3; 4 B×N, QP×B; 5 O—O, P—B3; 6 P—Q4, P×P; 7 N× P, P—QB4; 8 N—N3, Q×Q; 9 R×Q, B—Q2; 10 P—QR4, O—O—O; 11 B—K3, P—QN3; 12 N—B3, B—Q3; 13 P—R5, P—B5!; 14 P×P!?

A coffee house move. 14 N—Q4 is certainly safe but uninspiring.

14...P×N; 15 R×P, N—K2 !

Hoping to find time for ...N—B3.

16 R—R8 ch, K—N2; 17 R—R7 ch, K—N1; 18 N—Q5, N×N; 19 P×N, B—QB1?

Hoping for 20 P×P ch, B×P; 21 R—Q3 (threatening 22 R×P ch), P×P!; 22 R—N3 ch, B—N3!; 23 R—R1, R×P. But instead of the trappy text

move, Black could have won by 19... P×NP; 20 B×P, P×P!; 21 R(1)—R1 (or 21 R—QB1, B—KB4, with advantage to Black), 21...R—QB1 !

20 P×P ch, B×P; 21 P—QB4 !, B—N2; 22 R—Q3, R—Q2; 23 R×P, B—Q3; 24 R—R5, K—B1; 25 R(5)—N5, B—N1; 26 P—N3, R—K1; 27 P—B5, B—R2; 28 P—B6, B×P; 29 P×B, R—QB2; 30 R—N7!, Resigns

While on his way to Lugano for the 1968 Olympiad he stopped off in Yugoslavia to play in a tournament at Vinkovci. There he won by only two points but the opposition was stronger than at Netanya: Hort and Matulovic tied for second place with Gheorghiu and Ivkov half a point behind them. In his games with Minic and Wade, Fischer tried out the King's Gambit again after it had been missing from his games for five years.

56 FISCHER–MINIC
VINKOVCI 1968

King's Gambit Accepted

1 P—K4, P—K4; 2 P—KB4, P×P

A few rounds earlier Wade had declined the gambit with 2...N—KB3 and reached a satisfactory position after 3 P×P, N×P; 4 N—KB3, N—N4; 5 P—Q4, N×N ch; 6 Q×N, Q—R5 ch; 7 Q—B2, Q×Q ch; 8 K×Q (Fischer won in thirty-eight moves).

3 B—B4, N—K2 ?!

In the 1963/64 US Championship Evans had played the old fashioned 3...Q—R5 ch; 4 K—B1, P—Q3 ? (better 4... P—KN4, or 4...P—Q4); 5 N—QB3? (5 N—KB3 !), 5...B—K3 !; 6 Q—K2, P—QB3; 7 N—B3?! (7 P—Q4 prevents Black's queen from retreating without relinquishing the KBP) 7... Q—K2; 8 P—Q4, B×B; 9 Q×B, P—KN4, with equal chances (Fischer won in thirty-six).

4 N—QB3, P—QB3; 5 N—B3, P—Q4; 6 B—N3!, P×P; 7 N×P, N—Q4

It is important to block the vulnerable

diagonal since 7...N—N3 loses at once to 8 N(K4)—N5!, Q—K2 ch; 9 K—B2.

8 Q—K2 ?!

Trying for too much. 8 P—B4 !, N—B3; 9 N×N ch, Q×N; 10 O—O, B—K2; 11 P—Q4, is very strong, e.g. 11...N—Q2 (to prevent 12 N—K5); 12 Q—K2, P—KN4?; 13 N×P, Q×N; 14 B×P, with a winning attack – Fischer.

8...B—K2; 9 P—B4, N—B2; 10 P—Q4, O—O?

Black should play ...B—KN5 ! either now or on the next move so that ...N—K3 does not shut in the bishop. After 10...B—KN5; 11 P—B5, O—O; 12 QB×P, N—K3; 13 B×N(K3), P×B!; 14 B—Q6, the chances would be equal – Fischer.

11 B×P, N—K3; 12 B—K3, B—N5 ch?!

Better was 12...N—Q2 and then...N—B3.

13 K—B2, N—Q2; 14 P—B5 ?!

14 KR—KB1 !, followed by K—N1 was more active.

14...N—B3; 15 N×N ch, Q×N; 16 KR—KB1, N—B5 !

Not 16...R—K1?; 17 Q—B4 !, B—R4; 18 K—N1 !

17 B×N, Q×B; 18 P—N3

Or 18 K—N1, B—N5 !; 19 Q—K5, Q×Q; 20 N×Q, B—K3, with equal chances.

18...Q—R3; 19 K—N1?

19 Q—K7 forces 19...Q—B3; 20 Q×Q, P×Q, because on 19...B—KR6, White

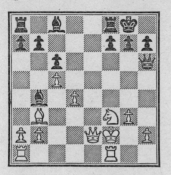

can keep up his attack against KB7 by 20 K—N1, B×R; 21 R×B, and if then 21...Q—B3; 22 Q×NP, followed by N—K5.

19...B—KR6 ??

Returning the compliment. 19...B—K3 ! neutralizes White's pressure against the KB2 square.

20 N—K5 !, B×R

Now 20...B—K3 loses to 21 N× KBP !, B×N; 22 B×B, R×R; 23 R—KB1, R—KB1?; 24 R×R, R×R; 25 Q—K8 mate – Fischer.

21 R×B, B—Q7

Threatening to exchange queens. If instead 21...P—KN3; 22 N×KBP, Q—N2; 23 N—Q8 dis ch, K—R1; 24 R×R ch, Q×R; 25 Q—K5 ch, and mate follows – Fischer. Fischer's next move is simple and decisive.

22 R—B3 !, QR—Q1?

Losing at once. The best defence was 22...K—R1; 23 N×KBP ch, R×N; 24 B×R, B—N4, 25 P—Q5, when Black is a pawn down with a bad game.

23 N×KBP, R×N; 24 Q—K7 Resigns

When Fischer inspected the playing conditions at Lugano, he found things to be far below the standard that he was prepared to accept. The playing hall was crowded – the players would be bunched too close to each other, and the spectators would be almost leaning over the boards. Coupled with the fact that there was no air conditioning it was quite obvious that the atmosphere in the hall would be oppressive. Also, the lighting was quite poor. These complaints were not only made by Fischer: many of the three hundred players were very dissatisfied with the conditions for the Olympiad.

Fischer demanded in vain to be allowed to play his games in a private room, away from all spectators. He was also not happy about the hotel assigned to the American team. But then many of the teams at Lugano were displeased with the hotels in which the players had been scattered. Some players were told that whole parts of their hotel's menu were available only to private guests and not to them. I moved out of the hovel assigned to my team after being told that I could only take a bath at certain times of the day, and then, only on payment of a fee. (The Lugano organizers had not provided us with any special 'bath money' so presumably they expected us to stagnate for four weeks.) Such are the tribulations of all international chess players from time to time. The difference between Fischer and the others is that he is not prepared to put up with anything less than reasonable treatment. And so, without playing a single game, Fischer took a train to Milan and went home.

By the end of 1968 he was probably thoroughly disgusted with the way that the chess world was treating him. Difficulties of communicating properly with the organizers at Sousse had led, possibly indirectly, to his withdrawal from the current World Championship cycle. Now, thanks to their attempts to run a successful Olympiad on a shoestring budget, the Swiss Chess Federation had created conditions in which he could not possibly play. If Fischer is anywhere near as paranoid as his public image, he must have felt that some gigantic Communist conspiracy existed with the express purpose of preventing him from participating in the premier events of the chess calendar. This feeling, in my opinion, prompted his third withdrawal from competitive chess.

7

FISCHER THE MACHINE

Fischer's active style of play has always kept to a minimum the number of difficult endgames with which he would be faced. From his early games there are no recorded instances of his reaching an endgame which required very intricate and exact play. It is almost certainly for this reason that during the early part of his international career he sometimes lacked the necessary technique to take full advantage of his endgame possibilities. In two of the games of his 1961 match with Reshevsky for example, Fischer dissipated half points in the endgame. And the famous game against Botvinnik from the Varna Olympiad (page 79) is another example of experience triumphing over Fischer's objective advantage. Nevertheless, by 1962 Fischer's endgame technique was not wholly lacking.

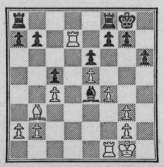

Fischer–Portisch, Interzonal Tournament, Stockholm 1962

This position arose after twenty-three moves of a Caro-Kann Defence (Two Knights variation). Fischer's strategy has revolved around his control of his K5 square and he managed to compel Portisch to exchange queens on that square, leaving White with a slight endgame advantage because of the constricting action of the pawn at K5, his control of the Q file, and his well placed rook on the seventh rank. On the other hand Black's well placed bishop seems to be able to hold his queen's side intact, and his pawn structure is so solid that White will experience difficulty in penetrating with his king.

24 B—R4

Otherwise 24...B—B3 ruins White's winning chances at once.

24 ...	QR—Q1
25 KR—Q1	R×R
26 R×R	P—KN4

This move not only hinders White's plan of P—KN4, followed by P—KN3 and K—B2—K3, but also prevents 27 R—B7, R—Q1; 28 K—B2, because of 28...P—N3; 29 R×RP (on 29 B—Q7, 29...P—QR4 gives Black a tenable position), R—Q7 ch, 30 K—K3, R—Q5; 31 B—N3, B×P; 32 R—R6, P×P; 33 P×P, P—R4!, when Black's outside passed pawn compensates for his Q-side pawn deficit.

27 B—Q1	B—B3

This must be played immediately otherwise 28 B—R5, B—B3; 29 R—K7, would leave Black's rook and king tied to the defence of his KBP.

28 R—Q6	R—B1
29 K—B2	K—B1
30 B—B3	B×B
31 P×B!	

31 K×B? would allow 31...K—K2!; 32 K—N4, P—B4 ch, and if 33 K—R5?, P—N5; 34 K×P??, R—R1 ch; 35 K—N6, R—R7, and Black will win.

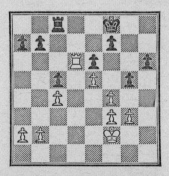

31 ...   P×P?

Black hopes to use his passed KRP to distract either White's rook (and then infiltrate with his own rook on the Q file) or his king (and then infiltrate on the KN file), but as we shall see, this plan is faulty. Correct was 31...K—K2, e.g. 32 P—B5 (otherwise Black could choose between 32...P—B4 and 32...R—Q1, both of which should suffice for equality), P×P; 33 R×P, R—B3 !. If White exchanges rooks the king and pawn ending is drawn, while if the rook retreats Black's position will be tenable, because his rook has much more freedom than in the game.

	32 P×P	K—K2

32...R—B3; 33 R—Q7, R—N3; 34 P—N3, R—R3; 35 R×NP, R×P ch; 36 K—N3, also gives White excellent winning chances.

	33 P—B5	P×P

Otherwise 34 P—B6 ch is very strong, e.g. (i) 33...R—Q1; 34 P—B6 ch, K—K1; 35 R×R ch, K×R; 36 K—N3, and White wins; or (ii) 33...R—KN1; 34 P—B6 ch, K—K1; 35 R—Q1, and Black is helpless against the long term plan of R—KR1, K—K3—K4 and P—B4—B5, eventually creating a passed pawn.

	34 R×P	R—Q1

The king and pawn ending after 34...R—B3; 35 R×R, P×R, is won for White, e.g. 36 K—N3, P—B3; 37 K—B4, K—K3; 38 P×P, K×P; 39 P—N3, K—K3; 40 K—N5, K—K4; 41 K—N6 !, K—B5; 42 K—B6, P—R3; 43 P—R3, P—R4; 44 P—R4, K×P; 45 K×P, K—K6; 46 K—K5, K—Q6; 47 K—Q6, K—B6; 48 K×P(B6), K×P; 49 K—N5 !!, winning.

	35 K—K2	R—KN1
	36 K—B2	R—Q1
	37 K—K3	R—Q8

37...R—Q5 is a logical looking alternative, but it does little to relieve Black's difficulties, e.g. 38 P—N3, P—B5 ch; 39 K—K2, K—K1 (what else? Black is virtually in zugzwang); 40 R—KB6, K—K2; 41 P—R4, K—K1; 42 P—R5, K—K2; 43 P—R6, P—N3; 44 R—B6, and White has complete control (44...K—Q2 ?; 45 R×NP !).

	38 P—N3	R—K8 ch
	39 K—B4	R—K7

If 39...R—KB8, then 40 R—R8 !, R—B7; 41 R—QN8, wins easily.

	40 K×P	R×P
	41 P—B4	

The next phase shows the superiority of a 2:1 pawn majority over a 3:2 one.

	41 . . .	R—K7

Preventing 42 P—K6 and threatening 42. . .R—K6.

	42 R—R3	R—K8
	43 R—Q3	R—QN8

Black's rook must leave the K file and thereby allow White to create a passed pawn, otherwise White will undermine his Q-side pawns, e.g. 43. . . R—K7; 44 R—Q5, P—N3; 45 R—Q3, R—K8; 46 R—R3, R—K7; 47 R— R8, R—K6; 48 R—R8, etc.

	44 R—K3	R—N7

On 44. . .P—QR3, White should not continue with 45 P—K6, because after 45. . .P—QN4 Black arrives in the text variation but with an extra tempo. Correct is 45 R—Q3 !, e.g. 45. . .P—QN4 (45. . .R—K8; 46 R— Q6 !); 46 K—K4 !, R—K8 ch (otherwise 47 P—B5 is very strong); 47 K— Q5, P×P; 48 P×P, R—KB8; 49 R—QR3, R×P; 50 R×P, R—Q5 ch; 51 K×P, and White's outside passed pawn will prove decisive.

	45 P—K6	P—R3
	46 P×P dis ch	K×P
	47 K—K5	R—Q7
	48 R—QB3	P—N3
	49 P—B5	R—Q8
	50 R—R3	P—N4

The scope of Black's king has been methodically reduced and it is now without a good move, e.g. 50. . .K—N2; 51 P—B6 ch, or 50. . .K—N1; 51 R—R6.

	51 R—R7 ch	K—N1

Or 51. . .K—K1; 52 K—K6 !.

	52 R—QN7	P×P
	53 P×P	R—Q5
	54 K—K6 !	R—K5 ch

If 54. . .R×P, White wins by 55 R—N8 ch, K—R2; 56 P—B6, R—K5 ch; 57 K—B5, R—K8; 58 P—B7, R—B8 ch; 59 K—K6, K—N2; 60 R—N8 ch, etc.

	55 K—Q5	R—B5
	56 K×P	R×KBP ch
	57 K—Q6	R—B3 ch
	58 K—K5	R—B2

Or 58. . .R—B8; 59 P—B5, R—QB8; 60 K—Q6, R—Q8 ch; 61 K—B7, P—R4; 62 P—B6, P—R5; 63 K—N8, and White wins.

	59 R—N6	R—B2
	60 K—Q5	K—B2
	61 R×P	K—K2
	62 R—K6 ch	K—Q1
	63 R—Q6 ch	K—K2

If 63...K—B1, then 64 R—QB6, and White reaches a king and pawn v king ending in which he has the opposition, e.g. 64. . .K—N2; 65

R×R ch, K×R; 66 K—B5.

64 P—B5	R—B1

64...R—R2 fails against 65 K—B6, R—R3 ch; 66 K—B7, R—R2 ch; 67 K—N6, R—R8; 68 R—Q2, R—N8 ch; 69 K—B7, etc.

65 P—B6	R—B2

Otherwise 66 R—Q7 ch and 67 K—Q6 is curtains.

66 R—R6	K—Q1
67 R—R8 ch	

Not 67 K—Q6 ??, R—Q2 ch!; 68 K—B5, R—Q8, with a book draw.

67 . . .	K—K2
68 R—R8 !	Resigns

Black must submit to 68...K—B2; 69 K—Q6, R—K2; 70 P—B7. This fine technical display by the nineteen-year-old Fischer is reminiscent of Capablanca or Lasker at their best. Fischer's performance in this game is all the more remarkable when one realizes that this was the first time in his career that he had been faced with a difficult rook ending.

And here, from later in the year, is another fine textbook ending.

Fischer–Tal, Candidates' Tournament, Curaçao 1962

Fischer is a pawn down but has more than enough compensation in the excellent position of his king and the weakness of Black's K-side pawn structure. Black's best course would be 33...R—B4; 34 B×P, K—Q2, followed by ...K—B3. By maintaining the knight on Q4 Black prevents White's king from entering the K side.

Instead, Tal decides to keep his extra pawn but as a result his rook and knight both become passively placed. Is it possible that Tal was playing for a win here?

33 . . .	N—B3 ?
34 K—B4	P—KN3

If 34...R—B7; 35 B—Q4!, and White's king runs amok among Black's pawns.

35 P—B3 !

Keeping the knight out of both K4 and KN4.

35 . . .	N—Q2
36 B—Q6	R—B7
37 P—N3 !	R—K7

If 37...R×P; 38 R—K1, K—Q1; 39 R—K6, followed by 40 R×P, etc. Any such ending with pawns racing on opposite wings will be won for White, because of the superiority of bishop over knight.

38 K—N5	R—K3
39 B—B4 !	

Threatening to win at once by 40 R—Q6.

39 . . .	N—B1
40 R—Q6	P—B1
41 K—R6 !	

Threat 42 K—N7.

41 . . .	R—K7
42 R—Q2	R—K2

After 42...R—K3, White wins by 43 K—N7, N—Q2; 44 R—QB2 ch, K—Q1; 45 B—N5 ch, K—K1; 46 R—B8 mate.

43 B—Q6	R—R2 ch
44 K—N5	R—KB2

If 44...N—Q2; 45 K×P, R—R1; 46 K—N7, R—K1; 47 K—B7 !!, and Black loses his rook to a discovered check, after 47...R—K6 or K8; 48 R—QB2 ch, K—Q1; 49 B—B7 ch, K—B1.

45 R—QN2 !!

Black is virtually in zugzwang and so . . .

45 . . .	P—B5
46 B×P	R—B4 ch
47 K—R6	P—QN4
48 B—Q6	P—N5

48...R×P; 49 R×P, is also without hope for Black.

49 P—N4	R×P
50 P—N5 !	N—K3

Otherwise 51 B×N, R×B; 52 K×P, leads to a quick win.

51 K×P	R—Q6
52 B—K5	R—K6
53 K—B5	

Now there is nothing to prevent the NP from promoting.

53 . . .	N—B1
54 R—N2 !	R—KB6 ch
55 B—B4	K—Q2
56 P—N6	N—K3
57 P—N7	R×B ch

Or 57. . .N×B; 58 P—N8(Q), N×R dis ch; 59 K—K4, R—B5 ch; 60 K—K5, R—B7; 61 Q—Q5 ch, K—K1; 62 Q—R8 ch, K—B2; 63 Q—R7 ch, picking up the rook.

58 K—K5	R—B1
59 P×R=Q	N×Q
60 K—Q5	P—R5
61 R—N7 ch	K—K1
62 K—Q6	P—N6
63 P—R3	Resigns

Sometimes endgames do not require long-term strategic plans: their technical problems can be solved by a quick tactical coup.

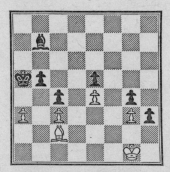

Bisguier–Fischer, US Championship 1966/67

69. . .B×P !; 70 B×B, K—R5; 71 B—B5, K—N6; 72 B×P, P—K5; 73 B×P, K×BP; 74 P—N4, K—Q7; 75 Resigns

I have mentioned in chapter five that from 1962 onwards Fischer was no longer willing to try to win as White and be content to draw as Black. His determination to squeeze the utmost out of every position puts his opponents under a kind of pressure that was hitherto unknown in master chess. Normally a Grandmaster can justifiably expect that one of his colleagues will agree to a draw in a drawn position, and that with the white pieces he can always draw quickly, simply by playing a quiet opening line and offering to split the point at an early juncture. With Fischer this is not so. He agrees draws in positions that are not only drawn but sterile. If there remains the slightest chance of victory he will not even contemplate sharing the point. His contempt of the draw is epitomized in his 'Of course not' refusal against Gheorghiu (see page 93).

After Fischer returned to action in 1970 it was noticeable that he considered other strong Grandmasters to be unable to play relatively easy endings. This facet of his attitude to his colleagues first came to my attention at the Siegen Olympiad. Evans had been showing me his ending against Polugayevsky, in which the Soviet Grandmaster had luckily escaped with a draw. At one point in the ending Evans had a chance to force a position with QRP, QBP and rook against rook – a well known theoretical draw. Instead of taking this line Evans chose another continuation which also drew, and when Fischer entered Evans' hotel room he criticized his teammate for not playing the ending with the two extra pawns. 'Polugayevsky is weak' said Fischer. 'You would probably win that ending against him!'

How ridiculous is this statement? Is it any more ridiculous, for example, than Fischer's hope of winning the following position against one of his most dangerous opponents?

Geller–Fischer, Interzonal Tournament, Palma 1970

This position was reached at the second time control. With plenty of time at his disposal Geller ought to have no problems in drawing, but ... 57 R—K4, R—KB4 ch; 58 K—K2, R—R4; 59 R—K3, K—R4; 60 R(3)—Q3, R(4)—R8; 61 R—Q8, P—B4; 62 K—B3, R—R6 ch; 63 R(2)—Q3, P—N5 ch; 64 K—B4, R × R; 65 R × R, R—KB8; 66 R—Q2. When Geller made this move the Soviet contingent was horrified. Their combined adjournment analysis had shown that 66 K—N3 was the easiest way to draw, and now Geller had forgotten. But not to worry, the position is still drawn. 66. . .K—R5; 67 K × P, P—N6. 'What was going on in Geller's mind is now the key to understanding the position. Geller had thought this to be impossible!! He thought to answer it with 68 P × P check to the black king, followed by white king TAKES black rook!!' – Wade. **68 P—B4 !, K—R6; 69 R—Q3, K—R5.** Or 69...K—R7; 70 K—N4, P—N7; 71 R—KR3 ch, K—N8; 72 P—B5, K—B7; 73 R—R2, drawing – Wade. **70 R—Q2.** 70 R—Q8 also draws. **70...R—QR8; 71 K—K5 ??.** White draws with 71 R—Q8, P—N7; 72 R—KR8 ch, K—N6; 73 R—KN8 ch, K—B6; 74 K—K6!! – Wade. **71...K—N5; 72 P—B5, R—R4 ch; 73 Resigns**

What happened to Taimanov in the second game of his match with Fischer is even more comical. Fischer had reached an ending of rook, bishop and four pawns against rook, knight and three – a relatively uncomplicated win. But then Fischer's concentration lapsed (he had earlier complained to the Yugoslav referee about Taimanov's pacing up and down the stage while he was thinking about his moves). In any event he messed up his position and when the game was adjourned for the second time the position was a clear draw.

Fischer–Taimanov, 2nd Match Game 1971

The daily Soviet sports newspaper even went so far as to state that it was an insult to his opponent for Fischer to continue the game. Tass, the Soviet news agency, had a similar comment: 'There can only be one result.'

But when the game was resumed ...

73	. . .	R—N2
74	R—B4 ch	K—Q4
75	R—R4	

Slightly better practical chances were offered by 75 R—B6, since after 75...N×B; 76 P×N, the rook ending is a win because Black's king is cut off.

75	. . .	N—N3

75...R—N1, and 75...N×B, also draw.

6	7R—R6	N—K4
77	K—B4	R—B2 ch
78	K—N5	R—N2 ch
79	K—B5	R—B2 ch

80 R—KB6	R×R ch
81 K×R	K—K5 ??

Incredible. 81...N—Q6; 82 P—R4, N—B5; 83 K—B5, K—Q3, leaves White a bishop and a pawn ahead in a totally drawn position. 81...K—Q3; 82 B—K2, N—Q2 ch; 83 K—B7, K—K4; 84 P—R4, N—B3, is also a draw.

	82 B—B8 !

Now Black's knight can only move to the useless square QB5 (82...N—Q6; 83 B—B5 ch, or 82...N—B6; 83 B—N7 ch), and his king is equally badly placed.

82 . . .	K—B5
83 P—R4	N—B6
84 P—R5	N—N4
85 K—N6	N—B6
86 P—R6	N—R5 ch
87 K—B6	Resigns

It is really impossible to have much sympathy with Taimanov for the manner in which he lost this game (or for his 0–6 score in the match), since his qualification from the Interzonal was assured by a $300 bribe to his last round opponent, the Yugoslav Grandmaster Milan Matulovic.

Fischer's win in the ending of the fourth game of the match was somewhat more convincing.

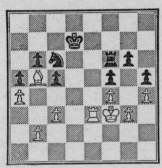

Fischer–Taimanov, 4th Match Game 1971

White's clear superiority in this position is undeniable. His rook is the more actively placed. The Q-side pawn structure and open nature of the position favour his bishop over Black's knight. And most important of all, his king has an entry route via QB4 and QN5 to QR6. It is this king march that wins the game for White. Afterwards Taimanov complained that in order to win, his opponent had to find seventeen successive 'only moves' and that Fischer found them all.

41 . . .	R—Q3
42 K—K2	

Not 42 R—Q3, R×R ch; 43 B×R, N—Q1; 44 B—B4, K—K2, and White cannot win because his king has no way of forcing an entry, e.g. 45

B—Q5 (or 45 K—K3, N—N2, and ...N—Q3), 45...N—B2; 46 B×N, K×B; 47 K—K3, K—K3; 48 K—Q3, K—Q4.

42 ...	K—Q1

42...K—B2 allows 43 R—K8, while if 42...R—B3, then 43 K—Q3, etc. Black must keep White's king out of QR6, and the rook out of his back rank.

43	R—Q3	K—B2
44	R×R	K×R
45	K—Q3	N—K2

If 45...K—Q4; 46 B×N ch, K×B; 47 K—B4 (zugzwang), K—B2; 48 K—N5, K—N2; 49 P—B4 (zugzwang), K—B2; 50 K—R6, K—B3; 51 K—R7, K—B2; 52 P—N3 (zugzwang), K—B3; 53 K—N8, and 54 K—N7, winning.

46	B—K8	K—Q4
47	B—B7 ch	K—Q3
48	K—B4	K—B3
49	B—K8 ch	K—N2
50	K—N5	N—B1

Threatening 51...N—Q3 mate!

51	B—B6 ch	K—B2
52	B—Q5	N—K2
53	B—B7 !	

If 53 B—N3, K—N2; 54 B—B7, K—R2!, and now 55 B×P, N×B; 56 K—B6, gives White only a draw. 53 B—B3, N—N1, is also unproductive.

53	...	K—N2
54	B—N3	K—R2
55	B—Q1	K—N2
56	B—B3 ch	K—B2

If now 56...K—R2; 57 B—N2, N moves; 58 K—B6.

57	K—R6	

The vital infiltration. Now White manoeuvres to a position in which he can sacrifice his bishop for three pawns.

57	...	N—N1
58	B—Q5	N—K2
59	B—B4 !	

59 B—B7 achieves nothing after 59...K—B3; 60 B—K8 ch, K—B2.

59	...	N—B3
60	B—B7	N—K2
61	B—K8	

Zugzwang.

61	...	K—Q1
62	B×P !	N×B
63	K×P	K—Q2

63...N—K2; 64 K×RP, is equally hopeless.

64	K×BP	N—K2
65	P—QN4	P×P
66	P×P	N—B1

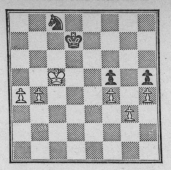

67	P—R5	N—Q3
68	P—N5	N—K5 ch
69	K—N6	K—B1
70	K—B6	K—N1
71	P—N6	Resigns

Although Fischer has occasionally made use of the services of a 'second', he has, in recent years, analysed his adjourned games in isolation. He wants to be solely responsible for his own successes: 'I don't want everyone saying that you helped me' he once said to Evans.

All Soviet players however are accompanied by analysts whenever they take part in important competitions. Even the Soviet entrant in the World Junior Championship usually has the help of a grandmaster. Undoubtedly this kind of help can be very useful. Botvinnik, for example, would almost certainly have lost to Fischer at Varna had he not had the help of Geller and a number of other leading grandmasters. But sometimes too many cooks can befuddle the mind. This is exactly what happened in the fifth game of the Fischer–Taimanov match.

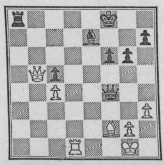

Taimanov–Fischer, 5th Match Game 1971

The game was adjourned in this position with Taimanov sealing the obvious move 42 B × P. After analysing all night (presumably while Taimanov was sleeping) Vasyukov and Balashov showed their man the fruits of their analysis over the breakfast table. After breakfast there were a few spare minutes before the car was ready to drive them to the playing hall, and so out came a pocket set and four Soviet hands flashed across the board, showing Taimanov once again what he had to do. When the Soviet trio arrived at the hall the same thing happened: five minutes were spent feverishly shifting the tiny pieces as though Taimanov was some university student hurriedly cramming for an examination. The result of all this hurried preparation was total confusion. Taimanov's mind was so mixed up that four moves later he made the worst blunder of his career: 42...B × B ch; 43 Q × B ch, K—N2; 44 R—KB1, Q—K5; 45 Q—B7 ch, K—R3; 46 R × P ??. After 46 R—B4 or 46 Q—B4 ch, the game would be drawn. 46...Q—Q5 ch; 47 R—B2, R—R8 ch; 48 Resigns

I have given this rather extreme example so that the reader might better appreciate what happened to Petrosian in the sixth game of the final Candidates' Match in Buenos Aires.

Petrosian–Fischer, 6th Match Game 1971

This adjourned position is clearly good for Black because he can eat White's QRP at will, yet the fact that the remaining pawns are on one side of the board means that Black's task is not at all simple. In fact, Korchnoy, Spassky and Tal all thought the position to be drawn (until the game was continued the next day).

42 N—K2

Petrosian's sealed move and the most natural one. An interesting alternative suggested by some of the kibitzers was 42 P—B4, NP × P; 43 N—B3, followed by P—R4 and P—N5, a plan designed to maintain an impregnable blockade. But as Shamkovitch points out this plan does not work: 43...P—R3 !; 44 P—R4, R × P; 45 R × R, K × R; 46 P—N5, BP × P; 47 P × P, P × P; 48 N × NP, B—R4; 49 N—B3, B—B2, and then Black marches his king along the QN file to QN8, along the back rank to K8, and then to KB7, when White's position collapses. The presence of bishop *v* knight gives Black all the extra tempi he needs to bring about zugzwang situations.

    42 . . .   B—R4
    43 R—N2 ch!

The Soviet team (Averbakh, Suetin and Petrosian, and maybe help from Moscow by telephone!?) found this move after several hours thought. They realized that 43 N—B1, R×P; 44 N—N3, R—R1! (if 44...K—N5; 45 N—R1!, R—B3; 46 N—B2 ch, K—N4; 47 N—R3 ch, K—B4; 48 N—B4, B—N5; 49 R—R8, with good drawing prospects); 45 R—R1, R—R2; 46 R—R2, K—N5!; 47 N—R1, R—B2!; 48 N—B2 ch, K—N6!; 49 R—R3 ch, K—N7, allows Black to make too much progress.

43 N—N3 is also good for Black: 43...K×P; 44 N—B5, R—QB2; 45 R—B2, R—QN2; 46 R—B6 ch, K—R2; 47 R—B5, B—K8; 48 K—K2, B—B6, with good winning prospects.

    43 . . .   K×P
    44 R—N1

Now the success of White's defence will depend on whether he can keep Black's rook out of its eighth rank.

    44 . . .   R—QB2
    45 R—N2

Probably 45 P—B3 was better, so that after a later R—N2, B—K7, White can return to QN1 without leaving his BP en prise.

    45 . . .   B—K8!

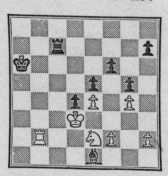

    46 P—B3?

Just as Taimanov was confused by too much adjournment analysis, so Petrosian forgets one of the vital points of the position. During the adjournment the Soviet camp had analysed the continuation 46 R—N1, B×P; 47 R—KB1, B—K6; 48 R×P ch, K—N4; 49 R—K6, R—R2; 50 R×P ch, K—N5; 51 N×P, R—R6 ch; 52 K—K2, B×N; 53 R×P, which is drawn since the KRP promotes on a square of the wrong colour. 48...K—R2 also fails to win: 49 R—K6, R—B4; 50 R—K7 ch!, K—N3; 51 R—K6 ch, K—B2; 52 R—KR6, R—N4; 53 K—B2, drawing.

Averbakh wrote: 'While analysing we were worried about the piece formation for Black – bishop on K8 and rook on QB3. Then the KBP will no longer be en prise. Just about an hour before the adjournment session began we came to the conclusion that in this case White would have to play 46 P—B3, but then then 46. . .B—B7 is not to be feared, because of 47 R—R2 ch, K—N4; 48 R—N2 ch, K—R5; 49 R—B2, R—K2; 50 R—R2 ch, and 50. . .K—N6 fails to 51 N—B1 ch.

'Apparently the analysis of this complicated position tired Petrosian out and he quite unexpectedly played 46 P—B3, when the rook was on QB2 and not QB3.'

46 . . .	K—R4
47 R—B2	R—QN2
48 R—R2 ch	K—N4
49 R—N2 ch	B—N5
50 R—R2	R—QB2
51 R—R1	R—B1 !
52 R—R7 ?	

A better defensive idea was 52 R—R2 !, P—R4; 53 P×P, e.g. 53. . .B—K8 ?; 54 R—N2 ch, K—R5; 55 R—N6, or 53. . .R—KR1 !; 54 N—N3, B—K8 (threat . . .B×N followed by . . .R×P winning); 55 R—QN2 ch, K—B3; 56 R—QB2 ch, K—Q2; 57 R—R2, B×N; 58 R—R7 ch.

Best play for both sides is probably 52. . .B—K8 (Korchnoy suggested 52. . .B—K2); 53 R—N2 ch, K—R5; 54 R—B2 !, when Black's task is still difficult.

52 . . .	B—R4
53 R—Q7	

If White captures the KRP his rook is left out of play for too long: 53 R×P, B—N3; 54 R—KB7, R—QR1; 55 R×P, R—R6 ch; 56 K—Q2, B—R4 ch, winning.

53 . . .	B—N3
54 R—Q5 ch	B—B4
55 N—B1	K—R5
56 R—Q7	B—N5

In comes the rook.

57 N—K2	K—N6
58 R—QN7	

Preventing 58. . .R—B7, but . . .

58 . . .	R—QR1 !
59 R×P	

59 N—B1 ch, K—N7; 60 R×B ch, K×N, leaves White with a lost rook ending.

59 . . .	R—R8

At last.

60 N×P ch	

60 N—N3, R—R7; 61 N—B1, R—KB7, is equally hopeless.

60 . . .	P×N
61 K×P	R—Q8 ch
62 K—K3	B—B4 ch

63 K—K2	R—KR8
64 P—R4	K—B5
65 P—R5	R—R7 ch
66 K—K1	K—Q6
67 Resigns	

Presumably Fischer will one day annotate this game, and we shall discover whether or not Black can force a win from the adjourned position if White defends accurately. Until then, we can probably do no better than to agree with Najdorf's assessment of the position: 'It is as difficult for White to draw as it is for Black to win!'

8

THE ROAD TO THE CHAMPIONSHIP

Solitude gives birth to the original in us, to beauty un-
familiar and perilous – to poetry. But also it gives birth to
the opposite: to the perverse, the illicit, the absurd.

THOMAS MANN

From the end of the Vinkovci tournament in September 1968 to the match between the USSR and the Rest of the World in March/April 1970, Fischer played only one serious game. He ignored all tournament invitations and even refused to take part in the 1969 US Championship that was the zonal tournament for the 1970/72 World Championship cycle. (He maintained that the tournament was too short and hence that it was too open to chance.)

The one game that he did play during this third dormant period tells us something about Fischer's creative attitude to chess.

57 SAIDY–FISCHER

MARSHALL *v* MANHATTAN MATCH 1969

English Opening

1 P—QB4, P—K4
Fischer normally prefers a quieter system against the English Opening. See for example his games against

Petrosian (59) and Smyslov (64) later in this chapter. It is interesting that he is willing to try out something that he obviously considers risky when he could mow down his opponent by virtue of his superior technique.

2 N—QB3, N—QB3; 3 P—KN3, P—B4; 4 B—N2, N—B3; 5 P—Q3, B—B4; 6 P—K3, P—B5 ?!

Around 1968 a similar system enjoyed a brief period of popularity against the Sicilian Defence: 1 P—K4, P—QB4; 2 N—QB3, N—QB3; 3 P—B4, P—KN3; 4 N—B3, B—N2; 5 B—B4, P—K3; 6 P—B5!?. The idea was that after 6...KP×P, White plays 7 P—Q3, sacrificing a pawn for attacking chances (particularly along the KB file). But this whole system is rather ineffectual against sound play by Black. All the more remarkable then that Fischer should choose to play the same idea with a tempo less!

7 KP×P, O—O; 8 KN—K2?

8 P×P was simple and strong. Black would have little to show for the pawn.

8...Q—K1; 9 O—O

Now 9 P×P can be met by 9...N—KN5.

9...P—Q3; 10 N—R4

Eliminating Black's strong bishop but at the cost of giving Black a very strong pawn at Q5.

10...B—Q5; 11 N×B, P×N; 12 P—KR3, P—KR4; 13 P—R3, P—R4; 14 P—N3

If 14 R—N1, B—Q2; 15 P—QN4, P×P; 16 P×P, N×P!.

14...Q—N3; 15 N—N2, B—B4; 16 Q—B2, N—Q2; 17 R—K1, N—B4; 18 B—B1, R—R3!; 19 B—Q2, R—N3; 20 B×P, R×P; 21 B—Q2, R—R1!

The reversed Benoni type pawn structure (White pawns at QB4 and Q3, Black pawn at Q5), splits White's position in two so that he cannot co-ordinate his pieces for a successful defence.

22 P—QR4, R—R3; 23 P—R5, K—R2; 24 R(K1)—Q1, P—N3; 25 B—K1

If 25 P×P, R(R3)×P; 26 R—R2, N×P.

25...P×P; 26 N—R4, R×P; 27 B×R, B×B; 28 Q—R2, N—N5; 29 Q—R3, N—B7; 30 Q—N2, N×R; 31 R×N, N×N; 32 R×N, Q—K5; 33 B×P

Losing at once, but otherwise the threat of 33...R—N3 proves fatal.

33...R×B; 34 R×R, Q—K8 ch; 35 K—R2, Q×R; 36 Resigns

Viewed objectively this game is a massacre. After failing to seize his chance in the opening, White quickly gets saddled with a passive position from which he finds it impossible to extricate himself. Yet in selecting the best games of the first six months of 1969, the *Informator 8* judges placed this game second, and Wade claimed that it would have merited first place had Fischer's sixth move been less dubious. To me it seems as though these judges were adulating Fischer's decision to play a game of chess when in a state of temporary retirement rather than the quality of the game itself (which is not very high).

Fischer's participation in the 'Match of the Century' was always in some doubt. Although the match was to be played in Yugoslavia where he had always been extremely popular, there were fundamental problems that for a long time appeared insoluble. In the period since Fischer's withdrawal from the Interzonal in Sousse, the winner of the Sousse tournament, Bent Larsen, had been achieving tremendous tournament results. While Fischer had been lying dormant he had been building up a claim to being the strongest player in the Western World. Because of this there was a great deal of controversy over who should play on top board in Belgrade for the Rest of the World team. Its captain, Dr Euwe, decided to put his team in the order of the current international rating list and in this list Fischer was ahead of Larsen. Furthermore, Larsen and Fischer both adopted the attitude that if they were not to be given top board they would not participate in the match (clearly the omission of either player would have enabled the Soviet Union to win by a massive margin).

When Fischer arrived in Belgrade he was extremely keen to play. He wanted his return to competitive chess to begin with an opportunity to defeat Spassky for the first time in his life. But Larsen remained adamant.

Eventually Fischer conceded. Larsen was right – his results during the previous two years or so had been spectacular, and entitled him to the position at the head of the team. So instead of meeting World Champion Spassky, Fischer faced the hardest man in the world to beat – Tigran Petrosian.

---

58 FISCHER–PETROSIAN
BELGRADE 1970 (1st game)

Caro-Kann Defence

Notes by Suetin

1 P—K4	P—QB3
2 P—Q4	P—Q4
3 P×P	P×P
4 B—Q3	N—QB3
5 P—QB3	N—B3

White plays this system very rarely nowadays. Fischer is, perhaps, its greatest enthusiast. [A peculiar comment since Fischer had only played this system once before – DNLL.] Black's last move leads to a closed position. Holmov recommends 5...P—K4; 6 P×P, N× P; 7 B—QN5 ch, N—B3.

6 B—KB4
On 6 P—KR3 comes 6...P—K4!, and Black equalizes easily. To 6 B—KN5, Fischer suggested an interesting variation: 6...N—K5; 7 B×N, P×B; 8 P—Q5, N—K4; 9 Q—R4 ch, Q—Q2; 10 Q×KP, Q—N4!?, which he thought was quite comfortable for Black. But if White continues 11 P—QN3!, N—Q6 ch; 12 K—B1, it isn't difficult to see that Black's task is not easy. 12...N—K4 dis ch is answered by 13 Q—K2.

Perhaps it is simpler to reply to 6 B—KN5 with 6...B—N5, and if 7 Q—N3, then 7...Q—Q2, with equal chances.
6 ...   B—N5
Positions of this kind are more common in the Slav Defence with colours reversed, e.g. 1 P—Q4, P—Q4; 2 P—QB4, P—K3; 3 N—QB3, P—QB3; 4 P×P, KP×P; 5 N—B3, B—KB4; 6 B—KN5. It is necessary to note that for about twenty years it has been a fashionable strategy for White to copy some of the active Black systems. At present, Larsen in particular favours such a strategy. There is his game against Botvinnik at Leiden 1970, which was a typical Scheveningen Sicilian with colours reversed.

How can one explain this tendency? Perhaps it is because for 'complete happiness' Black needs one tempo! But Black's 'happiness' consists first of all, in getting an equal game, whereas White's strategical task is far more complex – to hold the initiative and get even a slight advantage.

7 Q—N3   N—QR4
Petrosian believes in the richness of Black's resources. Simpler is 7...Q—B1, and if 8 N—QR3, then 8...P—QR3, with a strong position.

8 Q—R4 ch   B—Q2

Holmov recommends 8...N—B3; 9 B—QN5, B—Q2; 10 Q—B2, R—B1; 11 N—B3, N—QN5!, with a good game for Black. But this variation is far from being compulsory. Continuing 9 QN—Q2 and then 10 KN—B3, White harmoniously develops his forces.

9 Q—B2   P—K3

9...P—QR3 deserves consideration, intending the manoeuvre 10...B—N4.

10 N—B3   Q—N3

Black is being generous, neglecting to develop his K side. 10...B—K2 would have been better.

11 P—QR4!

A well timed reply, preventing ...B—N4.

11 . . .   R—B1

11...N—N6 doesn't win anything because of 12 R—R2, R—B1; 13 O—O, followed by QN—Q2, and White has a big lead in development. Even worse is 11...Q—N6, against which Fischer pointed out 12 Q—K2!, B×P?; 13 R×B, Q×R; 14 B—QN5 ch, winning.

12 QN—Q2   N—B3
13 Q—N1   N—KR4

According to Fischer, ...P—N3 would have been better.

14 B—K3

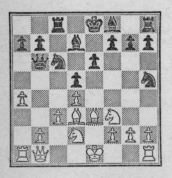

14 . . .   P—KR3

An important moment. The following possibilities were at Black's disposal:

(i) 14...P—B4, trying to close the game in the centre and on the K side. Fischer recommends the continuation

15 P—KN4, P×P; 16 N—N5, B—Q3; 17 B×P, assessing the position to White's advantage.

(ii) 14...B—Q3 is very complicated: 15 B×P, P—N3; 16 B×P, P×B; 17 Q×P ch, K—Q1; 18 P—KN4, N—K2 (of course not 18...N—B5, because of 19 B×N, B×B; 20 Q—B6 ch); 19 Q—N5, K—B2; 20 P—B4 (Holmov's recommendation. If 20 P×N?, QR—KN1; 21 Q—R4, N—B4; 22 Q—R3, N×B; 23 P×N, P—K4!, with an excellent game for Black.) 20...P×P; 21 P×N, QR—KN1. It seems that in this line Black has sufficient counter-chances, and he should therefore have gone into these complications by playing 14...B—Q3. In conceding his K4 square, Black comes under strong pressure.

15 N—K5   N—B3

Some commentators recommended the continuation 15...N×N; 16 P×N, B—B4; 17 P—R5, Q—B2; 18 P—KN4!?, B×B; 19 P×B, Q×KP; 20 P×N, Q×KP ch; 21 B—K2, B—N4; 22 Q—Q1, when Black has insufficient compensation for the piece. Playing R—R3, White defends against the attack, keeping the extra piece. It is interesting that Fischer, in his comments to the game, doesn't consider the move 18 P—KN4!?, preferring the positional 18 N—B3, which also gives White an advantage. After 18...B×B, White plays 19 P×B, P—KN3; 20 O—O, preparing a breakthrough in the centre with P—K4.

16 P—R3   B—Q3
17 O—O   K—B1

Fischer is right in thinking that 17...O—O would have been a lesser crime, although even then after 18 P—KB4, White has a very strong initiative.

Holmov analysed the interesting variation 17...P—QR4; 18 K—R1, O—O; 19 P—KN4, KR—Q1; 20 R—N1, B—K1; 21 P—N5, P×P; 22 B×P, K—B1; 23 P—KB4, and Black's position is very difficult.

18 P—KB4   B—K1
19 B—KB2

White is gradually developing an attack whereas Black is completely deprived of active counterplay.

19 . . .   Q—B2

In reply to 19...P—N3, Fischer gives 20 P—B5!, NP×P; 21 B×P, P×B; 22 Q×P, Q—Q1; 23 B—R4, and White wins.

20 B—R4   N—KN1
21 P—B5!

Although this forces the exchange of minor pieces, White's attack becomes stronger and stronger.

21 . . .   N×N
22 P×N   B×KP
23 P×P   B—KB3
24 P×P   B×KBP
25 N—B3   B×B

25...P—KN4 is not satisfactory because of 26 B—KB2 K—N2 27 B—Q4, and 26...N—K2 isn't good because of 27 B—Q4, B×B ch; 28 N×B, K—N2; 29 Q—K1, etc.

26 N×B   N—B3
27 N—N6 ch!

The most precise way. After the exchange on KN6, White's bishop is a dominating figure.

27 . . .   B×N
28 B×B   K—K2

The tactical complications are over, but it becomes clear that Black hasn't got a useful move. Petrosian desperately tries to unite the rooks.

29 Q—B5   K—Q1
30 QR—K1   Q—B4 ch
31 K—R1   R—B1

And after 31...R—B3; 32 Q—K5 (threatening 33 Q—N8 ch), Black is defenceless.

32 Q—K5   R—QB2

Black loses after 32...Q—B2; 33 Q×P ch, N×Q; 34 R×R ch, etc.

33 P—QN4!   Q—B3
34 P—B4!

Opening the central files decides the game very quickly.

34 . . .   P×P
35 B—B5   R(1)—B2
36 R—Q1 ch   R(KB2)—Q2

On 36...N—Q2, 37 KR—K1! is decisive.

37 B×R   R×B
38 Q—N8 ch   K—K2

38...Q—B1 is bad as well, because of 39 R×R ch, N×R; 40 Q—Q6!.

39 QR—K1 ch   Resigns

When Petrosian resigned the audience erupted. More than two thousand chess fans were in the Trades Union Hall in Belgrade to watch the games, and at least the same number were in the square outside, viewing the Fischer–Petrosian and Larsen–Spassky games on a large screen. Fischer's win was immediately proclaimed the best game of the first round and Fischer was awarded a special prize, donated by the newspaper *Politika*. They donated a special prize in each round for the best win. (It was generally agreed that Hort's first round win over Polugayevsky was a finer game, but naturally this did not affect the judges decision!)

Two days later came the second of the four rounds.

59 PETROSIAN–FISCHER

BELGRADE 1970 (2nd game)

English Opening

Notes by Petrosian

It is very rare to come across a game annotated by the loser. This is not accidental. One doesn't usually want to publish one's conclusions after analysing the game.

After I had lost the first game I had a difficult task: I had to work out my tactics for the next game. Trying to win at all costs could end catastrophically because of the small number of rounds. Should I try to draw with White? Absurd. What mood is my opponent going to be in? Peaceful or aggressive? I asked various people's opinion but I wasn't given much advice.

I decided to play aggressively, hoping to take advantage of the fact that Fischer would probably try to repeat his previous success. Shall I play 1 P—Q4? He will probably play the Grünfeld. So I'd better play 1 P—QB4 and disguise my plans a little.

    1 P—QB4   P—KN3

It seems that I have guessed correctly. Fischer leaves open the possibility of playing the Grünfeld, but perhaps he wants to transpose to the King's Indian Defence. No doubt he had noticed that I have recently had some bad spells against it.

    2 N—QB3   P—QB4

This is the secret. With this move order Black does not allow his opponent to advance with the QP. After 3 N—B3, B—N2; 4 P—Q4 Black replies 4...P× P; 5 N×P, N—QB3, when the exchange on QB6 and 6 N—B2, or 6 P—K3, do not promise White great advantages from the opening. It seems that Fischer was well prepared for the move 1 P—QB4.

My experience in this game was of use to me later. At Rovinj/Zagreb [one month later – DNLL] I played against Fischer in the last round. After 1 P—QB4, P—QB4, I played 2 N—KB3, and to 2...P—KN3, I played 3 P—K4, B—N2; 4 P—Q4, N—QB3; 5 P×P!, Q—R4 ch; 6 KN—Q2!, Q×BP; 7 N—N3, with advantage to White. [The game was drawn in forty-four moves – DNLL.]

    3 P—KN3   B—N2
    4 B—N2   N—QB3
    5 N—B3   P—K3
    6 O—O   KN—K2
    7 P—Q3   O—O
    8 B—Q2   P—Q4

Black has chosen a very stable defence. The strong pawn centre allows him to develop his pieces in peace. The secretive character of Black's QP is very important – it can either advance or, at a convenient moment, be exchanged on QB5.

White's plan in the centre is not so clear. Exchanging on Q5 or advancing P—K4 do not promise much. So White had to try the plan of forcing P—QN4.

    9 P—QR3   P—N3
    10 R—N1   B—N2
    11 P—QN4   BP×P
    12 RP×P   P×P
    13 P×P   R—B1

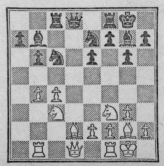

Black's position is now quite pleasant. The pawn at QB4 can cause White some difficulty, and then to the centralizing plan ...Q—Q2, followed by ...KR—Q1 it is not easy to find a refutation.

Of course if I was aiming for a draw I could have tried 14 N—QN5, and on 14...P—QR3, withdraw my knight to QR3, preparing to exchange Q-side pawns.

[It seems that White's opening strategy has proved such a failure that Petrosian ought to have been content with a draw at this stage. After the move played in the game he is always *fighting* for a draw – DNLL.]

14 P—B5?	P×P
15 P×P	N—QR4
16 N—QR4	B—QB3!

When I analysed the position after the thirteenth move I could not see any refutation of the plan 14 P—B5, although I didn't like it much. Black's sixteenth and seventeenth moves are very strong. It seems that it isn't easy to defend the QBP.

17 Q—B2	N—N2!

Of course not 17...B×N; 18 Q×B, R×P; 19 B—N4, and the rook cannot stay on the fourth rank.

18 KR—B1	Q—Q2
19 N—K1	N—Q4

Avoiding the variation 19...B×N; 20 R×N, Q×R; 21 B×Q, B×Q; 22 B×R, R×B; 23 R×B, N—B3, in which, in spite of great simplifications, Black has the better chances.

Instead Fischer continued to strengthen his position.

20 N—N2	B—N4
21 N(K1)—Q3	

After 21 N(N2)—Q3, B—Q5; 22 Q—N3, it becomes clear that it is not so easy for Black to win the QBP. But in the depths of my soul I really gave it up.

21 ...	B—Q5
22 Q—N3	N×P
23 N×N	R×N
24 R×R	B×R
25 N—Q3	B×N
26 Q×B	

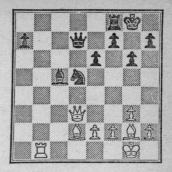

Black has a healthy extra pawn, but it is not so simple to make use of it. The journey from QR2 to QR8 is long, and to hope to gain some positional advantage on the other side of the board is difficult. White has not got any weaknesses, and his two bishops are worth something.

26 ...	R—Q1

Fischer is not very happy about the outcome of possible exchanges on his Q4 squares so he overprotects his knight. Now, after Black's queen leaves Q2 there are some tactical chances in connection with the knight.

27 B—KB3	

It is very difficult to refute this move. One has to wait patiently.

27 ...	Q—B2?

If I had now played 28 R—QB1!, Black would have had difficulty in meeting the threat 29 R×B, Q×R; 30 P—K4.

28 B—N5?	B—K2
29 B×B	Q×B

White loses the advantage of the two bishops, but Black's bishop, which 'worked' on both flanks (from QB4), vanishes.

30 Q—Q4?	

Really any other move would have been better. Now Fischer gradually brings his pieces on to the dark squares, and plays as if he has an extra piece because White's bishop is completely out of play.

[By now Petrosian was looking quite demoralised – DNLL.]

30 . . .	P—K4
31 Q—QB4	N—N3
32 Q—B2	

Before Black's pieces reached their ideal posts, I should have tried to exchange queens by playing 32 Q—QN4, in order to have some drawing chances in the endgame. Even if he had refused the exchange of queens it would have been a felicitous square for my queen.

32 . . .	R—QB1
33 Q—Q3	R—B5
34 B—N2	Q—B2
35 Q—R3	R—B6
36 Q—R5	R—B4
37 Q—R3	P—QR4
38 P—R4	N—B5
39 Q—Q3	N—Q3
40 K—R2	K—N2

Here the game was adjourned and I had to seal the move. The knight is beautifully placed on Q3, and in order to create some activity White must drive it away. That is why I sealed the text move instead of the better 41 Q—R6.

| 41 R—Q1 | N—K1 ! |

The knight is going to KB3 where it cannot be attacked. Moreover, after . . .N—KB3 the check on KN5 will be extremely unpleasant for White.

White's plight is illustrated by the variation 42 Q—R6, N—B3; 43 B—R8 (to free KN2 for the king), P—R5; 44 Q×P, R—R4; 45 Q—B6, Q—R2, and Black wins. That is why I now exchanged queens, but the endgame looks absolutely lost.

| 42 Q—Q7 | Q×Q |
| 43 R×Q | N—B3 |

This appears to be extremely strong but Fischer did not foresee everything.

44 R—R7	N—N5 ch
45 K—N1	R—B8 ch
46 B—B1	R—R8
47 P—K4	P—R5
48 K—N2	R—R7

Black's last move finishes the attack. To all Black's advantages is added the attack on the KBP. But White still has a chance to defend himself. After 49 K—N1 it is clear that the BP is untouchable. To take it with the rook is not possible because of 50 B—R3, and on 49. . .N×P; 50 B—B4 is very strong.

After the game (by the way, Fischer hadn't seen 49 K—N1) when we analysed the position quickly, we looked at the variation 49. . .N×P; 50 B—B4, N—R6 ch; 51 K—R1, R—KB7; 52 B—K6 ! (White's plan is based on this move). We decided that I was rescuing myself. Then somebody suggested 52. . . P—R6; 53 B×N, P—R7; 54 K—N1, R—QN7; 55 B—B1, P—N4, and the march of the black king decides the game.

So thanks to the fact that at the analysis a large number of chess journalists were present, this position was classified in chess periodicals as hopeless for White. But it isn't difficult to see that instead of 54 K—N1 ?, the correct move is 54 B—N2, followed by K—R2.

So it is questionable whether Black could have won after 49 K—N1. For White this would have been an excellent practical chance. The sad thing about it is that I saw all the possibilities and knew that what happened in the game was hopeless. [Petrosian still does not explain why he did not play 49 K—N1 – DNLL.]

49 R×P ch	K×R
50 B—B4 ch	K—K2
51 B×R	P—R6

It is a simple win for Black. The advanced QRP will tie White's king

down, and in the meantime Black will establish an advantage on the K side.
52 K—B3, N—B3; 53 K—K3, K—Q3; 54 P—B4, N—Q2; 55 B—N1, N—B4; 56 P—B5, N—R3; 57 P—N4, N—N5; 58 P×P, P×P; 59 P—R5, P×P; 60 P×P, K—K3; 61 K—Q2, K—B3; 62 K—B3, P—R7; 63 B×P, N×B ch; 64 K—N2, N—N5; 65 K—B3, N—B3; 66 K—B4, N—Q5; 67 Resigns

The third and fourth games between Fischer and Petrosian were both drawn, giving Fischer a 3–1 win in the series and the special prize of a Moscvitch car (which he sold).

Now that he had been coaxed back into the chess arena the Yugoslav organizers were determined to make the most of Fischer's presence in their country. Immediately following the Match of the Century, many of the grandmasters flew to the town of Herceg Novi for a 'World Blitz Championship', a double-round tournament with twelve players. The result: 1st Fischer 19 out of 22; 2nd Tal 14½; 3rd Korchnoy 14; 4th Petrosian 13½; 5th Bronstein 13; 6th Hort 12; 7th Matulovic 10½; 8th Smyslov 9½; etc. In view of this result it is hardly surprising that from about this time onwards Fischer often consumed an hour less than his opponents in regular tournament games.

By the time that Fischer had played in two normal tournaments it was apparent that during his hibernation he had been widening his opening repertoire. At Rovinj/Zagreb he played Alekhine's Defence for only the second time in his career (the first was in the 1965 Capablanca Memorial Tournament). And at Buenos Aires a couple of months later he branched out as far as opening 1 P—QN3, against Tukmakov. Another surprise came in his game against Minic at Zagreb. Having won with the Poisoned Pawn Variation against Parma in the first round, he unexpectedly switched back to a more popular line two rounds later.

---

60 MINIC–FISCHER
ROVINJ/ZAGREB 1970

Sicilian Defence

1 P—K4, P—QB4; 2 N—KB3, P—Q3; 3 P—Q4, P×P; 4 N×P, N—KB3; 5 N—QB3, P—QR3; 6 B—KN5, P—K3; 7 P—B4, B—K2 !
Surprise, surprise.
8 Q—B3, Q—B2; 9 O—O—O, QN—Q2; 10 P—KN4, P—N4; 11 B×N, N×B; 12 P—N5, N—Q2; 13 P—QR3

To me 13 P—B5 seems more natural. The frequently played text move weakens the area around White's king.
13...R—QN1; 14 P—KR4, P—N5; 15 P×P, R×P; 16 B—R3
In Gligoric–Tringov, Amsterdam 1964 in which this variation was employed for the first time, White played the somewhat dubious 16 P—R5?!, which allowed Black to get a good game: 16...N—B4; 17 P—N6, O—O; 18 P—

R6, BP×P; 19 P×P, R—B2. By
playing 16 B—R3, White prepares for a
sacrifice on K6, and therefore Black
usually plays 16...N—B4, but after
17 P—B5! White has a dangerous
looking attack. So Fischer played:
　　16...O—O

17 N—B5 ?!
Enterprising but unsound. White should
have sacrificed on K6: 17 N×P, P×
N; 18 B×P ch, K—R1; 19 N—Q5,
Q—B5!; 20 B×N, B×B; 21 N×B,
KR—QN1, and according to Gligoric,
Black has enough play to compensate
for his material deficit.

**17...N—B4!; 18 N×B ch, Q×N;
19 P—R5 ?**
This move is thematic but bad because
White's attack is too slow. Correct is
19 Q—K3, followed by R—Q4 and
KR—Q1, building up pressure on the
QP.
　　**19...B—N2; 20 P—R6, B×P; 21
　　N×B, N×N; 22 P×P, R—B1!**
The winning move. On 22...K×P,
White would win by 23 B—B5!; P×
B; 24 R×P ch, K×R; 25 Q—R5 ch,
K—N2; 26 R—R1, and mate.
　　23 R—R2
23 B—B5, P×B; 24 Q—R5, fails to
24...R×BP ch!; 25 K×R, Q—B2 ch;
26 K—N1, N—B6 ch; 27 K—B2, N×
R dis ch; 28 K×N, R—Q5 ch, and it is
Black who gives mate.
　　**23...R—R5; 24 K—N1, P—Q4; 25
　　P—B4**
Or 25 B—B5, P×B; 26 Q—R3, N—
B6 ch.
　　**25...R(R5)×P; 26 B—B1, R—N5;
　　27 Q—KR3, N—B6 ch; 28 K—B1,
　　N—R5 dis ch; 29 K—N1, R×NP ch;
　　30 R×R, N—B6 ch; 31 K—B1, Q—
　　R6; 32 B—Q3, Q—R8 ch; 33 K—
　　Q2, Q×R ch; 34 K—K1, N—K5; 35
　　Resigns**

As White, however, Fischer still had a big hole to be plugged in his repertoire
– the Winawer Variation. His eighteen month lay-off had not helped him to
find a satisfactory system for White, and he returned to an old variation,
popularized by Alekhine, that he had once played earlier in his career.

61　FISCHER–UHLMANN
ROVINJ/ZAGREB 1970

French Defence

**1 P—K4, P—K3; 2 P—Q4, P—Q4;
3 N—QB3, B—N5; 4 P—QR3**
This ultra sharp line was employed by
Alekhine in his first World Champion-
ship Match with Euwe.
　　**4...B×N ch; 5 P×B, P×P; 6 Q—
　　N4, N—KB3; 7 Q×NP, R—N1; 8
　　Q—R6, R—N3**

Two rounds later Kovacevic played 8...QN—Q2 against Fischer. The game continued 9 N—K2, P—N3 (Fischer–R. Byrne, US Championship 1966/67 went instead 9...P—B4; 10 N—N3, Q—B2; 11 Q—K3, Q—B3; 12 P—QR4, P—QR3; 13 P×P, Q×BP; 14 Q×Q, N×Q, and the game was eventually drawn); 10 B—KN5? (correct would have been 10 N—N3, with the plan of 11 B—K2 and 12 O—O), 10...Q—K2!; 11 Q—R4, B—N2; 12 N—N3, P—KR3!; 13 B—Q2? (better 13 B—B1), 13...O—O—O; 14 B—K2, N—B1!; 15 O—O, N—N3; 16 Q×RP, R—R1; 17 Q—N5, QR—N1; 18 P—B3, P—K6; 19 B×P, N—B1; 20 Q—N5, N—Q4; 21 K—B2, P—R3; 22 Q—Q3, R×P; 23 R—R1, Q—R5; 24 R×R, Q×R; 25 N—B1, R×P ch, and Black soon won.

A most creditable victory for the unknown Yugoslav were it not for the fact that he was being advised what to play by the Soviet players (via one of their wives). 'But they didn't tell him all the moves – just the killing ones' one of the other competitors told me!

9 Q—K3

9 Q—Q2 is probably better.

9...N—B3?

It is quite unnatural to block the QBP. Correct is 9...P—N3; 10 N—K2, B—N2; 11 N—B4, R—N1; 12 B—N2, QN—Q2. Now Black fails to get adequate counterplay.

10 B—N2, Q—Q3; 11 P—B3 ?!

Better is 11 P—QB4, P—K4; 12 P—Q5.

11...P×P ?

Black should open the centre before White has had time to complete his development. After 11...P—K4!; 12 BP×P, P×P; 13 P×P, N×KP; 14

O—O—O, P—B4, the position is unclear. But not 14...R—K3; 15 P—Q5, nor 14...B—B4; 15 B—K2, followed by P—N4.

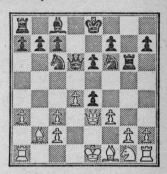

12 N×P, B—Q2; 13 O—O—O, O—O—O; 14 P—B4,

Already white is on top.

14... N—KN5; 15 Q—Q2, P—B4; 16 P—Q5 !, N—N1

If 16...N(B3)—K4; 17 N×N, N×N; 18 Q—Q4, and 19 Q×P; or 16...N—K2; 17 P—R3, N—KB3; 18 N—R4, N—K5; 19 Q—Q4.

17 P—R3, N—KB3; 18 N—K5

On 18 N—R4, Black can play 18...N—K5; 19 Q—K3, Q—N6.

18...N—K5; 19 Q—Q4, R—N6; 20 N—B7, Q—B5 ch; 21 K—N1, P—B4; 22 Q—K5 !

Neat. Black must lose material.

22...Q×Q; 23 B×Q, R(Q1)—N1

If 23...R—B1; 24 N—Q6 ch, N×N; 25 B×N, etc.

24 B—Q3, R×NP; 25 B×N(K4), P×B; 26 N—Q6 ch, K—B2; 27 N×KP dis ch, K—N3; 28 N—B6, B—R5; 29 N×R, B×P ch; 30 K—B1, N—Q2; 31 QR—N1, Resigns

The 1970 Olympiad was held in Siegen, West Germany. The playing hall was so beautifully arranged that not even Fischer could find fault with the conditions. The lighting was excellent, the players had plenty of room to move about inside their arenas, the spectators could not crowd near to the players as they had at Lugano, and carpets were laid over the whole of the enormous floor in order to cut out any sound that might emanate from the spectators' footsteps.

Although Fischer had not taken part in the previous year's US Championship, the US Chess Federation had decided to ask FIDE for special permission to allow him to be exempted to the Interzonal. Since the annual FIDE meeting was being held concurrently with the Olympiad and since Fischer's mere presence in Siegen was sufficient to bring him a good deal of sympathy from the FIDE delegates, this task was not nearly so difficult as one would expect. Even the Soviet delegation did not raise any serious objections. After all, Fischer had a poor record against Spassky (made worse by his loss to the World Champion in the finals at Siegen), and the American had yet to prove that in a match he would be as dangerous an opponent as in a tournament. The FIDE Congress decided that provided one of the qualifiers from the USA zone could be persuaded to withdraw, and that none of the non-qualifiers from the 1969 US Championship insisted on playing in the Interzonal, then Fischer could be given the vacant place. The obvious solution to this minor technical problem was money: Benkö was paid not to take his place at Palma (later he was paid again to go to Palma as 'second' for Addison and Reshevsky) and the remaining players from the zonal Championship all waived their right to replace him.

With so much speculation surrounding Fischer's participation in the World Championship cycle, it was natural that the greatest interest at Siegen centred around his game with Spassky. The two had not met since the Havana Olympiad where they had drawn.

62 SPASSKY–FISCHER
OLYMPIAD, SIEGEN 1970

Grünfeld Defence

Notes by Vasyukov

1 P—Q4	N—KB3
2 P—QB4	P—KN3
3 N—QB3	P—Q4
4 P×P	N×P
5 P—K4	N×N
6 P×N	B—N2
7 B—QB4	P—QB4
8 N—K2	N—B3
9 B—K3	O—O
10 O—O	Q—B2
11 R—B1	R—Q1

So far, the same as their game from Santa Monica 1966 (page 94).

12 P—KR3

Not a new move. It is true that after the game Gligoric–Smyslov, Yugoslavia–USSR Match 1959 (12...P—N3; 13 P—B4, P—K3; 14 Q—K1, B—N2; 15 Q—B2, N—R4; 16 B—Q3, P—B4) the text did not have a good reputation, but I think that Spassky was going to strengthen White's play with 15 P—B5 instead of the passive 15 Q—B2.

But Fischer chooses a move order which deprives White of this possibility.

12 ...	P—N3
13 P—B4	P—K3
14 Q—K1	

Behind his line of pawns White prepares to attack on the K side.

14 ...   N—R4

15 B—Q3   P—B4

By attacking the centre, Black is trying to limit his opponent's possibilities. A significant positional error would now have been 16 P—K5?, P—QB5!; 17 B—N1, B—N2, with fine prospects for Black.

16 P—N4!?

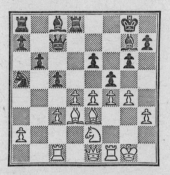

Despite weakening the K side this move is necessary. White cannot wait lest Black should snatch the initiative.

16 ...   P×KP
17 B×P   B—N2
18 N—N3   N—B5
19 B×B

After 19 B—KB2?, B×B; 20 Q×B, N—Q7; 21 Q×KP ch, K—R1; 22 KR—Q1, N—B6 ch; 23 K—R1, R—K1; 24 Q—Q5, N—R5, Black has the advantage because of the threats 25...QR—Q1 and 25...Q×P.

19 ...   Q×B
20 B—B2   Q—B3
21 Q—K2   P×P
22 P×P   P—QN4
23 N—K4

In positions where both sides have weaknesses the activity of one's pieces is very important. With the passive 23 KR—Q1?, R—KB1, White's advantage would have been dissipated.

23 ...   B×P

With the disappearance of the QP, Black gets chances of counterplay on the open Q file. If 23...R—KB1, then 24 N—B5, QR—K1; 25 P—QR4, P—QR3; 26 N×P, Q×N; 27 P×P, Q×P; 28 Q×N – draw. 27...Q—R6 (instead of 27...Q×P); 28 R×N, Q×RP, would lead to complications. It seems that White's position is dangerous, but Spassky could have kept the balance by 29 B—K1, R—Q1; 30 B—N4!, KR×P (or 30...R—B2; 31 Q—B3); 31 Q×KP ch, K—R1; 32 R×R, Q—N6 ch; 33 K—R1, Q×R; 34 R—B8.

24 N—N5   B×B ch

Annotating the game in '64' I. Zaitsev thought that the exchange of bishops was almost the decisive error. It is difficult to agree with this – the American Grandmaster made his mistake later.

25 R×B   R—Q3

Spassky thought that 25...R—K1 was stronger.

26 R—K1   Q—N3
27 N—K4

Also possible was 27 N×KP, R—K1; 28 P—B5, R—Q7; 29 Q—B3, P×P; 30 R—KB1 (30 P×P?, R×N!), threatening 31 P×P, R×R; 32 R×R, Q×N; 33 Q--B7 ch.

The text move is connected with a subtle trap.

27 ...   R—Q5

A sharp position. To try for the advantage Black could have played 27...R—B3, but having the initiative White would have replied 28 R—Q1, R—Q1; 29 R—Q3.

28 N—B6 ch   K—R1
29 Q×P!

I think that Fischer did not appreciate the strength of this move, otherwise he would have played 27...R—B3. Perhaps

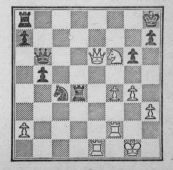

the American Grandmaster had now intended to continue with 29...R—Q8 when it appears that White loses a piece because of the threats of 30...Q×Q, and 30...R×R ch, followed by 31... R×N. What is the best answer to 29... R—Q8?

The World Champion had prepared a splendid combination involving a rook sacrifice: 30 Q—B7!!, R×R ch; 31 K—N2, N—K6 ch (this creates the most difficulties for White. If 31...Q—B3 ch?; 32 K—N3, R—KN8 ch; 33 K—R4, R×P ch; 34 K×R, N—K6 ch; 35 K—N5, Q—B4 ch; 36 P—B5, with inevitable mate); 32 K—B3! (32 K—N3, N—B4 ch!; 33 P×N, Q—K6 ch, and 34...Q—K2), 32...Q—B3 ch; 33 K—N3, R—KN8 ch; 34 K—R4, R×P ch; 35 P×R, Q—R8 ch; 36 K—N5, R—QB1 (after 36...N×P; 37 K×N, Q—KN8 ch; 38 K—R3, Q—KR8 ch; 39 K—N3, Q—KN8 ch; 40 R—N2, Q—K8 ch; 41 K—N4, Q—KR8; 42 R—N3, Black has run out of checks); 37 Q—Q7! (37 R—K2 is not so clear and R. Murei found an interesting draw: 37...Q—R6!; 38 R×N, R—B4 ch; 39 R—K5, R×R ch; 40 P×R, Q—K6 ch. If, instead of 39 R—K5, White plays 39 N—Q5, Black can still draw: 39...R×N ch; 40 Q×R, Q×R; 41 Q—B7, Q—QR6!; 42 K—R6, Q—R6 ch), 37...R—QN1; 38 Q—Q4, and White wins.

After realizing his mistake Fischer lost his confidence.

29 ...   R—Q3
30 Q—K4   R—KB1

Black could have equalized by 30... QR—Q1, e.g. 31 P—N5, R—Q7; 32 R(K1)—KB1 (32 R(K1)—K2, R×R; 33 Q×R, Q—K6; 34 Q×Q, R—Q8 ch; 35 K—N2, N×Q ch; 36 K—R2, R—Q7; 37 R×R, N—B8 ch), 32...R×R; 33 R×R, Q—K6; 34 Q×Q (34 Q—N7, Q—KN6 ch), 34...R—Q8 ch, and Black manages to draw.

But now White's initiative grows into a strong attack.

31 P—N5!   R—Q7
32 R—KB1!

32 ...   Q—B2?

Preventing the threatened 33 Q—K7, but missing the point of the coming attack. If 32...R×R; 33 R×R, and then 33...Q—B2, 34 R—K2, gives White complete control of the centre and an overwhelming position.

What possibilities did Black have instead of 32...Q—B2? We analyse the following variations:

(i) 32...N—Q3; 33 Q—K5! (33 Q—K7, R—B2), 33...Q—Q5; 34 Q—K7, with an easy win. Or 33...N—B2; 34 Q—B3, which is also a win for White (34...R×R; 35 N—Q5 dis ch, or 34...R—Q5; 35 N—Q7).

(ii) 32...K—N2; 33 P—KR4 (33 P—B5?, R×R; 34 R×R, Q—K6 and draws), 33...Q—Q5 (33...R×P?; 34 P—R5, R×R; 35 Q—K7 ch, R—B2; 36 P—R6 ch with advantage in the endgame).

(iii) 32...R×R; 33 R×R, Q—K6; 34 Q×Q (34 Q—N7, Q—KN6 ch, is a draw), 34...N×Q; 35 R—Q2, and White has the better ending.

33 R×R!   N×R
34 Q—Q4!

A sudden change. On 34...N×R; 35 N—K8 dis ch is decisive.

34 ...   R—Q1

This loses in a few moves but even after the better 34...Q—N3; 35 Q×Q, P×Q; 36 R—B1 (36 R—Q1, R—Q1; 37 K—N2, R—Q5), 36...N—B5; 37 P—QR4, Black hadn't got a chance.

35 N—Q5 dis ch   K—N1
36 R—B2!   N—B5

| 37 R—K2 | R—Q3 | 39 R—KB8 ch | Resigns |

If 37...Q—N3; 38 R—K8 ch.

38 R—K8 ch   K—B2

If 39...K × R; 40 Q—R8 ch, followed by N × Q.

Palma de Mallorca

Palma is the scene of one of the traditional annual tournaments in the chess calendar.[1] The tournaments are usually played at the Hotel Jaime 1 whose owner/manager is one of its leading patrons. But because of the increased size and importance of the 1970 event the hotel's facilities were deemed insufficient to provide the appropriate conditions of play. And so, although many of the players at the Interzonal and their seconds were happy to stay at the Jaime 1, a room of the Palma auditorium was used as the playing hall.

The auditorium did not provide an ideal venue but it was adequate. The main problem was the noise, caused by the ingoing and outgoing spectators leaving the door open, and so for the duration of the whole tournament the Executive President of the US Chess Federation sat by the door to keep it closed! Colonel Edmondson was also indispensible in helping to sort out one or two slight scheduling problems that were caused by Fischer's religious restrictions.

At Siegen, Fischer's play had seemed to lack some of its usual lustre, but at Palma he was extremely convincing, winning the tournament by the enormous margin of three and a half points. Against most of the tail enders he was absolutely merciless:

63 FISCHER–RUBINETTI
INTERZONAL TOURNAMENT, PALMA 1970

Sicilian Defence

1 P—K4, P—QB4; 2 N—KB3, P—Q3; 3 P—Q4, P × P; 4 N × P, N—KB3; 5 N—QB3, P—QR3; 6 B—QB4, P—K3; 7 B—N3, P—QN4; 8 O—O, B—N2; 9 R—K1, QN—Q2; 10 B—N5, P—R3; 11 B—R4, N—B4?

11...P—N4 is much stronger. Rubinetti said after the game that he knew the coming sacrifice was crushing, but he didn't know what else he could play!

12 B—Q5 !, P × B; 13 P × P dis ch, K—Q2; 14 P—QN4, N—R5; 15 N × N, P × N; 16 P—QB4, K—B1; 17 Q × P, Q—Q2; 18 Q—N3, P—N4; 19 B—N3, N—R4; 20 P—B5 !, P × P; 21 P × P, Q × P; 22 R—K8 ch,; K—Q2 23 Q—R4 ch, B—B3; 24 N × B, Resigns

Fischer spent only fifty minutes on this game.

[1] Since 1973 the venue has been changed to Madrid following the sale of the Hotel Jaime 1.

Fischer had some nasty moments at Palma. In the first round he narrowly escaped defeat at the hands of Hubner, and later in the tournament he was crushed by Larsen when using his favourite Sozin Variation against the Sicilian (this game was the beginning of the end for Fischer as far as the Sozin was concerned). But his overall performance was terrific. He won fifteen of the twenty-three games and scored three and a half out of four against the Soviet players. His game against Smyslov I consider to be his best of the tournament.

64 SMYSLOV–FISCHER
INTERZONAL TOURNAMENT, PALMA 1970

English Opening

Notes by Panov

1 P—QB4	P—KN3
2 N—QB3	B—N2
3 P—KN3	P—QB4
4 B—N2	N—QB3

The three previous games between these opponents ended in peace, but the total score in their games was to Fischer's advantage: two wins to one with five draws. Now Smyslov had an opportunity to level the score and the ex-World Champion chooses an aggressive continuation.

5 P—N3	P—K3
6 B—QN2	KN—K2
7 N—R4	

After this simplifying exchange White has lost all hope of an advantage from the opening. It is most interesting that Smyslov played the same move against Fischer in a similar position at Buenos Aires 1970: 1 N—KB3, P—QB4; 2 P—KN3, P—KN3; 3 B—N2, B—N2; 4 P—B4, N—QB3; 5 N—B3, P—K3; 6 P—N3, KN—K2; 7 B—N2, O—O; 8 N—QR4, P—K4! (9 N×P? is bad because of 9...P—K5!).

It seems to me that 7 N—B3, transposing to Reti's Opening, is better here. On 7 P—K4 the immediate 7...P—Q4 is good, or first 7...N—N5.

7 ...	B×B

8 N×B	O—O
9 P—K3	

More natural is 9 N—B3 and 10 O—O, with a calm position.

9 ...	P—Q4
10 P×P	

It would be better to avoid this exchange, which activates Black's pieces and opens the KB1–QR6 diagonal for Black's bishop.

10 ...	N×P
11 N—K2	P—N3
12 P—Q4?	

White wrongly assumes that his king is in no danger. He should have played 12 O—O, B—R3; 13 P—Q3, or 13 R—K1.

12 ...	B—R3!

A brilliant positional pawn sacrifice

in the style of the young ... Smyslov! White is forced to accept the sacrifice, because after 13 O—O, White loses the QP. If 13 R—QB1, R—B1; 14 QP×P, Q—B3; 15 N—QB4, Shamkovitch pointed out the variation 15...KR—Q1; 16 N—Q6, P×P!; 17 N×R, N(Q4)—N5!, with a very strong attack.

13 P×P   Q—B3
14 N—QB4

A bad mistake would be 14 N—Q4?, because of 14...P×P!; 15 N×N (or 15 B×N, P×N!; 16 B×N, P×P!), 15...Q×N, 16 R—QB1, N×P!

14 . . .   N—B6
15 N×N

The exchange of knights is forced, because after 15 Q—B2, N×N, Black either wins a pawn or has a strong attack, e.g. 16 K×N (or 16 B×N, QR—B1; 17 K×N, R×B; 18 P×P, KR—B1; 19 P—N7, B×P; 20 KR—QB1, Q—KB6 ch!; 21 K—K1, Q—R8 ch; 22 K—K2, Q×P, followed by 23...B—R3), 16...QR—B1; 17 P×P (or 17 KR—QB1, N—R4; 18 K—B1, R×P), 17...P×P; 18 KR—QB1, N—R4; 19 K—K1, N×N; 20 P×N, R×P; 21 Q—N3, KR—B1!.

15 . . .   Q×N ch
16 K—B1

Black has not only succeeded in preventing his opponent from castling, but has also paralysed his K side, excluding the KR from the game for a long time.

16 . . .   KR—Q1
17 Q—B1   B×N ch
18 P×B   Q—Q6 ch
19 K—N1   QR—B1
20 P×P   P×P
21 Q—N2   N—R4!
22 P—KR4

White hopes to activate his rook, creating tactical threats to the black king. He hardly had any better continuation. If 22 B—B1, then 22...N×P; 23 B×Q, N×Q, and the black rooks invade the second rank.

After 22 Q×P, N×P; 23 Q—N3, Q—Q7; 24 P—KR3, N—K4!, Black has a strong attack because of the threats 25...R—B7, 26...N—Q6, etc. If he returns the extra pawn in order to free the rook – 25 K—R2, Q×BP; 26 KR—KB1, then after 26...Q—K7!; 27 QR—B1 is no good because of 27...N—B6 ch, and again White cannot defend against the rooks coming in.

22 . . .   N×P
23 Q—B6

Not only maintaining the threat of P—R5, but also defending the very weak KBP. But Fischer is alert and finds the strongest move.

23 . . .   Q—B4!

This forces the better endgame.

24 Q×Q

The exchange of queens relieves White from the strong attack, and gives him some chances if his opponent doesn't play precisely. But Fischer does play precisely!

24 . . .   NP×Q

25 P—R5

25 K—R2 is weaker, because of 25...R—Q7; 26 KR—KB1, N—N7; 27 K—N1, R(1)—B7; 28 R—N1 (or 28 QR—B1, R×BP), 28...N—Q6; 29 R×P, N×P, and White's position is crumbling.

Now White's rook comes into the game but too late.

25 . . .   R—Q7
26 R—QB1   R—B4
27 R—R4   N—K4!

Obviously not 27...P—N4? because of 28 P—R4.

28 R×R	P×R
29 R—R4	P—B5
30 P—R6	K—B1
31 R—R8 ch	K—K2
32 R—QB8	

Otherwise Black queens his pawn.

32 . . .	R×RP
33 B—B1	R—B7
34 K—N2	

White has no good moves, e.g. 34 R—B7 ch, K—B3; 35 R—B8, N—B6 ch; 36 K—N2, N—K8 ch; 37 K—N1, P—B6; 38 B—N5, R—B8; 39 K—B1, P—B7; 40 K—K2 (or 40 B—R4, R—R8), 40...R—N8; 41 K—Q2, R—Q8 ch!.

34 . . .	N—N5

34...P—B6 is possible, but the move in the game is simpler. White cannot take the pawn at QB4 because of 35...

N×KP ch, winning a piece.

35 K—N1	R×P
36 B×P	

Not 36 R×P?, R×B ch.

36 . . .	R—B6
37 K—N2	R×KP
38 R—KR8	N×P
39 R×P	N—N5
40 B—N5	

Not only is Black two pawns ahead but White's pieces are on bad squares.

40 . . .	R—N6
41 B—B6	R—N7 ch
42 K—N1	

On 42 K—B3 there is mate in one.

42 . . .	N—K4
43 B—R8	R—N1
44 B—R1 and White resigned	

The young Grandmaster conducted the game in the true style of Capablanca.

Fischer's victory at Palma surprised nobody, but what was amazing was the apparent ease with which he disposed of Taimanov and Larsen at the Candidates' stage. Taimanov was obviously destined to lose the match, but the 6–0 score hardly reflects the difference in strength between him and Fischer. Nevertheless, it is rumoured that shortly before leaving for Vancouver, Fischer told a friend that he didn't see how Taimanov was going to score a single half-point!

Larsen's 6–0 catastrophe was not quite so surprising (he was suffering from high blood pressure throughout the match). The Danish Grandmaster is a very practical player who, once he had got off to a bad start, realized that to play for a draw in any game was merely to push Fischer half a point nearer winning the match. In the last two games of the match Larsen could have forced drawn positions had he so desired, but in each case he threw all caution to the winds.

The Petrosian match was quite a different story. In the first game Fischer was lost from the opening, but by careless play Petrosian frittered the game away. In the second game Petrosian did win, thereby stopping a run of nineteen successive wins (twenty if one counts Fischer's win by default over Panno in the last round of the Palma Interzonal). In the third game he should have won but the result was a draw. So from the first three games of the match Petrosian could easily have made three points but only managed to amass one and a half. After that came a short period of rest (two draws) while Fischer recovered from a cold, and then disaster for Petrosian – four losses in a row. (In Moscow some chess fans were said to be wondering in which century they were living, because they had been told that Petrosian loses two games in succession only once a century!)

Perhaps the most pleasing aspect of Fischer's play in the Candidate's matches is the precision with which he handled some of the endings (see the previous chapter). The overall quality of the games was not quite so high as one might have hoped, though this was almost entirely due to the nervous play of his three opponents. My favourite among these twenty-one games is the first game of the Larsen match, in which Fischer finally shows that he has come to grips with the Winawer Variation.

65 FISCHER–LARSEN
1ST MATCH GAME 1971

French Defence

1 P—K4	P—K3
2 P—Q4	P—Q4
3 N—QB3	B—N5
4 P—K5	N—K2
5 P—QR3	B×N ch
6 P×B	P—QB4
7 P—QR4	QN—B3
8 N—B3	B—Q2

The main alternative is 8...Q—R4; 9 Q—Q2, B—Q2; 10 B—K2, R—QB1; 11 P×P, N—N3 (so far, as in Hartston–Uhlmann, Hastings 1972/73); 12 Q—K3, P—Q5; 13 N×P, N×N; 14 Q×N, Q×P(B4); 15 B—K3!, with slightly the better endgame chances for White.

9 B—Q3	Q—B2
10 O—O	P—B5

Possibly better is the immediate 10...P—B3!?

11 B—K2	P—B3
12 R—K1	

Stronger than 12 B—R3, O—O; 13 R—K1, R—B2; 14 P×P, P×P; 15 B—KB1, R—K1; 16 N—R4, N—N3; 17 Q—R5, R—N2; 18 P—N3, Q—R4!, with approximately equal chances. Fischer–Mednis, US Championship 1962/63.

12 . . .	N—N3 ?!

Black should castle as his king now has no time to escape from the K file: 12...O—O (12...O—O—O; 13 B—R3, N—B4, is also possible); 13 B—R3, R—B2; 14 P×P, P×P; 15 N—R4,

N—N3; 16 B—R5, R—N2, with chances for both sides – Holmov.

13 B—R3 !	

Stronger than the sacrifice offered in the Mednis game, because White's KR is more actively placed.

13 . . .	P×P
14 P×P	N(B3)×P
15 N×N	N×N

Not 15...Q×N; 16 B×P, Q×BP; 17 B×P, O—O—O; 18 R—K3, and an attack on the Q side.

16 Q—Q4 !	

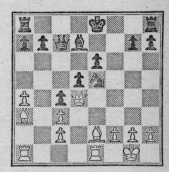

Now 16...O—O—O is absolutely out of the question because of 17 Q×RP, e.g. 17...N—B3; 18 Q—R8 ch, Q—N1; 19 Q×Q ch, K×Q; 20 B—Q6 ch, K—R2; 21 P—B4, with a clear advantage for White.

16 . . .	N—N3
17 B—R5	K—B2

17...O—O—O leads to variations similar to the previous note, but it might possibly have offered better chances than the text continuation.

18 P—B4

Threatening 19 P—B5, P×P; 20 R—K7 ch.

18 . . .   KR—K1
19 P—B5   P×P
20 Q×QP ch   K—B3

If 20...B—K3; 21 R×B, R×R; 22 Q×KBP ch, R—B3; 23 Q—Q5 ch, R—K3; 24 R—KB1 ch, or 20...R—K3; 21 Q×KBP ch, R—B3; 22 R—K7 ch!

21 B—B3 ?!

Stronger is 21 B—Q6, Q—Q1; 22 P—N4.

21 . . .   N—K4!

The only way to get counterplay. If 21...R×R ch; 22 R×R, R—K1; 23 Q—Q4 ch, K—B2; 24 R—N1, P—N3; 25 P—R5, with a very strong attack, or 21...B—K3; 22 Q—Q4 ch, K—B2; 23 QR—N1, and White wins the exchange.

22 Q—Q4   K—N3
23 R×N   Q×R
24 Q×B   QR—Q1
25 Q×QNP   Q—K6 ch?

After 25...Q×BP; 26 Q—B6 ch, K—N4; 27 B—B1 ch, P—B5; 28 P—R4 ch, K—B4 (if 28...K×P; 29 B×P, Q×R ch; 30 K—R2, and Black is in a mating net); 29 P—N4 ch, P×P e.p.; 30 K—N2!, Q—Q5!. White has no convincing continuation.

Also unclear after 25...Q×BP is 26 Q—N1, R—Q7 (26...R—K4, also appears adequate); 27 B—QN4, Q—Q5 ch; 28 K—R1, R×BP!; 29 B—B5!

26 K—B1   R—Q7
27 Q—B6 ch   R—K3
28 B—B5!   R—B7 ch
29 K—N1   R×NP dbl ch
30 K×R   Q—Q7 ch
38 K—R1   R×Q
32 B×R   Q×P(B6)?

The last chance was 32...P—QR4; 33 R—N1 ch (or 33 B—Q4, K—R3), 33...K—B2; 34 B—Q4, P—N4; 35 B—Q5 ch, K—N3; 36 B×P, Q×P(B7).

Larsen was very short of time at this point.

33 R—KN1 ch   K—B3
34 B×P   P—B5
35 B—N6   Q×P
36 P—R5   Q—QN7
37 B—Q8 ch   K—K3
38 P—R6   Q—R6
39 B—N7   Q—B4

39...Q—N7; 40 R—K1 ch, K—Q3, would have prolonged the game.

40 R—N1   P—QB6
41 B—N6   Resigns

By the time that he had qualified from the Candidates' Matches, Fischer had become a hero in the Soviet Union. Towards the end of his match with Larsen the telephone switchboard of the Moscow office of TASS was crammed with calls from chess enthusiasts who demanded to know the latest score. When the sixth game was over the operators did not bother to waste time by saying 'Hello. Can I help you?', they simply picked up the receiver, said 'six-nil' and put it down again without bothering to find out the nature of the enquiry. When Fischer defeated Petrosian in Buenos Aires the Soviet chess public started to doubt whether Spassky could retain his World Championship title. After all, Petrosian was the most difficult player in the world to defeat in a match, and he had just been brushed aside with four straight wins.

It is most rare for a foreign chess book to be translated into Russian – the Soviet Union has enough Grandmasters and chess writers of its own. But at the beginning of 1972 the games collections by Larsen and Fischer were published in Moscow (with one or two minor changes or omissions made necessary by occasional anti-Soviet statements). As a postscript to Fischer's *My Sixty Memorable Games*, the Soviet Grandmaster Alexei Suetin contributed an article on Fischer's style. The following translation by Bernard Cafferty was specially commissioned for this volume.

'Analysing the games played by Fischer in the last few years, i.e. those played after the ones given in *My Sixty Memorable Games*, one can discern the fruits of the immense amount of work which he put in during the 1967–70 lay-off. After Sousse he played 120 games (up to the end of 1971) and scored +86 =30 −4, about 85%. A very high percentage especially if one bears in mind that the majority (72) were against Grandmasters. Against Grandmasters he scored 82%, against masters about 90%. These figures are very eloquent and show why he emerged as the legitimate challenger to Spassky.

'A characteristic of modern mastery is universality, without however allowing this to exclude elements of individual style or creativity. Fischer is a true "universal", but he remains true to the principles of classic positional play, and is not an adherent of the new "irrational" style of play. In fact Fischer's style reminds me more (making due allowance for the time difference) of the rational and exceptionally effective style of Morphy.

'In fact the most notable feature of Fischer's play is his remarkable accuracy, concreteness, and rationality of thought. Even the strongest Grandmasters can be side-tracked, while analysing at the board, into side alleys. They are tempted by fantastic but unreal lines which prove a definite hindrance in the search for the truth. When, on the other hand, you study Fischer's games (even lightning games!) you are struck by the fact that he coolly, unhesitatingly, automatically rejects all these false if tempting beauties. All his efforts are directed towards finding the proper thread that leads towards the truth. This is one of the reasons for the absence of time trouble in his play.

'Korchnoy once told me a curious episode which occurred in one of his recent games with Fischer. After a long thought the Leningrad Grandmaster offered an original pawn sacrifice whose consequences were far from clear (it is generally known that Fischer likes capturing enemy pawns). On this occasion Fischer, after comparatively little thought, rejected the offer and chose a solid line instead. After the game Korchnoy asked him whether he had examined this line at all, and the answer was, "Hardly at all. I trusted you."

'This cannot be construed as laziness or superficiality on Fischer's part. It is his practicism. Yet despite this practicism [a rather derogatory word in Soviet semantics – BC], his play is not dry. His whole effort is directed towards gaining competitive success. His will to win is well known. He hardly ever has short draws, yet in playing for a win he never breaks positional principles. If a draw is the legitimate result and his opponent plays the right moves, then a draw it is. However it only needs his opponent to commit the slightest inaccuracy for the all discerning eye of the American to spot the error. Then he plays to exploit it, but again without breaking sound positional principles.

'The range of his play is very wide indeed, and he never avoids complications if they are demanded by the position. This can be seen both in his sharp opening repertoire as Black, and by a deep analysis of his games. In his matches with Taimanov and Larsen his opponents tried to draw him into irrational lines where the main rôle is played by intuition. Their attempts met with total failure. The reason for this failure was that he was superior to them in analysis and so in positions demanding very deep analysis he was able to drive them into regular time-trouble.

'Hence we conclude that we have before us a player of wide creative scope, with a clearly marked classical positional style. A player who loves clarity, but does not avoid complications. We must add to this his constant bent for active play, his fine fighting qualities and his superb technique. Nor must we forget that Fischer is young and healthy, that he follows a strict sporting routine, plays tennis and swims. All of which helps to ensure that he does not tire in the fifth hour of play and that he always keeps in tip top form. This is his strength.

'Does he have any weaknesses?... In his play with Black, Fischer does not often choose the more classical lines. His preference is for lines with considerable strategic risk, but it is well known that it is easier to take advantage of tactical risks taken by the opponent than strategical risks. However, such an approach makes immense demands on one's nerves and can only be regularly adopted by the younger players. It is quite possible that in years to come Fischer will start adopting the less strategically risky classical defensive lines when playing Black... There are a few tense, strategical situations in which the clear and energetic Fischer has proved insufficiently flexible and responsive to hardly noticeable changes in the situation. These rare losses show that he can be beaten.

'Summing up we can say that Fischer's style is remarkable for its high level of technique, its ability to exploit the slightest advantages present in a position, by its well perfected tactical art and by its marked practicism. Amongst his weak points one can point to a slightly too straightforward approach to the problems posed by modern openings, and to his rather mechanical decisions in the realm of strategy as well as a slight underestimate of the power of the opponent's attack on his king.

'Once again we stress that for all his wide scope Fischer stands firmly on a classical basis. It is of course true that the slight significance of the classical concept of chess as developed since the time of Morphy and Steinitz, has never been denied by any of the great leading modern players. Nevertheless, recently and particularly in the fifties, there have been signs of the emergence of a "neo-romantic" style of play, whose outstanding representatives are Tal, Korchnoy and Larsen. In opposition to the old logical positional school they opposed "irrational" play, which indulges in great positional and strategical risk. This sharp weapon was directed by them against the representatives of the sternly positional style with its clear distinctions between "better" and "worse" moves, between "correct" and "incorrect" ideas. Exploiting their superiority in combinative play and tactics the neo-romantics destroyed the soundest positional bastions, at times with fantastic boldness.

'As a result of this tendency we got a new type of genre – the sort of game in which, from the viewpoint of the classicists, there were many slight mistakes and inaccuracies, but which had a unity based upon a general idea, an original plan. This style became immensely popular in the fifties and sixties and was a very attractive one.

'However, thanks mainly to the achievements of the present World Champion Boris Spassky and his predecessor Tigran Petrosian there has been a noticeable reversion to classicism in recent years. After all, these two, and particularly Petrosian, have a penchant for strictly positional play, and they have many contemporaries who feel the same way.

'Returning to Fischer one can say that his striving for a clear classical style is based upon the modern, concrete understanding of it. By comparison, the play of Spassky is more complicated and more varied. This can be seen in Fischer's striving for clear plans, and his avoidance of anything that smacks of the irrational. His ideal is the exploitation of the opponent's mistakes, with the maximum accuracy, while never making a mistake himself. This is clearly opposed to the ideals of the irrationalists with their games which are rarely free from slight errors.

'Hence we have a player who never knowingly offends against the canons of correct play as he sees them, observing as it were a pact almost of a religious nature with the very game itself.'

9

THE PARADOX OF REYKJAVIK

At the beginning of 1972 I honestly expected Spassky to win the World Championship match. It wasn't that I thought that Fischer would not play, or that I believed Spassky to have the stronger physical stamina. It was because I felt that as Black Fischer had not yet found a defence to 1 P—Q4, with which he could be entirely happy.

Let us examine some of Fischer's more unfortunate moments from 1970 and 1971.

King's Indian Defence
The game Gligoric–Fischer from the Siegen Olympiad followed a game that Gligoric had won only a month or so earlier: 1 P—Q4, N—KB3; 2 P—QB4, P—KN3; 3 N—QB3, B—N2; 4 P—K4, P—Q3; 5 N—B3, O—O; 6 B—K2, P—K4; 7 P—Q5, QN—Q2; 8 O—O, N—B4; 9 Q—B2, P—QR4; 10 B—

N5, P—R3; 11 B—K3, N—N5; 12 B×N, P×B; 13 P—KR3, N—B3; 14 N×P, N×QP; 15 BP×N, B×N; 16 P—B4, B—Q5 ch.

Against Langeweg in the 1970 IBM Tournament in Amsterdam, Gligoric had played the correct 17 K—R2!, which leaves White with an excellent game. Afraid that Fischer had found some important improvement on Langeweg's play, Gligoric decided to vary, played 17 K—R1? and was immediately under pressure:

17...Q—R5; 18 Q—Q3, P—QB3; 19 Q—B3, P—R4; 20 P—B5, B—Q2; 21 B—B4, P—KN4; 22 QR—Q1, QR—K1; 23 QP×P, B×QBP; 24 B—Q5, R—K4 and Black eventually won.

After the game Gligoric asked Fischer what he had prepared as an improvement on the Gligoric–Langeweg game, and was shocked to learn that the IBM Tournament was so recent that Fischer had not yet seen the games!

In the first and third games of his match with Taimanov, Fischer employed the King's Indian and in both cases he was in great difficulties which were solved by his opponent's inaccurate play.

Had Fischer played the King's Indian against Spassky I think it most likely that he would have been faced with the Sämisch Variation. This is not only because of his bad record against the Sämisch during the earlier part of his career, but also because the Sämisch had always been Spassky's favourite anti-KID weapon. It was probably a combination of the two that decided Fischer against using the King's Indian in Reykjavik.

Grünfeld Defence
Fischer has lost two convincing games to Spassky in the Exchange Variation of the Grünfeld (see pages 94 and 140). And there are other systems against which he found great difficulty in equalizing:

Petrosian–Fischer, Belgrade 1970 (Game 4)
1 P—QB4, P—KN3; 2 P—Q4, N—KB3; 3 N—QB3, P—Q4; 4 N—B3, B—N2; 5 P×P, N×P; 6 B—Q2, P—QB4; 7 R—B1, and White had a very small advantage from the opening. (The game was drawn in fifty-two moves.)

Taimanov–Fischer, 5th Match Game 1971
4 B—N5, N—K5; 5 B—R4, N×N; 6 P×N, P×P; 7 P—K3, B—K3; 8 R—N1, P—N3; 9 B—K2, B—R3; 10 N—B3, P—QB3; 11 N—K5, B—N2; 12 P—B4, B—Q4; 13 O—O, N—Q2; 14 N×P(B4), O—O; 15 P—R4!, with the better game for White. Taimanov's advantage was eventually allowed to slip and in a completely drawn position (after the adjournment) he blundered away a rook (see page 125).

Petrosian–Fischer, 2nd Match Game 1971
4 B—B4, B—N2; 5 P—K3, P—B4; 6 QP×P, Q—R4; 7 R—B1, N—K5; 8 P×P!, N×N; 9 Q—Q2!, Q×RP; 10 P×N, Q—R4!; 11 B—B4, N—Q2; 12 N—K2, N—K4; 13 B—R2, B—B4?; 14 B×N!, B×B; 15 N—Q4!, with an excellent game for White. (Fischer lost horribly.)

Nimzo-Indian Defence

Fischer was extremely lucky to escape with a draw against Portisch at the Siegen Olympiad:

1 P—Q4, N—KB3; 2 P—QB4, P—K3; 3 N—QB3, B—N5; 4 P—K3, P—QN3; 5 KN—K2, B—R3; 6 N—N3, B×N ch; 7 P×B, P—Q4; 8 B—R3, P×P; 9 P—K4, Q—Q2; 10 B—K2, N—B3; 11 Q—B2, O—O—O; 12 O—O, P—R4; 13 KR—Q1, P—R5; 14 N—B1, N—KR4 ?; 15 P—Q5 !, N—K4; 16 P×P, Q—K1; 17 R×R ch, Q×R; 18 B×N, R×B; 19 P—B4, N—Q6; 20 P×P, P—B4; 21 Q—K2, R—R1; 22 P—K5, K—N1 !; 23 P—K6 !, Q—B3; 24 R—K1 !, B—N4; 25 B×P !!, P×B. If 25...N×B; 26 Q—K5 ch, Q×Q; 27 R×Q, R—KB1; 28 P—B5, followed by N—Q2—B3—R4 winning.

26 R—N1, P—R3; 27 P—R4, N×P; 28 Q—B3 ?. 28 Q—K4 ! was crushing. 28...N×KP; 29 Q×Q, P×Q; 30 P×B, P×P and the game was soon drawn.

Modern Benoni

Fischer played this defence three times during the Palma Interzonal. Against Portisch he had slightly the worse game until move twenty (drawn in twenty-nine). Against Uhlmann he was lucky enough to be given a pawn on move twelve in a simple opening trap. And against Gligoric:

1 P—Q4, N—KB3; 2 P—QB4, P—K3; 3 N—QB3, P—B4; 4 P—Q5, P×P; 5 P×P, P—Q3; 6 N—B3, P—KN3; 7 P—K4, B—N2; 8 B—K2, O—O; 9 O—O, R—K1; 10 N—Q2, QN—Q2 !?; 11 P—QR4, N—K4; 12 Q—B2, P—KN4!?; 13 N—B3, N×N ch; 14 B×N, P—KR3?. Better 14...N—Q2 and 15...N—K4.

15 B—Q2, P—R3; 16 B—K2, Q—K2; 17 QR—K1, Q—K4; 18 K—R1, Q—Q5; 19 P—B3, N—R4; 20 N—N5 ?. Putting his whole position en prise. 20 P—KN3 !, threatening N—Q1, followed by P—B4, would have left White with a clear plus.

20...P×N; 21 B×QNP, Q—K4 !. The move that Gligoric underestimated. Now White is lost.

This evidence proves, when taken in conjunction with his other games of the period, that in almost all of the games in 1970 and 1971 in which Fischer came out of the opening with a disadvantage, he was Black against 1 P—Q4. This led me to assume that as White Spassky would invariably open 1 P—Q4 and that he would make a big plus score with the white pieces. How wrong I was!

Fischer's preparations for the match with Spassky were extremely thorough. After defeating Petrosian in September/October 1971 Fischer declined all invitations to participate in tournaments. (In the Soviet Union he was criticized for declining to play in the Alekhine Memorial Tournament, December 1971, where the first prize was 1,000 roubles plus 1,000 dollars. Instead he gave a series of seventeen exhibitions in Argentina for a total fee of 8,500 dollars!)

On his return to the USA Fischer spent the next few months at Grossingers luxury hotel in the Catskill Mountains, improving his physical condition with a regime of swimming, tennis and working out in a gymnasium (several magazines and newspapers showed a photograph of him hitting a punch-bag). Amidst this physical build up and the problems surrounding the venue and conditions for the match, Fischer was widening his theoretical knowledge far more thoroughly than he had ever done before. He acquired a file of all of Spassky's published games and went over it diligently. By the time he arrived in Reykjavik he was no longer the same opponent against whom Spassky had been preparing to play.

There are three remarkable aspects of Fischer's opening play in Reykjavik. First, his plan to keep Spassky guessing by repeatedly switching opening systems; second, the number of (for him) new lines that he employed; and lastly, the strangest of all, the fact that two of his best loved and most often tested variations were severely punished.

The Reykjavik games have been sufficiently annotated in enough different books and publications. The games that I give here have, therefore, only been given the lightest of notes.

Game 1. A quiet Nimzo-Indian. The position was level until Fischer unnecessarily gave up a bishop in the ending (and even then it may have been drawn).

Game 2. Fischer forfeited.

Game 3. Fischer was 2–0 down. Would he content himself with a draw as Black (playing the same defence as in game 1)? No. He plays a very risky line of the Modern Benoni which has since been shown to be unsound. 1 P—Q4, N—KB3; 2 P—QB4, P—K3; 3 N—QB3, P—B4; 4 P—Q5, P×P; 5 P×P, P—Q3; 6 N—B3, P—KN3; 7 N—Q2, QN—Q2; 8 P—K4, B—N2; 9 B—K2, O—O; 10 O—O, R—K1; 11 Q—B2, N—R4; 12 B×N, P×B; 13 N—B4, N—K4; 14 N—K3, Q—R5 !; 15 B—Q2, N—N5; 16 N×N, P×N, and Black was not any worse off.

Shortly after this game, Gligoric twice demonstrated a very convincing line for White: 11 P—QR4, N—K4 (or 11. . .P—QR3; 12 Q—B2, N—R4; 13 B×N, P×B; 14 N—Q1 !, N—K4; 15 N—K3, Q—R5; 16 R—R3 !, and Black's counterplay was quashed. Gligoric–Browne, San Antonio 1972); 12 Q—B2, N—R4; 13 B×N, P×B; 14 N—Q1 !, Q—R5; 15 N—K3, N—N5; 16 N×N, P×N; 17 N—B4, with a clear advantage to White. Gligoric–Kavalek, Skopje Olympiad 1972.

Game 4. The first game of the match in which Fischer could make use of the white pieces. 1 P—K4, P—QB4; 2 N—KB3, P—Q3; 3 P—Q4, P×P; 4 N×P, N—KB3; 5 N—QB3, N—B3; 6 B—QB4. Of course. 6. . .P—K3; 7 B—N3, B—K2; 8 B—K3, O—O; 9 O—O. Fischer had not played the sharper Velimirovic Attack since his disastrous loss to Larsen at the Palma Interzonal: 9 Q—K2, P—QR3; 10 O—O—O, Q—B2; 11 P—N4 !, N—Q2 !; 12 P—KR4 ? (12 P—N5 !), N—B4; 13 P—N5, P—N4; 14 P—B3, B—Q2; 15 Q—N2, P—N5; 16 N(B3)—K2, N×B ch; 17 RP×N, P—QR4, and White was crushed on the Q side.

9...P—QR3. Larsen had played 9...B—Q2; 10 P—B4, Q—B1?!, in the 5th Match Game against Fischer. 9...N—QR4 and 9...N×N have also been played against Fischer. **10 P—B4, N×N; 11 B×N, P—QN4; 12 P—QR3.** Or 12 P—B5, P—N5; 13 N—K2, P—K4; 14 B—K3, B—N2, and Black does not stand badly. **12...B—N2; 13 Q—Q3, P—QR4!; 14 P—K5.** Naturally not 14 N×P, N×P, and Black has won the centre. **14...P×P; 15 P×P, N—Q2; 16 N×P, N—B4; 17 B×N, B×B ch; 18 K—R1, Q—N4**

19 Q—K2?. Correct was 19 Q—N3, Q×Q; 20 P×Q, B—R3; 21 P—QR4, B×N; 22 P×B, B—Q5; 23 P—B3, B×KP; 24 P—KN4, B—B2!, with a draw as the likely result. **19...QR—Q1; 20 QR—Q1, R×R; 21 R×R, P—R4!.** Also strong is 21...B—K6. 22 N—Q6, B—R1; 23 B—B4, P—KR5; 24 P—R3, B—K6; 25 Q—N4, Q×P?. Black can win by 25...Q×Q; 26 P×Q, B—B5; 27 R—K1, P—R6; 28 B—B1, P—B3; 29 N—B4, P×P, and if 30 N×RP?, B—N6; 31 R—Q1, R×B ch. **26 Q× RP, P—N4; 27 Q—N4, B—B4.** 27...R—Q1, fails to 28 N×P!, R× R ch; 29 Q×R, Q—K5; 30 B—B1, K×N; 31 Q—Q7 ch, K—B3; 32 Q—Q8 ch, K—K4; 33 Q—B7 ch, with a perpetual check. **28 N—N5, K—N2; 29 N—Q4, R—R1.** If 29...R—Q1; 30 P—B3, R—R1 (now White no longer has QB3 for his queen); 31 R—KB1, R—R3 (31...R—R5; 32 N—B5 ch!); 32 N—B3, B×N; 33 Q×B, and White is saved. **30 N—B3, B×N; 31 Q×B, B—Q3?.** 31...R—R5 (threat...R—B5 and...P—N5); 32 P—N4, B—Q3, gives Black better chances. **32 Q—B3!.** See the note to Black's 29th move. **32...Q×Q; 33 P×Q, B—K4; 34 R—Q7, K—B3; 35 K—N1, B×P; 36 B—K2, B—K4; 37 K—B1, R—QB1; 38 B—R5, R—B2; 39 R×R, B×R; 40 P—QR4, K—K2; 41 K—K2, P—B4; 42 K—Q3, B—K4; 43 P—B4, K—Q3; 44 B—B7, B—N6; 45 P—B5 ch, Draw agreed.**

Game 5. Another Nimzo-Indian, but this time a completely different variation by Fischer. Gligoric later discovered a flaw in Fischer's strategy, but over the board Spassky played aimlessly, drifted into an extremely

passive position and blundered. From a 2–0 deficit Fischer had levelled
the score in three games! Moreover, he had a plus score with Black
against 1 P—Q4.

Game 6. The opening of this game astounded the chess world. Barden and
I were commenting on this game for BBC TV and when Fischer's first
move came over the telex we asked for confirmation because we thought
that a careless operator had typed 1 c4 instead of 1 e4.

1 P—QB4!
No more Sozin Sicilians.
1...P—K3; 2 N—KB3, P—Q4; 3 P—Q4 !!
Fischer had played the English Opening before, but never the Queen's
Gambit. The psychological value of this switch was tremendous.
**3...N—KB3; 4 N—B3, B—K2; 5 B—N5, O—O; 6 P—K3, P—KR3;
7 B—R4, P—QN3; 8 P×P, N×P; 9 B×B, Q×B; 10 N×N, P×N;
11 R—B1, B—K3; 12 Q—R4, P—QB4; 13 Q—R3, R—B1; 14 B—N5 !,
P—QR3; 15 P×P, P×P; 16 O—O, R—R2 ?**
In Furman–Geller, Moscow 1970, Black played this awkward looking
move and fared rather badly. In his notes to the game, Geller suggested
as an improvement 16...Q—N2, and if 17 B—K2, N—Q2, or 17 B—R4,
Q—N3, with the idea of ...Q—R4. But although Geller was Spassky's
second in Reykjavik they would have been very unlikely to have analysed
this variation together, for the simple reason that it would be unthinkable
for Fischer to play the Queen's Gambit!
17 B—K2, N—Q2
Geller had played 17...P—QR4.
18 N—Q4, Q—B1 ?
18...N—B3; 19 N—N3, P—B5; 20 Q×Q, R×Q; 21 N—Q4, would
have been a lesser evil.
19 N×B, P×N; 20 P—K4 !

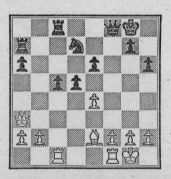

20...P—Q5 ? 20...P—B5; 21 Q—R3, N—B4, was obligatory. Now
White launches an irresistable attack. **21 P—B4, Q—K2; 22 P—K5 !,**

R—N1; 23 B—B4, K—R1; 24 Q—R3, N—B1; 25 P—QN3, P—QR4; 26
P—B5, P×P; 27 R×P, N—R2; 28 R(1)—B1, Q—Q1; 29 Q—N3, R—
K2; 30 P—KR4, R(1)—N2; 31 P—K6, R(N2)—B2; 32 Q—K5, Q—K1;
33 P—R4, Q—Q1; 34 R(1)—B2, Q—K1; 35 R(2)—B3, Q—Q1; 36 B—
Q3, Q—K1; 37 Q—K4 ! At this point we received a telex message to say
that Geller and Krogius were sitting in a car outside the playing hall in
readiness for Spassky's imminent defeat. 37. . .N—B3; 38 R×N !, P×R;
39 R×P, K—N1; 40 B—B4, K—R1; 41 Q—B4, Resigns. A beautifully
played game by Fischer.

Game 7. Fischer's first opportunity to play the Poisoned Pawn Variation.
Spassky never recovered the pawn, and should have lost at several
different points in the game (Najdorf claimed that Fischer overlooked ten
wins), but the game was drawn after enormous complications.

Game 8. Fischer again opened 1 P—QB4. The game took on a quiet
character until three blunders wrecked Spassky's position.

Game 9. Against 1 P—Q4 Fischer adopted the Semi-Tarrasch Defence. A
rather dull draw.

Game 10. The first Ruy Lopez of the match, this game was thought by
many to be the finest of the twenty. Spassky played his favourite Breyer
Defence and was steadily outplayed.

Game 11. Another Najdorf Sicilian. Fischer played the Poisoned Pawn
Variation but got a nasty shock. 1 P—K4, P—QB4; 2 N—KB3, P—Q3;
3 P—Q4, P×P; 4 N×P, N—KB3; 5 N—QB3, P—QR3; 6 B—KN5,
P—K3; 7 P—B4, Q—N3; 8 Q—Q2, Q×P; 9 N—N3, Q—R6; 10 B×N !,
P×B; 11 B—K2 !, P—KR4; 12 O—O, N—B3. Very dangerous. Black
should have tried 12. . .N—Q2, followed by . . .N—B4 to help the queen
escape from the Q side.
    13 K—R1, B—Q2 ?; 14 N—N1 !, Q—N5. Better was 14. . .Q—R5; 15
Q—K3, N—K2, and the queen can retreat. 15 Q—K3, P—Q4 ?; 16
P×P, N—K2; 17 P—B4 !, N—B4; 18 Q—Q3, P—R5. Threat . . .N—
N6 ch. 19 B—N4, N—Q3; 20 N(1)—Q2, P—B4 ?. Better was 20. . .R—
KN1, but Black's position is horrible in any case. 21 P—QR3, Q—N3;
22 P—B5 !, Q—N4; 23 Q—QB3, P×B; 24 P—QR4, P—R6. Or 24. . .
Q—K7; 25 QR—K1. 25 P × Q, and White won.

Game 12. Fischer played the Queen's Gambit again (by transposition from
the English Opening). Spassky adopted the Orthodox, instead of the
Tartakower Defence. A rather interesting struggle was drawn in fifty-five
moves.

Game 13. How would Fischer react to the thrashing of the eleventh game?
Another Poisoned Pawn Variation? No. He played Alekhine's Defence
which he had used only a few times before. Another hard fought game,
which Spassky was perhaps unlucky to lose, blundering in time trouble

on the sixty-ninth move. Fischer's continual switching of openings was costing Spassky a lot of time on the clock.

The score was now 8–5 in favour of Fischer and the struggle was virtually over. Although Spassky held the initiative many times during the duration of the match he was always unable to evaluate his advantages, and he never won another game. Right to the end Fischer kept him guessing about the openings. As Black, he chose to play the Najdorf Variation once more, but not the Poisoned Pawn. He used Alekhine's Defence again, but he also introduced two completely new defences into his opening repertoire – the Pirc Defence and the Kan Variation of the Sicilian. As White, he favoured 1 P—K4 during the final phase of the match, rejecting the Sozin Variation of the Sicilian for the Richter Rauzer (hardly surprising), and switching from the Closed Ruy Lopez to the Exchange Variation (with which he never looked like winning).

The psychological effect of switching openings so often, and choosing lines that he had never before played, was a masterpiece of judgement. Not only did Spassky's psyche have to survive the traumatic period before the match when nobody knew whether or not Fischer would actually come to Iceland, but it also had to recover from the surprise of playing a completely new opponent. The Bobby Fischer who played in Reykjavik was not the young man with consistent opening preferences, who never played a queen's pawn opening on principle. He had become a truly universal player, equally capable of handling a sharp Sicilian or a quiet Orthodox Defence.

From his results we can safely conclude that Robert James Fischer is the strongest chess player the world has ever known. From the diversity of openings that he has played with a profound understanding, it is clear that in that area of the game his knowledge has never before been equalled (and how much more there is to know now than there was even twenty-five years ago). The precision with which he plays the endgame is almost frightening. Even strong Grandmasters cannot treat a 'book draw' too lightly. His impeccable and often original handling of all types of middle game position leaves nothing lacking. At the time of writing, there is only one fault that I can find with Fischer's play: he is too strong! There is no point in his playing a match with any but one or two players. As Gligoric wrote in his excellent book on the 1972 World Championship Match: 'The new champion advocates the highest professional approach to the game, and sets new standards for Grandmasters, who will be obliged to give their best in international competition. Therefore, Robert Fischer enjoys the respect of the chess world.'

INDEX OF OPENINGS

The figures refer to page numbers
Bold figures indicate that Fischer played Black

INDEX OF OPPONENTS

The figures refer to page numbers
The opponents' colour is marked (W) or (B)